NORTHERN TOKYO
Pages 46–57

CENTRAL TOKYO
Pages 36–45

NORTHERN
TOKYO

CENTRAL
TOKYO

EYEWITNESS TRAVEL

TOKYO

EYEWITNESS TRAVEL

TOKYO

仲見世

DK

LONDON, NEW YORK,
MELBOURNE, MUNICH AND DELHI
www.dk.com

MANAGING EDITOR Aruna Ghose
EDITORIAL MANAGER Joseph Mathai
DESIGN MANAGER Priyanka Thakur
PROJECT EDITOR Arundhti Bhanot
PROJECT DESIGNER Rajnish Kashyap
DESIGNER Anchal Kaushal
SENIOR CARTOGRAPHIC MANAGER Uma Bhattacharya
CARTOGRAPHER Alok Pathak
SENIOR DTP DESIGNER Vinod Harish
SENIOR PICTURE RESEARCHER Taiyaba Khatoon
PICTURE RESEARCHER Sumita Khatwani

MAIN CONTRIBUTORS
Jon Burbank, Emi Kazuko, Stephen Mansfield, Robbie Swinnerton

PHOTOGRAPHER
Martin Hladik

ILLUSTRATORS
Richard Bonson, Gary Cross, Richard Draper, Paul Guest, Claire
Littlejohn, Maltings Partnership, Mel Pickering, John Woodcock

Printed and bound by L. Rex Printing Co. Ltd, China

First American Edition, 2008
13 14 15 16 10 9 8 7 6 5 4 3 2 1

Published in the United States by DK Publishing,
375 Hudson Street, New York, New York 10014

Reprinted with revisions 2010, 2013

Copyright © 2008, 2013 Dorling Kindersley Limited, London
A Penguin Company

Published in Great Britain by Dorling Kindersley Limited.

A CATALOG RECORD FOR THIS BOOK IS
AVAILABLE FROM THE LIBRARY OF CONGRESS.

ISSN 1542-1554
ISBN: 978-0-75668-563-8

FLOORS ARE REFERRED TO THROUGHOUT IN ACCORDANCE WITH
AMERICAN USAGE; IE THE "FIRST FLOOR" IS AT GROUND LEVEL.

Front cover main image: Tourists at Senso-ji in Asakusa, Tokyo

MIX
Paper from
responsible sources
FSC
www.fsc.org FSC™ C018179

**The information in this
DK Eyewitness Travel Guide is checked regularly.**
Every effort has been made to ensure that this book is as up-to-date
as possible at the time of going to press. Some details, however,
such as telephone numbers, opening hours, prices, gallery hanging
arrangements and travel information are liable to change. The publishers cannot accept responsibility for any consequences arising
from the use of this book, nor for any material on third party web-
sites, and cannot guarantee that any website address in this book
will be a suitable source of travel information. We value the views
and suggestions of our readers very highly. Please write to: Publisher,
DK Eyewitness Travel Guides, Dorling Kindersley, 80 Strand,
London WC2R 0RL, Great Britain, or email: travelguides@dk.com.

◁ **Cherry trees in full bloom along Nakamise-dori in Asakusa, Tokyo**

The expansive Yokohama Bay Bridge

1825 print by Hokusai depicting
the stages of wood-block printing

Imperial figure at Yomeimon
Gate, Tosho-gu shrine, Nikko

A typical selection of Japanese food
in a *bento* box

Tosho-gu shrine, Nikko

HOW TO USE THIS GUIDE

This guide helps you to get the most from your visit to Tokyo. It provides detailed practical information and expert recommendations. *Introducing Tokyo* maps the city and the region, sets it in its historical context, and guides you through the succession of significant cultural events. *Tokyo Area By Area* is the main sightseeing section, giving detailed information on all the major sights, with photographs, illustrations, and

detailed maps. *Farther Afield* looks at major sights of interest outside the city center, and *Beyond Tokyo* explores other places to visit within easy reach of the city. Carefully researched suggestions for restaurants, hotels, and shopping are found in the *Travelers' Needs* section of the book, while the *Survival Guide* contains useful advice on everything from changing money to traveling on the extensive Tokyo subway network.

TOKYO

The center of Tokyo has been divided into three sightseeing areas, each with its own chapter, color-coded for easy reference. Every chapter opens with an introduction to the part of Tokyo it covers, as well as an Area Map. This is followed by a Street-by-Street map illustrating the heart of the area.

Sights at a Glance lists the area's key sights by category, such as Notable Districts, Historic Buildings, Parks and Gardens, and Markets.

2 Street-by-Street map
This map gives a bird's-eye view of interesting and important parts of each sight seeing area.

A suggested route takes in some of the most interesting streets in the area.

1 Area Map
The sights are numbered and located on a map. City center sights are also marked on the Street Finder maps.

A locator map shows where you are in relation to other areas in the city center.

Each area has color-coded thumb tabs.

The Visitors' Checklist provides detailed practical information.

3 Tokyo's main sights
These are given two or more full pages. All top sights in Tokyo are described individually.

Stars indicate the sights that no reader should miss.

TOKYO AREA MAP

The colored areas shown on this map *(see inside front cover)* are the five main sightseeing areas used in this guide. Each is covered in a full chapter in *Tokyo Area by Area (see pp36–103)*. They are highlighted on other maps throughout the book. In *Tokyo at a Glance*, for example, they help you locate the top sights. They are also used to help you find the position of the three walks *(see pp78–83)*.

4 Farther Afield
This section covers those sights of interest to visitors that lie just outside the city of Tokyo and are easily accessible from the city center.

A key outlines the symbols used to read the map.

A map of the city shows the location of Farther Afield sights in relation to the city center.

The introduction outlines the areas covered in this section and their historical context.

5 Beyond Tokyo
Places worth visiting that are within a day's travel of Tokyo are described here. The general introduction is followed by a map which gives an illustrated overview of the region, with major roads marked and useful tips on getting around by bus and train.

Special features, such as this one on Zen Buddhist Temples, are highlighted with maps or illustrations.

6 Detailed Information
All the important sights are listed in order, following the numbering on the Area Map. *Practical information, including map references, opening hours, and telephone numbers, is also provided.*

INTRODUCING TOKYO

FOUR GREAT DAYS IN TOKYO

In little more than 400 years Tokyo has grown from being an impoverished fishing village to arguably the world's largest metropolis. These itineraries sample both the traditional sights of Edo *(see p25)*, such as the Imperial Palace and its moats, and the historically

Clay mask, Tokyo National Museum

important Sumida River, as well as taking in the city's famed futuristic architecture. They are designed to give a broad flavor of Tokyo and illustrate how this vibrant city preserves its past while striding boldly into the future. Prices mentioned include cost of travel, food, and admission fees.

Akihabara, or "Electric Town," lined with high-tech stores

to Yurakucho, site of the **Tokyo International Forum** *(see p43)*, one of the city's most striking examples of post-modernist architecture.

A FAMILY DAY

- **Fun at the Children's Castle**
- **Toys at Kiddyland**
- **Thrills at Tokyo Dome**
- **Sunset at a Shinjuku skyscraper**

FAMILY OF 4 allow at least ¥18,000

ARCHITECTURE AND ELECTRONICS

- **A museum of the future**
- **Majestic Rainbow Bridge**
- **Lunch in Akihabara**
- **Tokyo International Forum, an architectural marvel**

FAMILY OF 4 allow at least ¥10,000

Morning
Start at the **Miraikan** *(see p82)*, a superbly designed museum dedicated to science and the latest in cutting-edge Japanese technology. Follow the elevated railway across Dream Bridge to **Tokyo Big Sight** *(see p82)*, an exhibition and convention center. A gravity-defying structure, the center building consists of four inverted pyramids standing on a deceptively small base. Take the Yurika-mome Line to Daiba Station. Stop at one of the outdoor cafés at **Decks Tokyo Beach** *(see p83)*, where the walkways look down onto the sandy strip of Odaiba Marine Park and the picturesque Rainbow Bridge.

Afternoon
Take the Yurikamome Line to Shimbashi Station, changing to the JR Yamanote Line for **Akihabara** *(see p45)*, the electronics district. Enjoy a wonderful tempura lunch at **Nakase** *(see p135)*. Explore the area's electronic emporiums and mangaesque buildings before visiting the **Tokyo Anime Center** *(see p45)*, a colorful, interactive space dedicated to anime culture. Return to the station and take the Yamanote Line

Post-modernist masterpiece, Glass Hall, Tokyo International Forum

Morning
Begin this day, centered around kids and young-at-heart adults, at the **National Children's Castle** *(see p68)*. Each floor has a different theme from chutes and slides for the very young to music rooms where kids can try out musical instruments. Do not miss the rooftop play garden with its go-karts and jungle gyms. Take the JR Yamanote Line from Shibuya to Harajuku Station and then walk along Omotesando-dori to **Maisen** *(see p137)*, for a great lunch of *tonkatsu* (deep-fried pork cutlets) before checking out **Crayon House** *(see p145)*, an excellent children's bookstore.

Afternoon
Next stop is **Kiddyland** *(see p149)*, a multi-story toy shop. Take the train or subway to Suidobashi Station where the soaring **Tokyo Dome** *(see p153)* stands. Here you can watch exciting baseball games (Japan's de facto national sport). Tickets always sell out, so book in advance.

Evening

Take the Toei Oedo Line to Shinjuku Station and walk to the west exit of the **Tokyo Metropolitan Government Building** *(see pp14–15)*. Its high speed elevator goes up to the 45th-floor observation gallery for the city's best sunset and night views.

AN OUTDOORS DAY

- **A relaxing river cruise**
- **A grand tour of the historic Imperial Palace**
- **A stroll in Shinjuku-Gyoen Garden**
- **Shopping and a *shabu-shabu* dinner**

TWO ADULTS allow at least ¥10,000

Morning

Board the Suijo Bus (river cruise) at Asakusa's Azuma Bridge. The Sumida River provides the setting for one of the most interesting concentrations of bridges in Japan. On alighting walk straight into the grounds of the **Hama Detached Palace Garden** *(see pp40–41)*, a stunning, spacious, landscape garden dating from the 1650s that includes an elegant tea pavilion on the edge of its tidal salt pond. Walk through the Ginza district or take the metro to **Hibiya Park** *(see p43)*, a spacious, green Western-style park, full of shady arbors. Stroll along the outer moat of the Imperial Palace to the Marunouchi Building *(see p182)* and lunch at Kua'Aina, a popular Hawaiian burger restaurant.

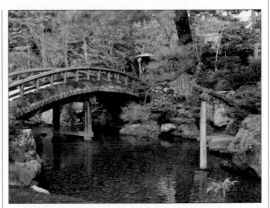
Imperial Palace Garden, a pleasant retreat in the heart of the city

The restaurant is right in front of **Tokyo Station** *(see p42)* and its redbrick, Queen Anne-style façade.

Afternoon

Return to the palace moat and Otemon gate, the main entrance to the **Imperial Palace Garden** *(see p43)*. The green of manicured lawns contrast with gigantic stones and a ruined keep that give a vivid sense of the grandeur of the original castle grounds. Head for JR Yurakucho Station to **Shinjuku-Gyoen Garden** *(see p183)*, a cherry blossom-viewing spot. The former estate of a feudal lord, this is the closest you can get to a great outdoors experience in Tokyo. Stroll over to **Takashimaya Times Square** and **Tokyu Hands** *(see p145)* for window shopping. It is worth walking to other side of the tracks to West Shinjuku for the superb *shabu-shabu* at **Yuan** *(see p138)*.

Exhibition of flag models at the Japan Folk Crafts Museum

ART BROWSING

- **Treasures at the Tokyo National Museum**
- **A fine art museum and garden**
- **A craft museum**

TWO ADULTS allow at least ¥10,000

Morning

Begin this day of museums, galleries, and cultural sights with the world's largest collection of Japanese art and antiquity at the **Tokyo National Museum** *(see pp50–53)*. The cafés around nearby Shinobazu Pond, with the Benten shrine sitting on an islet surrounded by lotuses, are a good place for a coffee break. Take the Ginza Line to Omotesando for the next cultural treat, the **Nezu Museum of Fine Arts** *(see p68)*. Finally, experience an authentic sushi-train at **Heirokuzushi** *(see p136)*.

Afternoon

It is just two stops from Shibuya on the Keio-Inokashira Line to Komaba-Todaemae and the **Japan Folk Crafts Museum** *(see p77)*, housed in a wonderful 1936 residence. Return to Shibuya Station and the **Bunkamura** *(see p66)* cross-cultural center, which houses regular exhibitions. After spending an hour or two here, you will be well positioned for a night out in Shibuya.

Putting Tokyo on the Map

Tokyo, Japan's official capital city since 1868, lies on the Japanese archipelago's largest island, Honshu. This island chain is situated to the east of mainland Asia, in the northwest of the Pacific Ocean. Tokyo is located at the southern end of the Kanto Plain, on Tokyo Bay, and is bordered by Chiba, Yamanashi, Kanagawa, and Saitama prefectures.

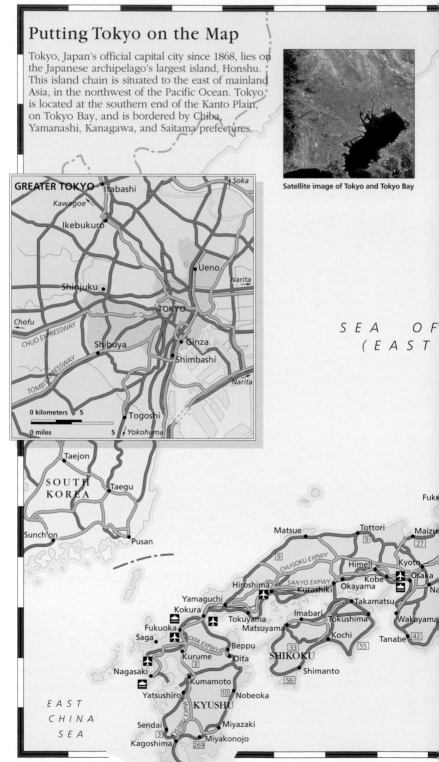

Satellite image of Tokyo and Tokyo Bay

GREATER TOKYO

Itabashi
Soka
Kawagoe
Ikebukuro
Ueno
Narita
Shinjuku
Chofu
TOKYO
CHUO EXPRESSWAY
Shibuya
Ginza
Shimbashi
TOMEI EXPRESSWAY
Narita

0 kilometers 5
0 miles 5

Togoshi
Yokohama

SEA OF
(EAST

Taejon
SOUTH
KOREA
Taegu

Sunch'on
Pusan

Fuk

Matsue
Tottori
Maizu
9
27

CHUGOKU EXPWY

9
Himeji
Kyoto
SANYO EXPWY
Kobe
Osaka
Hiroshima
Kurashiki
Okayama
Na

Yamaguchi
Takamatsu

Kokura
Tokuyama
Imabari
Tokushima
Wakayama

Fukuoka
Matsuyama

Saga
OITA EXPWY
Beppu
Kochi
Tanabe
42

Nagasaki
Kurume
Oita
33
55

3
SHIKOKU
Shimanto

Kumamoto
56

Yatsushiro
10
Nobeoka

EAST
CHINA
SEA
KYUSHU

Sendai
Miyazaki
3

Kagoshima
Miyakonojo
269

Wakkanai ✈

Otoineppu

40

Nayoro

Abashiri

Kitami

Asahikawa   39

HOKKAIDO

Nemuro

Kushiro

38

Sapporo

Obihiro

Urahoro

DOO EXPWY

5

234

Tomakomai

Oshamanbe

Muroran

Mori

Hakodate

Aomori

Hirosaki

7

Kuji

4

Akita   46

Morioka

Yokote   45

Sakata   7

TOHOKU EXPWY

TOHOKU SHINKANSEN

13

Ishinomaki

Tsuruoka

Yamagata   Sendai

Ryotsu

Niigata

Sado Island

Fukushima

BAN-ETSU EXPWY

Kashiwazaki

Aizu-Wakamatsu   6

4

Nagano   Nikko

Toyama   Maebashi   Utsunomiya

nazawa   18

Takayama   Chino   Mito

41   Kawagoe   **TOKYO**

Kofu   Kawasaki   Funabashi

TOHOKU EXPWY

JOBAN EXPWY

ONSHU   Yokohama   Chiba

gifu   CHUO EXPWY   Kamakura

Nagoya   Hakone

hashi   Shizuoka

23

se

PACIFIC

OCEAN

(J A P A N   S E A)

PACIFIC

OCEAN

KEY

✈	Airport
⛴	Major ferry port
═	Expressway
━	Major road
—	*Shinkansen* (bullet train) line
-·-	International border

SOUTHEAST AND EAST ASIA

RUSSIAN FEDERATION

MONGOLIA

N. KOREA   **JAPAN**

CHINA   S. KOREA

Tokyo

MYANMAR

THAILAND

VIETNAM

PHILIPPINES

MALAYSIA

INDONESIA   PAPUA NEW GUINEA   SOLOMON ISLANDS

AUSTRALIA

0 kilometers   200

0 miles   100

Architecture in Tokyo

Tokyoites have been obliged to rebuild their city so many times that what meets the eye is a mishmash of architectural styles. First impressions suggest chaos, but there is a dynamism, perhaps even a hidden order, to Tokyo's macramé of older wood and mortar buildings and its hi-tech modernity. From the splendid futuristic creations of Odaiba *(see p75)* to the triangulated rooftops and glass sheets of Tadao Ando's 21_21 Design Sight in Roppongi *(see pp68–9)*, visitors sense perpetual renewal. In the midst of innovation are traditional structures, but Tokyo's heart, one suspects, is firmly in the future.

Prada Aoyama, *the dazzling creation of Jacques Herzog and Pierre de Meuron, has tinted, diamond-shaped outer panels which reveal a stylish interior.*

SHINJUKU SKYSCRAPER DISTRICT

Shinjuku district in Tokyo epitomizes the modern Japanese urban labyrinth. Most skyscrapers are clustered to the west of Shinjuku Station. Built of materials such as aluminum, steel, and concrete, the buildings use flexible-frame technologies to withstand powerful earthquakes.

Tokyo Opera City Tower is an impressive 768-ft (234-m) high octagonal building with 54 floors.

NTT Docomo Building, 800-ft (240-m) high, holds the title of the tallest four-faced clock tower in the world.

Tokyo Metropolitan Government Office Building Two lacks the height of its bigger namesake but has similar post-modernist angles.

Shinjuku Park Tower, with its three cascading towers, designed by Kenzo Tange, blends with the skyline.

Asahi Super Dry Hall, *an amusing cartoon-like building, was built by French architect Philippe Starck in 1989 for the Asahi beer company.*

St Mary's Cathedral, *an early Kenzo Tange masterpiece, is covered in sparkling sheets of stainless steel, designed to symbolize the light of Christ.*

Fuji-TV Building, *another Kenzo Tange creation and a signature building of Odaiba, is a design marvel of girders, sky corridors, and a titanium-clad sphere.*

TRADITIONAL ARCHITECTURE

Traditional Japanese architecture is based on the use of wood, combined with interiors consisting of paper screens, paper and wood doors, and *tatami* mat flooring *(see p108)*. In Tokyo's older temples and shrines, architectural aesthetics survive in the polished wood floors, ceramic roof tiles, movable partitions, and the sliding panels and opaque screens that create an interaction between the exterior and interior. Gokoku-ji temple *(see p73)*, which dates from 1681, remains gloriously intact, as does the even older Sanmon gate at Zojo-ji temple *(see p41)*. Though a post-war reconstruction, the Meiji shrine *(see p64)*, located at the centre of a sacred forest, keeps faith with the pure, austere lines and aesthetics of traditional Shinto architecture.

Famous Sanmon gate, Zojo-ji temple

Tokyo Metropolitan Government Office, with its stunning walls of granite and digital like windows, towers above the Citizen's Plaza. Its 45th-floor observatory is a great sightseeing spot.

The Olympic Pavilion's *sweeping curved roof of tensile steel helped Kenzo Tange to win architecture's most coveted award, the prestigious 1967 Pritzker Prize.*

Sumitomo Building has an impressive atrium running the entire height of the building.

Sompo Japan Building

Tokyo International Forum, *one of Tokyo's architectural marvels designed by New York-based architect Raphael Viñoly, has a soaring 197-ft (60-m) high glass atrium, crisscrossed by walkways and curving walls resembling a crystal ship.*

Aoyama Technical College, *a sci-fi montage of posts, lightning rods, poles, and capsules by contemporary architect Makoto Watanabe, is an example of just how far Tokyo can go into the architectural beyond.*

Japanese Traditional Theater

Four major types of traditional theater are still
performed regularly in Japan – Noh, Kyogen, Kabuki,
and Bunraku *(see pp154–5)*. Originating in Shinto rites,
Noh was first performed by Kan'ami Kiyotsugu (1333–
84) and developed by his son Zeami. Adopted by the
daimyo (feudal lords), Noh became more ritualistic
and ceremonial. Gradually its farcical elements were
confined to a separate form, Kyogen. By the 17th
century, people wanted a more comprehensible and
entertaining form of drama, and Kabuki evolved from
Noh, starting in Kyoto. A form of puppet theater,
Bunraku, was aimed at the general populace.

A Noh play *is being performed
for the imperial household in
this 1863 woodblock print by
Taiso Yoshitoshi.*

The backdrop is a single pine tree,
epitomizing the simplicity of Noh staging.

Slow rhythmic movements, subtle
expressions, and sonorous music
characterize a Noh performance.

NOH

An austere, restrained, and powerful theatrical
form, Noh is performed on a bare, three-sided
cypress-wood stage roofed like a shrine, with an
entrance ramp to one side. One or two masked
characters appear at a time. Their slow, choreographed actions *(kata)* are performed to music.

Musicians playing
traditional drums and
flutes sit at the back
of the stage and
accompany the actors.

Noh actors may be men or
women but the majority
are men.

Kyogen *evolved from comic interludes
devised as relief from the demanding
nature of Noh. A down-to-earth, colloquial form, its characters highlight
human foibles and frailties. Masks are
rarely used, and costumes are plain.
The actors wear
distinctive yellow
tabi socks.*

Noh masks *are worn by the leading
characters; the greatest masks are
classified as National Treasures. The
mask on the right represents a samurai,
and on the far right, a demon.*

Noh costumes *are
usually richly deco-
rated and heavy. Many
layers are worn to make
the actors seem larger
and more imposing.*

Kabuki actors *were popular subjects for Edo-era woodblock prints. The tradition can still be seen in this modern poster advertising a Kabuki play.*

BUNRAKU

Bunraku puppets are about 1.2 m (4 ft) tall with carved wooden heads, movable hands, and elaborate costumes. The main puppeteer wears traditional formal dress; his two assistants, one on each side, are clothed in black. *Shamisen (see p155)* music accompanies the action, and a narrator both tells the story and speaks all the parts. Many Kabuki plays were originally written for puppets; Bunraku has in turn borrowed a number of of Kabuki dramas.

Bunraku puppet with his manipulator

Stage right is where less important characters are usually located.

Costumes and wigs are highly elaborate, indicating the status and personality of each character.

The pine trees on Kabuki stage backdrops are a reference to its evolution from Noh.

KABUKI

Kabuki is flamboyant and colorful with a large stage and cast. The major actors are stars, often from famous acting dynasties. Elaborate make-up replaced Noh masks, and a curtain allowed set changes. The musicians and chorus sit behind screens on either side or on stage.

Stage sets often incorporate special effects including trapdoors, revolving sections, and overhead cables for flying.

Stage left is usually occupied by characters of high rank or importance.

The hanamichi *(flower path) is a raised walkway running from the stage right through the audience and is used for dramatic entrances and exits.*

Aragoto, *or "rough-style" acting, is used in certain plays by male characters who move in exaggerated, choreographed ways and wear stylized makeup. Eye and facial movements are crucial to an actor's success.*

Although Kabuki *was founded by a woman, Izumo no Okuni, female actors were soon banned as immoral. All actors are now male, and female roles are played by highly skilled onnagata.*

Sumo and the Martial Arts

A karate kick

Now more of a professional sport than a martial art, sumo traces its origins back 2,000 years to Shinto harvest rites, and retains strong links with Shinto in many of its rituals. There are six sumo tournaments in Japan every year *(see p152)*, broadcast live on TV and followed enthusiastically. Training is a way of life for sumo wrestlers, and if a tournament is not on, it may be possible to watch practice sessions. Martial arts are known as *budo*, or the "martial way." They aim to cultivate balance, control, speed, and accuracy in a spiritual, mental, and physical sense. Kendo and *kyudo*, the least changed since the days of the samurai, are seen as the purest of the martial arts.

Sumo wrestlers *were a highly popular subject for Edo-period wood-block prints.*

Throwing salt *to purify the ring and the fight to come is part of a complex pre-match ritual that the wrestlers undertake. They also stamp, clap, and raise their hands before crouching down in front of their opponent ready to start.*

The gyoji (referee) wears traditional court costume and uses a fan to signal when to begin.

Grand champions (yokozuna) *perform pre-match rituals wearing a richly decorated ceremonial apron and a white hemp-rope belt hung with folded paper (as seen at Shinto shrines). This champion is performing shiko, lifting his leg and stamping his foot to banish evil spirits and intimidate his opponent.*

A referee pours an offering *of sake onto the ring as part of the dedication ceremony before a tournament. The ring is a platform of clay edged by a square of sunken rice-straw bales, with an inner ring (where the match is fought) also marked by sunken bales.*

SUMO WRESTLING

Despite their size – there are no weight restrictions – sumo wrestlers *(rikishi)* move quickly and with agility, and so matches are often short (10 seconds or so). The loser is the first to touch the ground with any part of his body, except the soles of his feet, or to step out of, or be pushed from, the ring. The referee declares the winner.

Banners *announce a sumo tournament – here at the National Sumo Stadium in Tokyo (see p153). Each tournament lasts 15 days. The lower-ranking wrestlers fight early in the day, while higher-ranking ones appear from mid-afternoon onward.*

The wrestlers' hair is oiled and fastened into a topknot *(mage)*.

Only 48 winning techniques are commonly used, but many more have been identified.

MARTIAL ARTS

Originally developed as traditional arts of war by the samurai, the martial arts have evolved into forms of austere discipline *(shugyo)* aimed at spiritual improvement; some are also competitive sports. The modern forms of kendo and kyudo trace their origins to methods practiced in Japanese antiquity.

Kendo *means the "way of the sword." Originating from samurai fencing, kendo now uses bamboo swords. Contestants wear extensive padding and protection. In a match, points are gained for hitting the head, torso, forearm, or throat.*

Kyudo, *or the "way of the bow," has close associations with Zen Buddhism. Although accuracy in hitting a target is important, the emphasis is also on concentration of mind and body.*

Judo *developed from jujitsu. A system of self-defense, it is well established as a sport in which throwing and grappling techniques are used to subdue an opponent.*

A loincloth *(mawashi)* is worn for bouts, along with a thin belt *(sagari)* hung with threads similar to those seen at Shinto shrines.

Karate *("empty hand") reached Japan in 1922 from Okinawa. A form of self-defense as well as spiritual and physical training, it has become a sport, consisting of explosive yet controlled kicks, punches, or strikes, and blocking moves.*

The ring stands *under a suspended roof resembling that of a Shinto shrine. A different-colored tassel hangs from each corner of the roof, representing the four seasons.*

Aikido – *the "way of harmonious spirit" – uses an opponent's strength and speed against them. Training unites spiritual awareness and physical flexibility.*

THE HISTORY OF JAPAN

F*rom the origins of the Japanese race to its military behavior in World War II, Japan's history is still subject to conjecture. What is indisputable is that the people of this archipelago were able to avail themselves of the fruits of continental civilization even as their isolation protected them from attack. As a result, Japan has one of the most distinct of all the many Chinese-influenced cultures in Asia.*

During glacial epochs when the sea level was low, Japan's first inhabitants may have reached the archipelago overland from Sakhalin and Siberia, China and Korea, or the Okinawa islands. Crude stone tools found at sites across Honshu, Japan's main island, may date back 40,000 years.

Recent discoveries posit the emergence of the hunting and gathering society known as Jomon around 14,500 BC. Jomon pottery is among the world's oldest and includes vessels and figurines, particularly of women. Mounds of shells and other evidence indicate that the diet included fish, shellfish, deer, wild pigs, and wild plants and seeds. In the Kanto Plain (near Tokyo), the Jomon culture in its later stages included village-like groupings.

Rice agriculture and bronze, iron, and other crafts are believed to have reached Japan via Korea during the Yayoi period. The Yayoi people spread from the southern island of Kyushu to Honshu over time, pushing the earlier inhabitants north. Chinese histories record a visit by an envoy of Himiko, queen of Yamatai,

Clay figurine from the Kofun period

to the Chinese kingdom of Wei in 239, but Yamatai's location is open to debate. Aristocratic orders emerged, including that of the emperor, said to be descended from the sun goddess Amaterasu. Figures of high rank were buried in massive *kofun* (tumuli), along with clay sculptures, armor, mirrors, and jewelry.

By the late 6th century, tribes that had migrated to the fertile lands of the Yamato Plain in Western Honshu were engaged in a power struggle over the introduction of Buddhism. Prince Shotoku, appointed regent by Empress Suiko in 593, helped seal victory for the pro-Buddhist camp.

In 701, the Taiho code, a penal and administrative system based on the Chinese model, was in place. Founded in 710 on the Yamato Plain, the city of Nara became the grand diocese of Buddhism and one of Asia's most splendid cities in its 74-year spell as Japan's first capital. With the completion of the *Man'yoshu*, the earliest known Japanese poetry, in 759, the culture began to establish a clear voice of its own.

PERIODS AT A GLANCE

Jomon	14,500–300 BC
Yayoi	300 BC–AD 300
Kofun/Asuka	300–710
Hakuho	645–710
Nara	710–794
Heian	794–1185
Kamakura	1185–1333
Muromachi	1333–1568
Momoyama	1568–1600
Tokugawa (Edo)	1600–1868
Meiji	1868–1912
Taisho	1912–1926
Showa	1926–1989
Heisei	1989–present

TIMELINE

300 BC–AD 300 Continental methods of farming, metalworking, pottery, and other skills reach southwestern Japan via Korea, and spread through the islands

710 Heijo-kyo (Nara) made capital

701 Taiho code put in place, the basis of the first Japanese legal system

| AD 1 | 200 | 400 | 600 |

Yayoi earthenware

239 Himiko, queen of Yamatai, sends envoy to kingdom of Wei in China

587 Power struggle over introduction of Buddhism from China

712 *Kojiki*, Japan's oldest historical account, complete

◁ **Detail from a 16th-century screen painting, showing customs month-by-month in the Momoyama period**

COURT LIFE AND THE TALE OF GENJI

Court life in the Heian period focused on romance, aesthetic pursuits, and fastidious observation of precedent and ritual, as documented in the *Pillow Book* of court lady Sei Shonagon in the late 10th century. The *Tale of Genji*, written in the early 11th century by Sei Shonagon's rival, Murasaki Shikibu, a court lady of the Fujiwara clan, is possibly the world's oldest novel. It depicts the loves and sorrows of a fictitious prince, Genji, and, after he dies, the amorous pursuits of a man whom Genji thought was his son. The story has been illustrated in countless scrolls.

Tale of Genji scroll

HEIAN PERIOD

The Fujiwara family and Emperor Kammu built a new capital in Western Honshu known as Heian-kyo, now Kyoto, in 794. The new system, also based on Chinese models, held that the land and people were the property of the emperor. Tax-exempt status was granted to Buddhist institutions, large landholders, and settlers who would expand the state's frontiers. Meanwhile, the Fujiwara clan gained influence by acting as regents, and intermarriage with the imperial family. A pattern emerged in which emperors would abdicate, name a younger successor, enter a monastery, then exercise power from behind the scenes.

Buddhism's immense influence continued as proponents such as the Japanese Buddhist monk Saicho adapted it, launching hundreds of separate movements and sects. Powerful temples grew militant in faceoffs with other temples and the government, creating armies of warrior-monks. Ironically, Buddhism's abhorrence of killing fed the nobility's contempt for the farmer-warriors – the early samurai – on the frontier, who battled the indigenous people and each other. After 1100, the court could no longer control infighting, and tensions rose between two clans of farmer-warriors from the northeast – the Taira and the Minamoto. By 1160, the ruthless Taira Kiyomori was the most powerful man in Japan. But the Minamoto, led by the brothers Yoshitsune and Yoritomo, fought back to defeat the Taira and establish the first military shogunate at Kamakura *(see pp90–93)* in 1185.

Heian-period fan

Wooden statue of Minamoto no Yoritomo

KAMAKURA SHOGUNATE

Deliberately basing his government far from the imperial court in the village of Kamakura, Minamoto no Yoritomo carefully crafted a system that benefited his *bushi* (warrior) peers and brought 150 years of relative peace and stability. Yoritomo's direct heirs were shoguns only in name, however, as they were dominated by hereditary regents from the military Hojo family of Kamakura. The Hojo assumed the prerogatives of power while granting the imperial institution and nobility the privilege of signing off on policy.

TIMELINE

794 Heian-kyo (Kyoto) becomes capital, which it remains until 1868

823 Kukai, leading proponent of Shingon Buddhism, appointed head of Toji temple

985 Genshin writes tract promoting Pure-Land Buddhism

1087 Emperor Shirakawa abdicates and becomes first cloistered emperor

| 800 | 900 | 1000 | 1100 |

801 Warriors sent to Northern Honshu to battle Ezo tribes

866 First Fujiwara regent assumes post

940 First uprising by a warrior member of the Taira clan

Toji temple

c.1000 Court lady Murasaki Shikibu writes *Tale of Genji*

Portuguese in Kyushu – the "Southern Barbarians" who introduced firearms and Christianity to Japan

The *Tale of the Heike*, a chronicle of the war between the Taira and Minamoto clans, was first recited to *biwa* (lute) accompaniment at this time. Temples and works of art were created in Kamakura, reflecting Yoritomo's warrior ideals of stoicism, self discipline, frugality, and loyalty. Zen Buddhism as imported from China was popular with the samurai, while the Pure-Land, True-Pure-Land, and Nichiren Buddhist sects promoted salvation to the common people.

Mongol invasions were repelled twice in the 13th century, but weakened the resources and command of Kamakura. The end came in 1333, when the Ashikaga clan, led by Takauji, toppled the Kamakura shogunate. However, the power systems instigated by Yoritomo and the Hojo influenced Japanese life for five more centuries.

Muromachi-period sword guard

MUROMACHI SHOGUNATE

With military power back with the imperial court in Kyoto, arts such as Noh drama and the tea ceremony flowered under the patronage of Shogun Ashikaga Yoshimasa. However, a succession dispute split the court into southern and northern factions. With leaders engaged in power struggles, chaos and famine were common. The nadir was reached during the Onin War (1467–77), when arson and looting destroyed much of Kyoto.

The Muromachi period, named for the Kyoto district where the Ashikagas built their palace, was a time of craven ambition that unleashed every class in society to vie for advantage. Warfare, once the exclusive business of samurai, now involved armies of footsoldiers *(ashigaru)* recruited from the peasantry, who could hope for promotion based on success in the battlefield.

In 1542, a trio of Portuguese from a shipwrecked junk emerged in Tanegashima, an island off Kyushu, and introduced firearms to Japan. Francis Xavier, a founding member of the Society of Jesus, established a Jesuit mission on Kyushu in 1549. The contact with Europeans further destabilized the political situation and set the stage for the first of the great unifiers, Oda Nobunaga, who entered Kyoto in 1568.

1180–85 Minamoto clan defeats the Taira and establishes Kamakura shogunate

Great Buddha statue at Kamakura

c.1400 Noh theatrical form flourishes under Shogun Ashikaga

1467 Devastating Onin War begins. Vast sections of Kyoto are burned over the next decade

| 1200 | 1300 | 1400 | 1500 |

1160 Ascendant Taira clan under Taira Kiyomori suppresses its rivals, the Minamoto, and dominates court life

1281 Second Mongol invasion

1274 First Mongol invasion

1242 Emperor Shijo dies without naming an heir, setting off succession dispute

1560–80 Oda Nobunaga victorious in battles for hegemony of Japan

1428 Peasant uprising in Kyoto

1401 Formal relations with China reestablished

Screen depicting the Battle of Nagashino in 1575, won by Oda Nobunaga's 3,000 musketeers

MOMOYAMA PERIOD

After Japan had been racked by over a century of debilitating, inconclusive warfare, Oda Nobunaga, who rose through military ranks in the provinces, set out to unify the nation under his rule. From 1568–76 Nobunaga defeated rival warlord Asai Nagamasa; burned down Kyoto's main temple complex, where militant monks had long challenged the court and their Buddhist rivals; drove Ashikaga Yoshiaki into exile; and deployed 3,000 musketeers to massacre the Takeda forces at the Battle of Nagashino. In 1580, in his last great military exploit, Nobunaga

Momoyama-period detail at Nishi Hongan-ji, Kyoto

obtained the surrender of Ishiyama Hongan-ji, a nearly impregnable temple fortress in today's Osaka in Western Honshu. The temple had been the power base of the Buddhist True-Pure-Land sect. By 1582, when he was forced to commit suicide by a treasonous vassal, Nobunaga was in control of 30 of Japan's 68 provinces. Nobunaga's deputy, a warrior of humble birth named Toyotomi Hideyoshi, continued the work of unification, launching epic campaigns that brought Shikoku (1585), Kyushu (1587), the Kanto region (1590), and Northern Honshu (1591) under his control. He followed up by destroying many of the castles and forts belonging to potential rivals, confiscating weapons belonging to peasants, and devising a system in which peasants held their own small plots and paid a fixed tax directly to the central government.

In his later years, Hideyoshi ordered two unsuccessful invasions of Korea and persecuted the Portuguese missionaries and their Japanese converts. Like Oda Nobunaga, however, Hideyoshi never claimed the title of shogun but became obsessed with ensuring the perpetuation of his line after his death. Two years after his death in 1598, however, dissension among his retainers led to the Battle of Sekigahara, in which Tokugawa Ieyasu emerged victorious.

THE TOKUGAWA SHOGUNATE

Named shogun by the emperor in 1603, Ieyasu split the population into rigidly defined hereditary classes. To end turf wars, samurai were forbidden to own

TIMELINE

Osaka Castle

1615 Siege of Osaka Castle

1635 All foreign commerce confined to the artificial island of Dejima in Nagasaki Bay. From 1641, only Dutch and Chinese allowed access

1689 Haiku poet Basho departs on his journey to the north

1707 Last erupt of Mc Fuji

| 1600 | 1625 | 1650 | 1675 | 1700 |

1590 Hideyoshi controls all Japan

1597 Violent persecution of Christians in Nagasaki

1614 Christianity banned

1600 Tokugawa Ieyasu wins battle of Sekigahara, achieves hegemony over Japan

1657 Meireki fire in Edo kills over 100,000

Statue of Basho

1703 Suic of the 47 *ronin*

:

land and could reside only within certain quarters of castle towns. Farmers were allotted small plots, which they had to cultivate. Artisans formed the next class, merchants the bottom. Movement between regions was regulated, and families or whole villages could be punished for crimes by their kin or neighbors.

The *daimyo* or lords who governed regions, now subject to Tokugawa authority, were shuffled to different regions if their service was not approved. After 1635, the *daimyo* and their samurai retinue were forced to reside every other year in the city of Edo (Tokyo), the new seat of the shogunate.

Fireman official's garment in Edo

ISOLATION AND THE RISE OF EDO
William Adams, an Englishman who reached Japan on a Dutch ship in 1600, served Ieyasu in various capacities over the next two decades (as portrayed in James Clavell's 1976 book *Shogun*). During this time, the English,

Dutch, Portuguese, Spanish, and New World governments made overtures to the shogunate on trade. However, the increasingly xenophobic Tokugawa regime restricted all foreign shipping to Nagasaki on the island of Kyushu from 1635; only Chinese and Dutch traders were allowed from 1641. This heralded 200 years of isolation from the rest of the world.

While Kyoto remained the official capital through the Tokugawa period, Edo eclipsed it in size and was probably the largest city in the world by around 1700. Edo also hosted an explosion of arts such as Kabuki and Bunraku theater *(see pp16–17)* and the *ukiyo-e* works *(see p55)* of Utamaro, Sharaku, Hokusai, and Hiroshige. Patrons included the merchant class and samurai.

In 1853 Commodore Matthew Perry steamed into Edo Bay with four US vessels to challenge Japan's refusal to enter into international relations. Weakened by unrest from within its own and other ranks, the shogunate could only accede to Perry's demands. Samurai from the Satsuma, Choshu, and Tosa domains in Kyushu, Western Honshu, and Shikoku became the driving force behind a successful restoration of imperial power and a reorganization of the government carried out in 1868.

Early map of Edo, which outgrew Kyoto under the Tokugawa shogunate

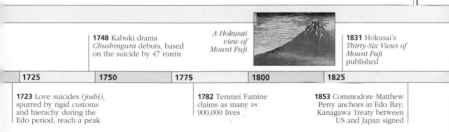

1748 Kabuki drama *Chushingura* debuts, based on the suicide by 47 *ronin*

A Hokusai view of Mount Fuji

1831 Hokusai's *Thirty-Six Views of Mount Fuji* published

1725	1750	1775	1800	1825

1723 Love suicides *(joshi)*, spurred by rigid customs and hierachy during the Edo period, reach a peak

1782 Tenmei Famine claims as many as 900,000 lives

1853 Commodore Matthew Perry anchors in Edo Bay; Kanagawa Treaty between US and Japan signed

Wood-block print of Sino-Japanese War of 1894–5

MEIJI RESTORATION

Emperor Meiji (1852–1912) was 16 when the restoration of imperial rule was declared on January 3, 1868. Tokyo was swiftly made the new capital.

A new centralized system pressed for changes that would render Japan capable of competing with the West. Military conscription and the elimination of the hereditary samurai class were undertaken to create a modern fighting force, provoking furious resistance from samurai in 1874–6. *Daimyo* domains were gradually transformed into prefectures, although *daimyo* and court nobles lingered in the form of a new class called *kazoku*. Universal literacy became a goal. By 1884, tax and banking reforms, and an industrial strategy aimed at exports were underway. The Meiji Constitution of 1889, promulgated by the emperor, allowed the military direct access to the throne while creating a house of peers and a lower house.

Following disputes over control of the Korean peninsula, the Sino-Japanese War of 1894–5 ended with Japan's victory over China, but showed that greater military strength would be needed

Emperor Meiji (1852–1912), first emperor of modern Japan

for the nation to contend as an imperial power equal with the West.

By the turn of the century, the transformation to an industrial economy, with textiles the chief export, was well underway. A second imperialist conflict, the Russo-Japanese war of 1904–5, ended with Japan aggrandizing its claims to Korea, which was annexed in 1910, and southern Manchuria in China.

During the final decade of Meiji's reign, the home ministry stressed reverence for the emperor, the family, the Shinto religion, and military and national heroes. Suppression of groups seen as enemies of the state became the government's prerogative.

WAR WITH CHINA AND WORLD WAR II

The attempt to transform Japan from a feudal to a modern industrial state caused severe dislocation. By 1929, when the stock market collapsed, resentment against those who had prospered from exports intensified. Young officers, chafing to restore national pride, began assassinating rich moderates, while militarists and oligarchs in the government believed that seizing land from China and Russia would secure raw materials and improve national security. At the same time, a pan-Asianist movement, which saw Japan on a mission to lead Asia out of servility, construed the Chinese resistance to Japanese domination as an insult. By 1937, the country was embroiled in an unwinnable war with China that further estranged it from the rest of the world.

TIMELINE

1868 Meiji Restoration; Edo is renamed Tokyo and made capital

1869 Colonization of Hokkaido begins

1889 Imperial constitution promulgated

1890 Imperial Diet convenes for first time

Diet Building

1865 | **1880** | **1895** | **1910** | **1925**

1895 China cedes territory to Japan, ending war. Russia, France, and Germany force Japan to relinquish the territory

1910 Korea becomes Japanese colony

1932 In the May 15 incident, young naval officers assassinate prime minister and attempt coup

1904 Russo-Japanese war begins

1905 Treaty of Portsmouth ends war. Korea becomes a Japanese protectorate

1894 Sino-Japanese war begins

1933 Japan withdraws from League of Nations

1923 Great Kanto Earthquake

Aftermath of the bombing of Tokyo in 1945

When the US cut off Japanese access to oil, Tokyo made the desperate decision to seize Pacific territory in a sneak attack on Pearl Harbor, Hawaii, in December 1941. A few months later, Japan took Southeast Asia.

By 1944, American bombers were decimating Japanese cities, but the Japanese army was determined not to surrender unconditionally, opting instead for a suicidal defensive strategy. In August 1945, the US dropped atomic bombs on Hiroshima and Nagasaki, and the Soviet Union entered the war in the Pacific. Emperor Hirohito ordered the cabinet to sue for peace.

Akihito, who was made emperor in 1989

JAPAN SINCE 1945

After World War II the Allied Occupation Force began arriving as millions of homeless Japanese returned to bombed-out cities. The emperor renounced his divine status; land reform was implemented; and war-crimes trials were soon underway.

By 1952, the occupation had ended and the Korean war had turned into a boon for the Japanese economy. Industrial production surged as the average household wanted to own a TV, washing machine, and refrigerator.

In 1960, protests against the ratification of the US-Japan Security Treaty rocked Japan. The prime minister resigned. His successors focused on economic growth. By the time of the 1964 Tokyo Olympics, annual growth was around 10 percent and rising. Prosperity based on exports such as cars, electronics, and technological products made Japan one of the world's richest nations.

The recession of the 1990s was marked by unemployment, plummeting land values, and deflation. The effects of a shrinking economy were further conflated by the breakdown of the family, and rising crime. These days the products and artifacts of fashions, styles, and tastes are magnifying Japan's presence in the world, one which is elevating Japanese popular culture to a rank second in global terms only to that of the United States. As ever, Tokyo is the engine driving much of this change.

On March 11, 2011, a devastating 9.0-magnitude earthquake and subsequent tsunami caused massive destruction in parts of northeastern Japan. Despite suffering major damage and loss of life, Japan is recovering.

Tokyo skyline as seen from the Sumida River

1937 Sino-Japanese war of 1937–45 begins; 140,000 Chinese massacred in Nanjing

1945 Atomic bombs dropped on Hiroshima and Nagasaki; Japan surrenders

1995 Great Hanshin Earthquake in Kobe; fanatical cult releases sarin gas on Tokyo Subway

1997 Economic recession in Southeast Asia, spreading to Japan

2007 Shintaro Ishihara re-elected Tokyo Governor

| 1940 | 1955 | 1970 | 1985 | 2000 | 2015 |

Prayers of a soldier

1964 Tokyo Olympics; first "bullet train"; government begins to promote computer industry

1989 Emperor Hirohito (Showa) dies; Akihito is new emperor

2008 Economy surges; Tokyo undergoes construction boom

Shinkansen ("bullet train")

1941 Japan enters World War II

TOKYO THROUGH THE YEAR

The seasons are closely observed in Japan. Many ritual observances are founded on traditional rural *matsuri* (festivals). There is nothing solemn about these events however, as hard-working, hard-playing Tokyoites enjoy nothing more than a good festival. The festivals, sports events, trade shows, flower exhibitions, and blossom-viewing all

New Year's sumo dedication ceremony

add up to a full cultural calendar. Each suburb also organizes its own festivals, more so during the summer months, when dancers in kimonos and Japanese drum groups perform, and clear skies explode with spectacular fireworks. In contrast, the winter months are devoted to travel, especially around New Year, and religious ceremonies.

SPRING

Spring symbolizes many important things in life. It is when the new economic year begins, students graduate, and projects are launched. While March and April can be rainy, May is usually sublime. The Japanese tend to value spring for its transience and the cherry, more than any other flower, embodies the imper-manence of life. However, there is nothing mournful about the vibrant cherry blossom-viewing parties held at parks throughout the city.

Bugaku dancer, Meiji Shrine Festival

MARCH

Hina Matsuri *(Girls' Day and Doll Festival, Mar 3).* Dolls dressed in traditional Heian-period imperial costumes are displayed in homes and public places.
Golden Dragon Dance *(Mar 18).* This colorful event takes place thrice in the day at Senso-ji temple in Asakusa.

APRIL

Hanami *(Cherry blossom-viewing, late Mar to Apr).* A glorious spring rite celebrated wherever there are cherry trees, but most famously in Chidorigafuchi, Ueno Park, and Sumida Park.

Meiji Shrine Spring Festival *(Apr 2–May 3).* An extensive compendium of traditional cultural events attended by devotees, including colorful court dances, *yabusame* (horseback archery), and music performances.
Hana Matsuri *(Buddha's Birthday, Apr 8).* Devotees pour sweet tea over a small image of the Buddha to honor his birth. Services are held at some temples.
Azalea Festival *(Apr 10–May 5).* Held at various venues, the best known being Nezu Shrine, where countless bushes grow along an embankment.
Tokyo International Anime Fair *(late Mar or early Apr).* One of the world's largest anime events for fans of animation and manga. It is held at Tokyo Big Sight.

MAY

Kodomo no hi *(Children's Day, May 5).* Focusing largely on boys, families fly colorful *koi nobori* (carp streamers), symbolizing strength and determination.
Summer Sumo Tournament *(mid-May).* This 15-day event is held in the Kokugikan hall in Ryogoku.
Kanda Matsuri *(Sat & Sun before May 15, alternate odd-numbered years).* One of the city's three big festivals. Floats and *mikoshi* (portable shrines) parade through the streets around Kanda Myojin Shrine.
Sanja Matsuri *(3rd Fri–Sun in May).* A wild and heady mix of dance, music, ritual, and the jostling of heavy portable shrines, near Asakusa Jinja.
Design Festa *(mid–late May).* Asia's biggest art event. Thousands of people set up displays at this two-day fair at Tokyo Big Sight.

Visitors at the resplendent Azalea Festival

AVERAGE DAILY HOURS OF SUNSHINE

Hours
10
8
6
4
2
0

Jan Feb Mar Apr May Jun Jul Aug Sep Oct Nov Dec

Sunshine Chart
The amount of sunshine per month in Tokyo does not vary greatly, even in the winter months. Winters can see temperatures drop to freezing but the clear skies are rarely disturbed by rain or snow.

Spectacular fireworks display on the Sumida River

SUMMER

When restaurants serve shaved ice, cold noodles, and glasses of chilled barley tea you know the humid summer days are upon the city. The clammy June rains can seem relentless. In August, as people return to their hometowns to celebrate O-Bon, the city is pleasantly quiet. Spectacular firework festivals along the banks of the Sumida and Edo rivers during the O-Bon festival add a splash of vivid color to the season.

JUNE

Iris Viewing *(early to mid-Jun)*. The iris garden in the grounds of Meiji-jingu shrine and at the Horikiri Iris Garden, Katsushika ward, offer the best viewing.

Sanno-Sai *(mid-Jun)*. In a festival that dates back to the founding of Edo, locals in historical costumes take out processions of *mikoshi*, accompanied by music and dancing at Hie Shrine.

JULY

Asagao Ichi *(Morning Glory Fair, Jul 6–8)*. Dozens of merchants set up stalls outside Iriya Kishibojin temple to sell flowers associated with the horticultural tastes of the Edo era.

Tanabata Matsuri *(Star Festival, Jul 7)*. Based on a Chinese legend; this is said to be the only day when two stars can meet as lovers across the Milky Way. Branches of bamboo are decorated with paper streamers inscribed with scribbled wishes, sometimes in the form of poetry.

Sumidagawa Hanabi Takai *(last Sat in Jul)*. A fireworks display on the Sumida river near Asakusa. The river turns into a sheet of red, green, and violet as lantern-lit boats take to the water.

AUGUST

O-Bon *(Festival of the Dead, mid-Aug)*. Family members return home at a time when, according to a Buddhist belief, the spirits also return to earth. Ancestral graves are visited and tended, and there are joyful Bon-Odori dances and festivals.

Koenji Awa Odori *(late Aug)*. Thousands of participants gather along Koenji's main street to join in the amusing Fool's Dance.

Samba Festival *(last Sat in Aug)*. Dancers from Rio join local samba devotees along Asakusa's Kaminarimon-dori, for an event that draws over half a million spectators.

Vibrantly costumed dancer at the Samba Festival

AVERAGE MONTHLY RAINFALL

MM												Inches
300												12
240												9
180												6
120												3
60												0
0	Jan	Feb	Mar	Apr	May	Jun	Jul	Aug	Sep	Oct	Nov	Dec

Rainfall Chart
*Tokyo's rainy season
lasts all through
June and into the
early days of July.
September and
October typhoons
can bring squalls.
Fall is generally
a dry season. April
has unpredictable
rain showers.*

FALL

Although the summer heat
continues into September,
fall is a gentle season, with
many fine, clear days and
little rainfall. The ginkgo leaf
is the symbol of Tokyo and
avenues of the yellow-leaved
trees can be seen throughout
the city. Chrysanthemum
festivals are held in temples
and gardens. Open-air food
stands called *yatai*, and
convenience stores start to
prepare *oden* (potpourri
hotpot) toward the end of
the season signaling cooler
days to come.

Women in traditional costumes at the Jidai Matsuri Festival

Visitors try the latest technology
at the Tokyo Game Show

SEPTEMBER

Tokyo Game Show *(mid-Sep)*. Held at the gigantic
convention center at
Makuhari Messe on Tokyo
Bay, the three-day event
attracts thousands of visitors.

Hachiman-gu Festival *(Sep
14–16)*. Horseback archery
and a procession of floats
draw a large crowd to this
important Kamakura shrine.
Ningyo-Kuyo *(late Sep)*.
Hopeful couples pray for
children by offering dolls at
the Kiyomizu Kannon-do
temple in Ueno Park. Priests
make a ritual fire, placing
last year's dolls on the pyre.

OCTOBER

**Tokyo International Film
Festival** *(late Oct)*. The
largest in Asia, the
focus is on films from
Asia and Japan.
**Chrysanthemum
Viewing** *(late
Oct–mid-Nov)*.
Chrysanthemum
pavilions are erected
in Shinjuku Gyoen
Garden; flower dolls
are displayed at
Yushima Tenjin shrine.
Edo Tenka Matsuri
*(late Oct, alternate,
odd-numbered
years)*. A parade to comme-
mmorate the birth of Edo.

Sony's humanoid
robot exhibit

NOVEMBER

Tokyo Designer's Week *(early
Nov)*. Art enclaves dotted
around the city showcase
the latest trends in the field
of fashion, video graphics,
furniture, and interior design.
Tokyo Jidai Matsuri *(Festival
of the Ages, Nov 3)*. Locals in
period costumes representing
figures from Japanese history
parade around Asakusa's
Senso-ji temple. This is a
great photo opportunity.
Shichi-Go-San *(Seven-Five-
Three Children's Festival,
Nov 15)*. Children of
these ages are dressed
up in kimonos for
visits to shrines in
appreciation of their
health and to pray
for further blessings.
**International Robot
Exhibition** *(late Nov to
early Dec, alternate,
odd-numbered years)*.
Billed as the world's
largest trade show
focusing on robotics,
it brings together an
exciting array of the latest in
technology and products.

AVERAGE MONTHLY TEMPERATURE

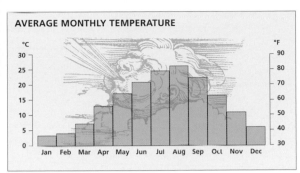

Temperature Chart
Spring is comfortable for most visitors. Summer temperatures can be misleading. June to September are muggy with high levels of humidity. Winter temperatures can drop to freezing. May and October are the most pleasant months with crisp, clear skies.

WINTER

Winter can be cold in Tokyo, however there is only a day or two of snowfall. The return of *mochi* (rice cakes) and little jars of warmed up sake are seasonal signs. An exodus takes place at Oshogatsu (New Year), which is one of the year's peak travel times. For those who remain at home, it is a chance to enjoy traditional New Year dishes and to offer prayers for the coming year.

DECEMBER

Hagoita Ichi
(Battledore Fair, Dec 17–19). Ornate battledores, sold in the precincts of Senso-ji temple, feature the faces of famous Kabuki actors, celebrities, and sports stars.

Joya-no-Kane *(midnight Dec 31).* Temple bells begin to toll at midnight, 108 rings representing the 108 human sins that must be expunged.

JANUARY

Oshogatsu *(New Year's Day).* Japan's most important festival. The first few days are family-oriented. People visit Shinto shrines to offer their wishes for the coming new year. **Water Purification Rituals** *(Jan 10–12).* A ritual cleansing by both young and old. The best places to catch this event are at Kanda Myojin and Teppozu Inari shrines.
Seijin no hi *(Coming-of-Age Day, 2nd Mon in Jan).* Young people turning 20 this year celebrate their passage to adulthood.

Kabuki actor in costume

FEBRUARY

Setsubun *(Feb 3 or 4).* Marking the first day of spring on the old lunar calendar, temple priests and celebrities throw dried soy beans into crowds of onlookers, symbolizing the casting out of bad spirits.
Plum Viewing *(late Feb).* Yushima Tenjin shrine is a famous spot, though there are few plum trees here. Open-air tea ceremonies and floral exhibits are displayed, and plum bonsai are sold.

PUBLIC HOLIDAYS

If a public holiday falls on a Sunday, the following Monday is also a holiday.

New Year's Day (Jan 1)
Coming-of-Age Day (2nd Mon in Jan)
National Foundation Day (Feb 11)
Vernal Equinox Day (around Mar 20)
Showa Day (Apr 29)
Constitution Memorial Day (May 3)
Greenery Day (May 4)
Children's Day (May 5)
Marine Day (3rd Mon in Jul)
Respect-for-the-Aged Day (3rd Mon in Sep)
Fall Equinox Day (around Sep 23)
Health-Sports Day (2nd Mon in Oct)
Culture Day (Nov 3)
Labor Thanksgiving Day (Nov 23)
Emperor's Birthday (Dec 23)

Braving the icy waters during a purification ritual

TOKYO AREA
BY AREA

Tokyo at a Glance

Japan's capital is situated on the banks of the Sumida River, by Tokyo Bay. As the fishing village of Edo it became the shogunate's center of power in 1590. The Shitamachi (low city) of merchants and artisans served the political and intellectual elite in the Yamanote (high city) on the hills to the west. Renamed Tokyo and made capital in 1868, the city was devastated by the Great Kanto Earthquake of 1923, followed by World War II bombing. It has since reinvented itself as one of the world's most modern, exciting, and energizing cities. Transportation is efficient – the easy-to-use JR Yamanote Line circles the city, subway lines crisscross the center (*see* Back End Paper), and *shinkansen* lines link it with the rest of the country. It can be difficult to find individual buildings by their addresses (*see p171*). The Tokyo Street Finder (*see pp180–89*) locates all the sights, restaurants, and hotels mentioned in this guide.

LOCATOR MAP

West Shinjuku (see pp62–3) *is an area of soaring skyscrapers, providing a visible manifestation of the corporate wealth of Tokyo. The most impressive buildings are the Tokyo Metropolitan Government Offices, designed by Kenzo Tange.*

WESTERN TOKYO
(see pp58–69)

Shibuya (see pp66–7) *is a mixture of large department stores and smaller shops, all catering to young consumers. Adjacent to Shibuya are the equally fashion-oriented areas of Harajuku and Minami-Aoyama.*

East Shinjuku (see pp60–61) *comes alive when West Shinjuku shuts down. It encompasses a red-light area, countless bars, and various forms of entertainment from movies to pachinko parlors.*

◁ A bustling shopping street in Shinjuku

Ueno Park (see pp48–9) *is one of Tokyo's most extensive green spaces, always crowded with locals. Spectacular in the cherry blossom season, it also merits an unhurried visit at other times of the year for its boating ponds and many temples, shrines, and museums.*

Tokyo National Museum (see pp50–53) *consists of four main buildings, dominating the northern reaches of Ueno Park, which exhibit a stunning array of Japanese art, and archaeological artifacts. It is the largest such collection in the world and includes some fascinating items from elsewhere in Asia including China and Korea.*

NORTHERN TOKYO
(see pp46–57)

CENTRAL TOKYO
(see pp36–45)

Senso-ji Temple (see pp56–7) *offers an insight into the traditional side of Tokyo. Still attracting thousands of worshipers daily, it also has many craft shops lining its main approach.*

0 kilometers	2
0 miles	1

Ginza (see pp38–9) *provides the archetypal Tokyo shopping experience, with its venerable department stores and small, exclusive shops, which have been joined by various international designer boutiques. Some excellent restaurants are also located here.*

CENTRAL TOKYO

Situated to the north and west of the Sumida River, this area has been at the heart of Tokyo since the first shogun, Ieyasu, built his castle and capital where the Imperial Palace still stands today. Destroyed by a series of disasters, including the Great Kanto Earthquake of 1923 and the Allied bombing in World War II, the area has reinvented itself several times over. Ginza and Nihonbashi were commercial centers and are still prosperous, offering a mix of department stores and

A kimono-clad woman at Kanda Myojin Shrine

side-street boutiques. The Shiodome skyscraper development is another prominent commercial center. For more down-to-earth shopping, there is the Jimbocho area for books, Akihabara for electronics, and the early-morning Tsukiji Fish Market. Central Tokyo's continuing political importance is evident in the Hibiya and Marunouchi districts, and the area is also home to two very different shrines – Kanda and Yasukuni. A selection of green spaces provides a respite from the bustle elsewhere.

SIGHTS AT A GLANCE

Notable Districts
Akihabara Electronics District ⑰
Ginza see pp38–9 ①
Hibiya District ⑩
Jimbocho Booksellers' District ⑭
Marunouchi District ⑨
Nihonbashi District ⑦

Historic Buildings
Diet Building ⑩
Imperial Palace ⑪
Kabuki-za Theater ②

Shrines
Kanda Myojin Shrine ⑯
Yasukuni Shrine ⑬

Modern Architecture
Shiodome ⑤
Tokyo International Forum ⑨
Tokyo Tower ⑥

Parks and Gardens
Hama Detached Palace Garden ④
Kitanomaru Park ⑫
Koishikawa Korakuen Garden ⑮
Shiba Park ⑥

Market
Tsukiji Fish Market ③

KEY

▦	Street-by-Street map pp38–9
Ⓢ	Subway station
▣	Train station
▣	Long-distance bus station
ⓘ	Tourist information

GETTING THERE

The best ways to get around are by Yamanote Line or subway, or, for smaller distances, on foot. The Yamanote Line stops at Akihabara, Kanda, Tokyo, and Shimbashi stations, while a number of subway lines crisscross the area.

◁ **The Imperial Palace with the landmark Nijubashi bridge in the foreground**

0 kilometers 1
0 miles 0.5

Street-by-Street: Ginza ❶

銀座

When Ieyasu moved his military capital to Edo in 1590, Ginza was all swamp and marshland. Once filled in, the area attracted tradesmen and merchants. The silver mint that provided Ginza's name, "silver place," was built in 1612. In 1872 fire destroyed everything and, with the Meiji Restoration in full swing, the government ordered English architect Thomas Waters to rebuild the area in red brick. From then on it was the focus for Western influences and all things modern, and is still one of Tokyo's prime market centers. Tiny shops selling local crafts mix with galleries, department stores, and the ultra-modern Sony showroom for an unrivaled shopping experience.

Shoppers at the landmark Ginza Yon-chome crossing

Mullion Building, housing Hankyu and Seibu department stores

Hankyu and Seibu department stores focus on fashions, with a mix of Japanese and international labels.

Gallery Center Building

On the second floor of this modern building are a number of exclusive galleries showcasing Japanese and Western art. On the fifth is an auction house, and the sixth has the Youkyo Art Hall, with exhibits by artists working in different media.

HARUMI-DORI

SOTOBORI-DORI

NAMIKI-DORI

MIYUKI-DORI

SUZU

Ginza Noh Theater

Namiki-Dori and Chuo-Dori are now called "Brand Street" with boutiques such as Gucci, Dior, Louis Vuitton, and Cartier.

The Asahi Building contains a traditional kimono shop, silversmiths, and several boutiques.

Sony Showroom

Sony's latest technology and electronic gadgets are on display on several floors here, and many can be tried out.

KEY

- – – Suggested walk route
- ▬▬ Train line

Printemps is a branch of the French department store. Parisian influence came to Ginza in the 1930s and can also be seen in the nearby French cafés and boutiques.

LOCATOR MAP
See Tokyo Street Finder map 5

Wako Department Store
Opposite the San'ai Building, this enduring landmark was originally built in 1894. Its clocktower is a popular symbol of Ginza, and the window displays are always entertaining.

Matsuya department store is another huge store stocking everything from food to bonsai plants. Restaurant City offers a large range of cuisines.

Nihonbashi

DORI

IKI-DORI

CHUO-DORI

Mikimoto
Visit the glittering interior of this shop, the original producer of cultured pearls.

Mitsukoshi Department Store
This classic Tokyo store retains an aura of glamor – some people still dress up to shop here. Do not miss the particularly luxurious kimono department.

Kabuki-za Theater *(see p40)*

Ginza Yon-chome crossing, one of the busiest in the world, is Ginza's main intersection.

San'ai Building
Made of glass, this building is at its best at dusk when the lights and neon signs inside shine through the glass, creating a magical effect.

0 meters   100
0 yards   100

Kabuki actors performing at the Kabuki-za Theater

Kabuki-za Theater ❷

歌舞伎座

Map 5 C3. 4-12-15 Ginza.
Tel (03) 3541-3131. **S** Higashi-
Ginza stn, Toei Asakusa & Hibiya
lines. 🖥 www.shochiku.co.jp/play/
kabukiza/theater/index.html

Tokyo's principal theater for
Kabuki *(see p17)* opened
in 1889 during the reign of
Emperor Meiji – a part of
Kabuki's shift from popular
daytime entertainment for the
Shitamachi masses in Asakusa
to a more highbrow art form.
 The building was one of the
striking examples of the use
of Western building materials
and techniques in traditional
Japanese style. Partially
destroyed by the Allied
bombing of 1945, the theater
was rebuilt in 1951, only to

be demolished completely in
2010. A brand-new structure
is scheduled to open in 2013
(see pp154–5).

Tsukiji Fish Market ❸

築地中央卸売市場

Map 5 C4. **S** Tsukijishijo stn, Toei
Oedo line; Tsukiji stn, Hibiya line.
◯ 5:30am–noon Mon–Sat.

Officially known as Tokyo
Central Wholesale Market, the
world's largest fish market
moved to this location from
Nihonbashi in 1935, after the
1923 Great Kanto earthquake
and its subsequent fires
destroyed the old one.
 Auctions are held daily
(except Sunday), from about
5:30 to 10am. During this
time, 15,000 restaurateurs
and food sellers from all

over the city buy 450 types
of sea produce from about
1,700 stalls. The market itself
resembles a huge hangar
filled with a maze of tiny
stalls, each crammed with
fish. Despite the rush, people
are tolerant of casual visitors.
On the same site is a large
wholesale vegetable market.
 A small bridge marks the
entrance to the market. Just
before the bridge is **Namiyoke
Inari Jinja** (Wave-repelling
Fox Shrine), where fishermen
and traders come to pray for
safety and prosperity. Opposite is a street lined with shops
selling everything from dried
tuna to porcelain dishes. In
the alleys to the right are more
shops and food stalls selling
excellent sushi and tempura.
 When leaving the market,
turn left before the bridge
for a line of shops and small
restaurants. The river wharf,
where boats unload, is over
the bridge to the left.
 The wholesale fish market
is moving to the Toyosu
district in 2013; however,
there are plans to keep a
fish market at this location.

A box of fish from Tsukiji market

Hama Detached Palace Garden ❹

浜離宮庭園

Map 5 B4. **Tel** (03) 3541-0200.
S Shiodome stn, Oedo line.
🚉 Shimbashi stn, Yamanote line.
🚢 Sumida River Trip. ◯ 9am–
5pm. (Last adm 30 mins before
closing.) 🖥

Situated where the Sumida
River empties into Tokyo
Bay, this 62-acre (25-ha)
garden was built in 1654 as a
retreat for the shogun's family
and opened to the public in
1945. Former US President
Ulysses S. Grant stayed in a
villa in the gardens during
his visit in 1879 and sipped
green tea with Emperor Meiji
in Nakajima teahouse.

TUNA FISH SUPPLIES

Tsukiji Fish Market specializes in *maguro* (tuna) from as
far away as New Zealand and the North Atlantic. Japan
consumes about 30 percent of the annual global 1.7 million
ton tuna catch, and eats 80 percent of its tuna raw, as sashimi,
which requires the best cuts of fish. Suppliers can demand
prices of up to 10–20 times that of the lower-grade tuna.

The Pacific Ocean's South
Blue Fin tuna, a favorite for
sashimi, is endangered. The
catch is managed and tuna
numbers currently seem
stable, although reduced
tuna sales may be due to the
recession of the 1990s and the
late 2000s. If the economy in
Japan starts to boom, South
Blue Fin stocks could once
again be put under pressure.

Rows of frozen tuna at Tsukiji
Fish Market

For hotels and restaurants in this region see pp110–12 and pp132–4

The lovely garden grounds surrounding the duck ponds are still a pleasant place to stroll and sit. All of the original teahouses and villas, trees, and vegetation burned down after a bombing raid on November 29, 1944. **Nakajima Teahouse** has been rebuilt, seeming to float over the large pond. Green tea and Japanese sweets are available here.

Nakajima teahouse in Hama Detached Palace Garden

Shiodome ❺

汐留

Map 5 C4, 4 F3. **S** Shiodome stn, Toei Oedo line. **R** Shimbashi stn, Yamanote line, Toei Asakusa line. **R** Shiodome stn, Yurikamome line.

Before industrialization, the ocean-facing parts of Tokyo Bay were famous for their *nori* (seaweed) cultivation. In the late 1980s, waterfront development became Tokyo's new frontier. The **Shiodome City Center** complex, opened in 2003, is one of the more successful of these waterfront developments. Within this grove of ultra-modern sky-scrapers are the impressive, triangular **Shiodome Media Tower**, headquarters of Kyodo News, and **Acty Shiodome**,

the tallest residential building in Japan. Indoor malls and a spacious outdoor piazza provide exciting places to dine or shop. Nearby is **ADMT**, the Advertising Museum of Tokyo, located in the basement of the **Caretta Shiodome**, which has the offices of the world's largest advertising agency – Dentsu. Beyond the northern boundary of Shiodome is the **Nagakin Capsule Tower**, a curious apartment complex based on the manned rocket designs of the 1970s. For greater exploration of the Tokyo Bay area, take the Yurikamome Line from Shiodome Station toward **Rainbow Bridge**, and enjoy great views of the Sumida River and the futuristic island of Odaiba *(see p75)*.

Shiba Park and Tokyo Tower ❻

芝公園と東京タワー

Map 5 A4, 2 F5. **S** Shiba-koen stn, Toei Mita line. **S** Akabanebashi stn, Oedo line. **Tel** (03) 3433-5111. ◯ 9am–10pm daily. 🎫 (extra for higher viewpoint).

Shiba Park is a rather fragment-ed green space. A large part of it is a golf driving range, but a portion in the east is pleasantly landscaped with woods and a water course. The park used to be the Tokugawa family's graveyard and at its center is **Zojo-ji**, the family temple. It was founded in 1393, and Ieyasu moved it here in 1598 to protect his new capital. The

The soaring Tokyo Tower, inspired by the Eiffel Tower in Paris

present-day temple dates from 1974; nearby are the rebuilt Daimon (big gate) and the Sanmon (great gate), built in 1622, the oldest wooden structure in Tokyo.

To the west of the park, on the edge of the Roppongi District *(see pp68–9)*, is the striking **Tokyo Tower**. Completed in 1958, at 1,093 ft (333-m) tall, it is higher than the Eiffel Tower in Paris, on which it is based. The ground floor has an aquarium and elevators to the observation deck. Other floors house amusements. Two viewpoints – the main one at 492 ft (150 m) and a higher one at 820 ft (250 m) – offer spectacular views of Tokyo Bay, the nearby districts of Shimbashi and Ginza, and Mount Fuji on a clear day. As a lofty symbol of the city, Tokyo Tower has been usurp-ed by the 2,080-ft (634-m) Tokyo Sky Tree, in Sumida.

The Shidome skyline from the vantage point of the Sumida River

View of Mitsukoshi's central hall in Nihonbashi

Nihonbashi District ❼

日本橋地区

Map 5 C1–2, 6 D1. **S** *Tokyo stn, Marunouchi line; Nihonbashi stn, Ginza, Tozai & Toei Asakusa lines; Mitsukoshimae stn, Ginza & Hanzomon lines.* **R** *Tokyo stn, many lines.* **Tokyo Stock Exchange** *Tel (03) 3665-1881.* ◯ *9am–4pm Mon–Fri.* **Kite Museum** *Tel (03) 3271-2465.* ◯ *11am–5pm daily.* **Bridgestone Museum of Art** *Tel (03) 3563-0241.* ◯ *10am–7pm Tue–Sat, 10am–5:30pm Sun & public hols.* 🖫

Once the mercantile center of Edo and Meiji Tokyo, Nihonbashi means "Japan's bridge," after the expansive bridge over the Nihonbashi River that marked the start of the five major highways of the Edo period. After the destruction of the 1923 earthquake, shops, businesses, and banks started relocating to Marunouchi and Ginza.

Although the area never regained its original stature, it is still a thriving commercial center, with dozens of bank headquarters as well as huge department stores and smaller traditional shops. **Mitsukoshi** *(see p142)* has its main store here, on Mitsukoshimae. It started as a kimono shop in 1673. Head for the basement food market with its free samples, and the sixth-floor bargain counters where you can jostle with Tokyo's thrifty elite. To the west of the store, the **Bank of Japan**, built in

1896 and modeled on the Neo-Classical Berlin National Bank, was the first Western-style building designed by a Japanese architect, Kingo Tatsuno.

On the north bank of Nihonbashi River, just before **Nihonbashi Bridge**, is the bronze marker from which distances to and from Tokyo are still measured. The bridge here today dates from 1911.

On the south bank of the river, east of the bridge, is the **Tokyo Stock Exchange**, which lists more than 2,000 companies, and is one of the world's top five. This is a great place to see how important commerce remains in Tokyo. The visitors' observation deck overlooks the trading floor and has interesting exhibits comparing stock markets worldwide.

West of the Stock Exchange is the **Kite Museum**, located on the fifth floor of a well-known eatery, Tameikan. The restaurant's former owner, a kite enthusiast, founded the museum which exhibits kites from China and other Asian countries. To the south of Nihonbashi bridge, the **Bridgestone Museum of Art** holds one of Japan's best collections of Western art, including works by Manet, Picasso, Rouault, and Brancusi. To its north, the **Pokemon Center** is a shop devoted to the famous animation characters.

South of the museum, the **National Film Center** *(see p151)* hosts regular screenings of Japanese and foreign films. There are permanent exhibits of film equipment, and other film-related items. Books, film posters, and archival material are easily available in the center's bookstore and public library.

Marunouchi District ❽

丸の内地区

Map 5 B1–2. **S** *Tokyo stn, Marunouchi line.* **R** *Tokyo stn, many lines.* **Tokyo Station Gallery** *Tel (03) 3212-2485.* ◯ *10am–7pm daily.*

This district lies to the south and west of Tokyo Station. During the Edo era, it earned the name "Gambler's Meadow" as its isolation made it an ideal place to gamble secretly. In the Meiji period it was used by the army, who sold it in 1890 to Mitsubishi. The arrival of the railroad increased Marunouchi's appeal as a business site.

Tokyo Station, designed by Kingo Tatsuno and completed in 1914, is a brick building based on the design of Amsterdam station. Its handsome dome was badly damaged in the 1945 air raids and subsequently replaced by the polyhedron here today. It houses the small **Tokyo Station Gallery**.

Facing the station, the striking **Marunouchi Building** is an important local landmark, housing shops, restaurants, and offices. A short walk west of the station over Wadakura Bridge leads to the **Wadakura Fountain Park**, with interesting water features. Returning over the bridge, cross Hibiya-dori and turn right to the **Meiji Seimeikan Building** (1934), with its huge Corinthian columns. Hiroshige, the wood-block print artist, was born on this site in 1797. Beyond, the **Imperial Theater** *(see p181),* founded in 1910, shows Broadway musicals and Japanese popular dramas.

Tokyo Station's Western-style façade

Tokyo International Forum ⑨

東京国際フォーラム

Map 5 B2. **S** *Yurakucho stn, Yurakucho line; Tokyo stn, Marunouchi line.* **R** *Tokyo & Yurakucho stns, many lines.* ◯ *7am–10:30pm daily.*

Designed by New York-based architect Rafael Viñoly, and completed in 1996, the Forum is one of downtown Tokyo's most distinctive buildings *(see p15)*. A cultural center, it is made up of two buildings – a curved, glass atrium soaring 200 ft (60m), and a cube-like, white structure housing four halls (the largest seating 5,012). A tree-shaded courtyard separates the two, while glass walkways provide an overhead link.

The interior of the huge atrium has a ceiling resembling a ship's hull. Inside the Forum are a number of shops, cafés, and restaurants, all with state-of-the-art facilities. The Cultural Information Lobby within the complex offers Internet facilities and has an audio-visual library highlighting Tokyo's attractions.

The airy glass-and-metal interior of Tokyo International Forum

The imposing granite exterior of the Diet Building

Hibiya District and the Diet Building ⑩

日比谷地区と国会議事堂

Map 2 F3, 5 A2, 5 B2. **S** *Kokkai-Gijidomae stn, Chiyoda & Marunouchi lines; Hibiya stn, Toei Mita, Chiyoda & Hibiya lines.* **Hibiya Park** ◯ *24 hrs daily.* **Diet Building** ◯ *9am–5pm Mon–Fri.* 🎟 *(compulsory, by reservation).* **Idemitsu Museum of Arts** *Tel (03) 5777-8600.* ◯ *10am–5pm Tue–Sun (to 7pm Fri).*

Central Tokyo's only large, Western-style park, **Hibiya Park** is the focus of Hibiya district. The park's location, close to political centers, makes it a favorite place for public protests. The large bandstand is also used for concerts. Completed in 1936, the **Diet Building** houses the legislature of the Japanese government, originally established as the Imperial Diet in the Meiji era. Tours (in Japanese only) cover the Diet chamber, where you can see the deliberations of Diet members, and the extravagantly decorated rooms used by the emperor for official functions. Overlooking the Imperial Palace, in the Tei Geki building, the **Idemitsu Museum of Arts** features one of the city's finest displays of Japanese and Asian art.

Imperial Palace ⑪

皇居

Map 3 A5, 3 B5, 5 A1, 5 B1. **S** *Nijubashi stn, Chiyoda line.* **R** *Tokyo stn, many lines.* **Imperial Palace** ◯ *Jan 2, Dec 23.* **East Garden of the Imperial Palace** *Tel (03) 3213-2050.* ◯ *9am–4:30pm Tue–Thu, Sat, Sun (Nov–Feb: to 4pm).*

Ieyasu, the first Tokugawa shogun, started building his castle here in 1590. In the Edo period his successors made this into the world's largest castle; now only the inner circle remains. The emperor and his family still live in the western part of the grounds in the **Imperial Palace**, rebuilt after the previous one was bombed during World War II. Public access is allowed twice a year – at New Year and on the emperor's birthday. The rest of the grounds, bounded by the moat, are divided into public parks.

The most famous landmark is the **Nijubashi**, a double-arched stone bridge, east of the palace. Completed in 1888, it was the palace's main entrance. The huge **Otemon** (Big Hand Gate), rebuilt in 1967, was the main gate before Nijubashi was built. Now it is the entrance to the **East Garden of the Imperial Palace**. Just inside is **Sannomaru Shozokan**, a collection of art and artifacts of the Showa Emperor. Beyond is the Edo-era **Hyakunin Basho**, where 100 samurai lived while standing guard in shifts. Behind is the **Honmaru**, the castle's main keep, now just massive stone walls with good views from the top. To the east of the Honmaru is the **Ninomaru** garden, landscaped by shogun Iemitsu in 1630.

A glimpse of the Imperial Palace over the stone bridge Nijubashi

Tokyoites enjoying an outdoor summer picnic in Kitanomaru Park

Kitanomaru Park ⑫
北の丸公園

Map 3 A5. **S** *Kudanshita stn, Hanzomon, Toei Shinjuku & Tozai lines; Takebashi stn, Tozai line.* **National Museum of Modern Art** *Tel (03) 5777-8600.* ☐ *10am–5pm Tue–Sun.* 🖳 **www**.momat.go.jp/english **Crafts Gallery** *Tel (03) 3211-7781.* ☐ *10am–5pm Tue–Sun.* 🖳 **Science and Technology Museum** *Tel (03) 3212-8544.* ☐ *9:30am–4:50pm daily.* 🖳 **www**.jsf.or.jp/english

Lying to the north of the Imperial Palace, Kitanomaru Park is reached through the massive **Tayasumon** gate. A former ground for the Imperial Palace Guard, the area became a park in 1969. Before entering, walk past with Tayasumon on the left to reach **Chidorigafuchi** (the west moat), one of Tokyo's most beautiful cherry blossom-viewing spots. Row boats can be rented here.

Within Kitanomaru's pleasant grounds are a number of buildings. Near Tayasumon is the **Nippon Budokan** *(see p152).* Built for the 1964 Olympics martial arts competition, it is now used mostly for rock concerts. A short walk farther on is the **Science and Technology Museum**. Some of the interactive exhibits are

fun, including virtual bike rides and electricity demonstrations (all explanations are in Japanese).

Five minutes beyond, over a main road, and left down the hill, is the **National Museum of Modern Art**. The permanent collection comprises Japanese works from the 1868 Meiji Restoration to the present day; visiting exhibits are often excellent. Nearby is the National Museum of Modern Art's **Crafts Gallery**. Inside this 1910 Neo-Gothic brick building is an exquisite collection of modern workings of traditional Japanese crafts – pottery, lacquerware, and damascene (etched metal artifacts). Some pieces are for sale.

Yasukuni Shrine ⑬
靖国神社

Map 2 F1. *Tel (03) 3261-8326.* **S** *Kudanshita stn, Hanzomon, Tozai & Toei Shinjuku lines.* ☐ *24 hours daily.* **www**.yasukuni.or.jp/english **Yushukan** ☐ *9am–5pm daily.* 🖳

The 2.5 million Japanese, soldiers and civilians, who have died in war since the Meiji Restoration are enshrined at Yasukuni Jinja (Shrine of Peace for the Nation), which was dedicated in 1879. Its history makes it a sobering place to visit.

Until the end of World War II, Shinto was the official state religion, and the ashes of all who died in war were brought here regardless of the families' wishes. Unsettling for some of Japan's neighbors, the planners and leaders of World War II and the colonizers of China and Korea are

also enshrined here, including wartime prime minister, Tojo Hideki, and eight other Class-A war criminals. Visits by cabinet ministers are controversial.

Beside the shrine is the **Yushukan**, a museum dedicated to the war dead. Many exhibits put a human face to Japan at war; under a photograph of a smiling young officer is a copy of his last letter home, and there are mementos of a nurse who died from overwork. Romanticized paintings of Japanese soldiers in Manchuria and displays of guns, planes, and even a locomotive from the Thai-Burma Railroad may be disturbing to some.

Jimbocho Booksellers' District ⑭
神保町古本屋街

Map 3 B4–5. **S** *Jimbocho stn, Toei Mita, Hanzomon & Toei Shinjuku lines.*

Three of Japan's prestigious universities, Meiji, Chuo, and Nihon, started out in this area in the 1870s and 1880s, and soon booksellers sprang up selling both new and used books. At one time 50 percent of Japan's publishers were based here. Although only Meiji University is still here, dozens of bookshops, several selling *ukiyo-e* prints, remain, all clustered around the junction of Yasukuni-dori and Hakusan-dori. For books in English on Oriental subjects try **Kitazawa Books** or **Issei-do**; for *ukiyo-e* prints, visit **Oya Shobo** – all are on the south side of Yasukuni-dori, walking away from Hakusan-dori.

The change in the economic status (and priorities) of students is evident here. Shops selling surf- or snowboards are everywhere. Music shops selling electric guitars seem as numerous as the bookshops.

Browsing in one of Jimbocho's bookshops

Tsutenkyo bridge in Koishikawa Korakuen Garden

Koishikawa Korakuen Garden ⑮

小石川後楽園

Map 3 A3–4. **Tel** (03) 3811-3015. **S** Korakuen stn, Marunouchi & Namboku lines. ☐ 9am–5pm daily.

Meaning "garden of pleasure last," Korakuen is one of Tokyo's best traditional stroll gardens, a delightful place to spend a few restful hours. The name Korakuen comes from the Chinese poem "Yueyang Castle" by Fan Zhongyan – "Be the first to take the world's trouble to heart, be the last to enjoy the world's pleasure."

Construction of the garden started in 1629 and finished 30 years later. Once four times its present size of almost 20 acres (8 ha), it belonged to the Mito branch of the Tokugawa family. An exiled Chinese Scholar, Zhu Shun Shui, helped design the garden including the **Engetsukyo** (full-moon) **Bridge**, a stone arch with a reflection resembling a full moon. **Tsukenkyo Bridge** is a copy of a bridge in Kyoto; its vermilion color is a striking contrast to the surrounding deep green forest.

The garden represents larger landscapes in miniature. Rozan, a famous Chinese sightseeing mountain, and Japan's Kiso River are two famous geographic features recreated here. In the middle of the large pond is **Horai Island**, a beautiful composition of stone and pine trees.

Kanda Myojin Shrine ⑯

神田明神

Map 3 C4. **Tel** (03) 3254-0753. **S** Ochanomizu stn, Marunouchi line. ☐ Ochanomizu stn, Chuo & Sobu lines. ☐ 24 hours daily. **Museum** ☐ 10am–4pm Sat, Sun & public hols. ☑ ☑ Kanda Matsuri (Sat & Sun closest to May 15 in alternate, odd numbered years).

Myojin is over 1,200 years old, although the present structure is a reproduction built after the 1923 earthquake. The gate's guardian figures are two beautifully dressed archers – Udaijin on the right and Sadaijin on the left. Just inside the compound on the left is a large stone statue of Daikoku, one of the *shichi-fuku-jin* (seven lucky gods). Here, as always, he is sitting on top of two huge rice bales.

Lions on the gate to Kanda Myojin Shrine

The vermilion shrine itself and its beautiful interior, all lacquer and gold and ornate Chinese-style decoration, are impressive. Early morning is the best time to glimpse the Shinto priests performing rituals. The Kanda Matsuri (*see p28*) is one of the grandest and greatest of Tokyo's festivals – come early and be prepared for crowds.

Behind the main shrine is a **museum** containing relics from the long history of Myojin. There are also several small shrines, hemmed in by the surrounding office blocks.

Akihabara Electronics District ⑰

秋葉原電気店街

Map 3 C4. **S** Akihabara stn, Hibiya line. ☐ Akihabara stn, Yamanote, Chuo & Sobu lines.

Akihabara Electronics District surrounds Akihabara Station. Under the station are tiny shops along narrow aisles selling any electronic device, simple or complex. The market grew out of the ruins of World War II, when the Japanese army had surplus radio equipment it wanted to dispose of on the black market.

Akihabara and electronics have been synonymous ever since. The focus then changed to household electronic goods, and now the emphasis is on computers, cell phones, and video games. On Chuo dori, Laox (*see p142*) is a great source of tax-free goods. **Radio Kaikan**, the site that housed the original radio spare parts dealers, remains with small operators. A redevelopment north and east of the station features flagship stores such as the Akihabara UDX and the Yodobashi Akiba Building.

The **Tokyo Anime Center** is a showcase for the very latest in Tokyo's popular anime culture. Its 3D digital theater holds regular screenings, live concerts, and other anime-related events.

Colorful shop fronts and advertisements in Akihabara district

NORTHERN TOKYO

In festival costume at Senso-ji temple

The northern districts of Ueno and Asakusa contain what remains of Tokyo's old Shitamachi (low city). Once the heart and soul of Edo culture (see p25), Shitamachi became the subject of countless ukiyo-e wood-block prints (see p55). Merchants and artisans thrived here, as did Kabuki theater (see p17) and the Yoshiwara pleasure district near Asakusa. One of the last great battles in Japan took place in Ueno in 1868, when the Emperor Meiji's forces defeated the Tokugawa shogunate. Ueno and Asakusa are the best parts of Tokyo for just strolling and observing. Life in Asakusa still revolves around the bustling Senso-ji temple, its main approach packed with shops. Ueno is dominated by its huge park containing, among others, the National and Shitamachi museums. It is still possible to find pockets of narrow streets lined with tightly packed homes, especially in the Yanaka area, which escaped destruction by war and earthquake. Shopping is a pleasure in Northern Tokyo. As well as the traditional arts and crafts shops near Senso-ji temple, there are specialists in plastic food in Kappabashi-dori, religious goods in neighboring Inaricho, and electronic items at Ameyoko Market.

SIGHTS AT A GLANCE

Temples
Senso-ji Temple pp56–7 ❼

Parks and Gardens
Ueno Park pp48–9 ❶

Notable Districts
Inaricho District and Kappabashi-dori ❺

Museums
Drum Museum ❻
Shitamachi Museum ❸
Tokyo National Museum pp50–53 ❷

Markets
Ameyoko Market ❹

KEY
Ⓢ Subway station
Ⓡ Train station
🛈 Tourist information

GETTING THERE

Ueno Station is on the Yamanote Line; most of the sights in this area can be reached from here on foot. The Ginza subway line links Ueno with the sights of Asakusa to the east.

0 meters   500
0 yards   500

◁ Lanterns hanging on Ueno Park's cherry trees to celebrate the cherry blossom-viewing festival

Ueno Park ①

上野公園

Ieyasu, the first Tokugawa shogun, built the Kanei-ji temple and subtemples here in the 17th century to negate evil spirits that might threaten from the northeast. Judging by how long the Tokugawas lasted, it was a wise move. In 1873, five years after the Battle of Ueno, when the last supporters of the shogun were crushed by imperial forces, the government designated Ueno a public park. A favorite since its earliest days, the park has figured in many popular wood-block prints and short stories. Shinobazu Pond (actually three ponds) is an annual stop for thousands of migrating birds. Several museums and temples are dotted around the park, and Japan's oldest zoo, which is also one of the country's best, is here.

Boating on the Shinobazu pond

The Tokyo Metropolitan Art Museum, in a modern red-brick building, has a large collection of contemporary Japanese art, plus special exhibitions.

Ueno Zoo

★ **Pagoda**
This landmark five-story pagoda dates from the 17th century and is a survivor from the original Kanei-ji temple complex. Today it stands in the grounds of Ueno Zoo, a popular destination for Japanese schoolchildren, among others, thanks to its giant pandas.

★ **Tosho-gu Shrine**
This ornate complex of halls is one of Tokyo's few remaining Edo-era structures. Ieyasu was enshrined here and later reburied at Nikko (see pp98–9).

The Great Buddhist Pagoda was built in 1967. A Buddha statue formerly stood on the site; only its head remains.

Gojo shrine is reached through a series of red *torii* (gates). Inside, red-bibbed Inari fox statues stand in an atmospheric grotto.

Benten Hall

Shinobazu Pond

Shitamachi Museum *(see p54)*

KEY

ℹ️ Tourist information

STAR SIGHTS

★ Pagoda

★ Tosho-gu Shrine

★ Tokyo National Museum

KANEI-JI
TEMPLE

★ **Tokyo National Museum** (*see pp50–53*)

UGUISUDANI
STATION

Rinno-ji
Temple
Imperial
Cemetery

National Science Museum
A steam engine and life-sized blue whale model mark this museum's entrance. Inside are exhibits on natural history, science, and technology.

Baseball
ground

Tokyo
Metropolitan
Festival Hall

The main walkway is lined with hundreds of cherry trees. Boisterous *hanami* (blossom-viewing) parties are held here each spring.

UENO STATION

National Museum of Western Art
Rodin's massive Gate of Hell *stands outside this building by Le Corbusier. On display are various Impressionist works, plus paintings by Rubens, Pollock, and others.*

Japan Art
Academy

Ueno Royal
Museum

The Tomb of the Shogi Tai is a small, leafy area containing two tombstones to the many samurai who died in the 1868 Battle of Ueno.

Saigo Takamori Statue
The leader of the victorious Meiji forces, Saigo subsequently instigated the Satsuma rebellion against the emperor in 1877, but killed himself when it failed. He was posthumously pardoned, and this statue was erected in 1899.

| 0 meters | 100 |
| 0 yards | 100 |

Kiyomizu Hall
Part of the original Kanei-ji temple, this dates from 1631 and is dedicated to Senju (1,000-armed) Kannon. Kosodate Kannon, the bosatsu of conception, is also here, surrounded by numerous offerings of dolls.

Tokyo National Museum ❷

東京国立博物館

The group of buildings that makes up the Tokyo National Museum is in a compound in the northeast corner of Ueno Park; tickets to all buildings are available at the entrance gate. The Honkan is the main building. To its east is the Toyokan *(see p52)*. Temporarily closed, the 1908 Beaux-Arts Hyokeikan is mainly used for special exhibitions. Behind it is the Gallery of Horyu-ji Treasures, containing stunning objects from Horyu-ji temple, near Nara, and the Heiseikan *(see p53)*. More than 110,000 items make up the collection – the best assembly of Japanese art in the world – and the displays change frequently.

**MUSEUM COMPLEX
LOCATOR MAP**

Noh and Kabuki

One of the exquisite kimonos that form part of the textile and mask collection, this dates from the 16th century, when it was used in a Noh play (see p16). *The kimono depicts lilies and court vehicles.*

Heiseikan

First floor

The museum shop in the basement can be reached via twin staircases outside and a central one inside.

This building dates from 1938 and combines Japanese and Western features.

GALLERY OF HORYU-JI TREASURES

When the estates of the Horyu-ji temple complex near Nara were damaged during the Meiji reforms, the impoverished temple gave a number of its exquisite treasures to the imperial family in exchange for money to finance its repairs. Over 300 of those priceless treasures, including rare and early Buddhist statues, masks used for Gigaku dances, and beautifully painted screens, are housed in this gallery designed by architect Yoshio Taniguchi.

Entrance

7th-century gilt-bronze Kannon statue

Steps down to museum shop

Rikishi mask, used for Gigaku dances, 8th century

For hotels and restaurants in this region see pp112–13 and pp134–5

★ Ukiyo-e and Costumes
Popular from the mid-17th through the 19th century, these wood-block prints depicted everything from Kabuki stars to famous landscapes, details of market life to scenes from the pleasure quarters, like this 18th-century print of "Two Beauties."

VISITORS' CHECKLIST

Map 3 C2, 4 D2. **Tel** (03) 3822-1111. S *Ueno stn, Hibiya & Ginza lines.* ⊞ *Ueno stn, many lines; Uguisudani stn, Yamanote line.* ◯ *9:30am–5pm Tue–Sun.* 🖼 ♿ **www**.tnm.go.jp/en

Courtly Art
This collection includes scrolls, wood-block prints, and screens. This 16th-century gold screen is illustrated with a procession of noblemen, a scene from the Tale of Genji *(see p22).*

★ National Treasures
The themed exhibition in the National Treasures room changes about every five weeks. Exhibits may be of calligraphy, Buddhist statues, tea utensils, or even armor, like this 16th-century Muromachi period domaru *armor.*

Second floor

★ Sculpture
This serene, wooden 12th-century sculpture of the Juichimen Kannon Bosatsu (11-faced goddess of mercy) is about 10 ft (3 m) high. Mainly Buddhist, the pieces in the sculpture collection range from miniature to monumental.

KEY TO FLOOR PLAN

- Donations Gallery
- Thematic Exhibition
- Sculpture
- Lacquerware and ceramics
- Swords and Metalwork
- Folk Culture and Historic Materials
- Modern Art
- Japanese and Buddhist Art
- National Treasures
- Courtly and Tea Ceremony Art
- Military Attire
- Interior Furnishings and Painting
- Ukiyo-e Costumes, Noh & Kabuki

GALLERY GUIDE: HONKAN
The collection is on two floors. The second floor is a counterclockwise, chronological arrangement of Japanese art as it developed from Jomon-era (from 10,000 BC) clay figures to 19th-century Ukiyo-e wood-block prints. In between is everything from calligraphy and tea utensils to armor as well as textiles used in Noh and Kabuki. The first floor also works best when viewed counterclockwise. Its rooms are themed, with stunning exhibits of sculpture, lacquerware, swords, and Western-influenced modern art.

STAR COLLECTIONS

- ★ Sculpture
- ★ Ukiyo-e and Costumes
- ★ National Treasures

Tokyo National Museum: Toyokan

The Toyokan (Asian Gallery) has an eclectic collection of non-Japanese Eastern art, including textiles, sculpture, and ceramics. Many exhibits are from China and Korea – a result of their long ties with Japan. The layout of the three floors is in a rough spiral; a well-marked route takes visitors from the sculpture on the first floor up to the Korean collection at the top. The museum is closed for refurbishment until 2013.

★ Korean Art
Dating from the Bronze Age (100 BC–AD 300), this dagger is one of the older pieces on display in the Korean collection.

★ Chinese Ceramics
Ceramics, such as this 8th-century Tang-dynasty camel, feature in the Chinese art section, along with bronzes, scrolls, jade, textiles, and glassware.

Chinese Sculpture
One of a number of beautiful Buddhist statues on the first floor, this 11-faced Avalokitesvara from Xian in China dates from the 11th century.

Entrance

Third floor

Second floor

First floor

Vietnamese Ceramic Bowl
This delicately decorated 15th- to 16th-century bowl is part of the collection of Asian art on the first floor, which also includes fabrics and statuary.

KEY TO FLOOR PLAN

- Chinese and Indian Sculpture
- Egyptian and West, Southeast, and South Asian Art
- Chinese Art and Antiquities
- Korean and Central Asian Art and Antiquities
- Non-exhibition space

STAR EXHIBITS

- ★ Korean Art
- ★ Chinese Ceramics

Indian Sculpture
This 2nd-century figure of a seated Bodhisattva, from Gandhara in Pakistan, is grouped with the Indian sculptures on the first floor.

Tokyo National Museum: Heiseikan

The Heiseikan was purpose-built to house major temporary exhibitions and a superb collection of Japanese archaeological artifacts. Its modern facilities do full justice to the fascinating displays. The first floor houses the Japanese archaeology gallery, with items from 10,000–7,000 BC onward. The temporary exhibitions on the second floor are of mainly – but not only – Japanese art. Captions are in English and Japanese.

★ Haniwa Male Figure
This haniwa *is dressed as a warrior. Other human figures that have survived include singers, dancers, and farmers.*

KEY TO FLOOR PLAN

- Archaeological exhibits
- Temporary exhibitions
- Non-exhibition space

First floor

Second floor

Entrance

Honkan

★ Haniwa Horse
Haniwa (meaning "clay ring") is used to describe earthenware sculptures that were made for 4th- to 7th-century tombs and were thought to protect the dead. Many forms have been found, including horses and other animals.

STAR EXHIBITS

★ Haniwa Sculptures

★ Jomon Figures

Fukabachi Bowl
This large cooking pot is a fine example of Jomon pottery, which is among the oldest in the world. The curved, deep sides allowed the fire to be built up around it, while the flattened base ensured it could be balanced when in the hearth.

★ Jomon Figures
The prehistoric Jomon period (14,500–300BC) produced Japan's first pottery, including dogu. This figurine is one of several female figures characterized by bulging eyes.

Shitamachi Museum ❸

下町風俗資料館

2-1 Ueno-koen, Taito-ku. **Map** 3 C3.
Tel (03) 3823-7451. Ⓢ Ueno stn,
Hibiya & Ginza lines. 🚆 Keisei-Ueno
stn, Keisei line; Ueno stn, many lines.
◯ 9:30am–4:30pm Tue–Sun. 🌐

Dedicated to preserving the
spirit and traditional artifacts
of Shitamachi *(see p47)*, this
hands-on museum is both
fascinating and fun. On the
first floor are re-creations of
Edo-era shops such as a candy
store and a coppersmith's.
Second-floor exhibits include
traditional toys, tools, and
photographs. All the exhibits
were donated by Shitamachi
residents. *Kamishibai* performances (storytelling using
large, hand-painted cards)
take place on weekends. The
nearby **Shitamachi Museum
Annex** (north of Ueno Park)
is in the traditional style of
shop-houses of the mid-Edo
period (late 17th century).

Ameyoko Market ❹

アメ横

Map 3 C3. Ⓢ Ueno stn, Hibiya &
Ginza lines; Ueno-Okachimachi stn,
Oedo line. 🚆 Okachimachi stn,
Yamanote line; Ueno stn, many lines.

One of the great bazaars in
Asia, Ameyoko is a place
where almost anything is
available, at a discount. In Edo
times, this was the place to
come and buy *ame* (candy).
After World War II black-
market goods, such as liquor,
cigarettes, and nylons started
appearing here, and *ame*
acquired its second meaning
as an abbreviation for
American (*yoko* means alley).
An area of tiny shops packed
under the elevated train
tracks, Ameyoko is no longer
a black market, but it is still
the place for bargains on
foreign brands. Clothes and
accessories are concentrated
under the tracks, while food,
notably seafood, lines the
street that follows the tracks.
Tropical fruits and exotic
imports fill the stalls inside
the **Ameyoko Center Building**.

Appetizing colorful beer and food
models on display, Kappabashi-dori

Inaricho District and Kappabashi-dori ❺

稲荷町地区とかっぱ橋通り

Map 4 D3, 4 E2–3. Ⓢ Inaricho &
Tawaramachi stns, Ginza line.

Inaricho District is the Tokyo
headquarters for wholesale
religious goods. Small wooden
boxes to hold Buddhas and
family photos, paper lanterns,
bouquets of brass flowers
(jouka), Shinto household
shrines, and even prayer beads
can be found here. Most of
the shops lie on the south
side of Asakusa-dori, in the
stretch between Inaricho
and Tawaramachi stations.
  Kappabashi-dori, named after
the mythical water imps
(kappa) who supposedly
helped build a bridge *(bashi)*
here, is Tokyo's center for
kitchenware and the source of
the plastic food displayed in
almost every restaurant window.
Although the "food", such as

dessert dishes and palettes
of plastic sushi, is for sale,
prices are much higher than
for the real thing. Connoisseurs hold two Kappabashi
stores, **Maizuru** and **Biken**,
in high esteem.

Drum Museum ❻

太鼓館

Map 4 E3. Ⓢ Tawaramachi stn,
Ginza line. **Tel** (03) 3844-2141.
◯ 9am–6pm Wed–Mon. 🌐

Over 600 drums from across
Japan and the world are on
display at the Drum Museum,
set up by Miyamoto Unosuke
Shoten, manufacturers of
wadaiko, traditional Japanese
drums used in festivals.
  Although none of the text
describing the instruments is
in English, it is not difficult to
identify the Djembe drums
from Mali, Cuicas from Brazil,
Chimes of Chinese origin, or
the complete set of wedding
drums from Benin. A world
map on the wall shows the
provenance of each drum.
  The museum has special
attractions for kids allowing
a hands-on appreciation of
many of the instruments on
display. All the unmarked
drums can be played with the
sticks and mallets provided. A
blue dot warns that a more
delicate handling is required;
a red dot signifies "do not
touch." The museum's first-
floor gift shop sells a good
selection of local handicrafts,
traditional souvenirs, and
even a few drums. Look out
for flyers put up on the walls,
listing forthcoming drum
events around the country.

A worldwide collection of traditional drums, Drum Museum

For hotels and restaurants in this region see pp112–13 and pp134–5

The Floating World of Ukiyo-e

In the Edo period, wood-block prints, called *ukiyo-e*, or pictures of the pleasure-seeking "floating world," became the most popular pictorial art of Japan. They had a profound influence on artists such as Matisse and Van Gogh. Although today they are credited to individual artists, they were in fact a cooperative effort between the publisher, responsible for financing and distributing the work; the artist, who produced a fine line drawing; the carver, who pasted the drawings onto blocks of wood and

Two Kabuki actors by Sharaku

carved away what was not to appear on the print, making one block for each color; and the printer, who inked the wooden blocks and pressed them onto the paper – one for each color, starting with the lightest. Editions were limited to 100–200 copies. The first artist known by name was Moronobu, who died in 1694. The golden age of *ukiyo-e* lasted from about 1790 to the 1850s. Beautiful women, Kabuki actors, scenes from Tokyo, including Shitamachi, and the supernatural were recurring themes.

A full-color *calendar of beautiful women published by Suzuki Harunobu in 1765 marked a transition from the earlier black-and-white techniques. The calendar was a great success and attracted both financiers and artists to the medium.*

Depictions of women *were eroticized by artists such as Kitagawa Utamaro and Torii Kiyonaga, after Harunobu's calendar. This print is by Utamaro.*

Landscape *prints were dominated by Hokusai (1760–1849) and his younger rival Hiroshige (1797–1858). This print is from the latter's* Fifty-Three Stations of the Tokaido.

This 1825 print *by Hokusai shows the carving and printing stages of wood-block print making. Printers relied on vegetable dyes, some of which were very expensive. The red dye* beni, *derived from safflowers, could be worth more than its weight in gold. Some prints required up to a dozen colors.*

Ghosts and goblins *were a favorite theme, especially in summer (to be scared was thought to be cooling). Utagawa Kuniyoshi (whose print is shown here), Taiso Yoshitoshi, and Kobayashi Kiyochika were masters of the genre, which marked the end of* ukiyo-e's *golden age.*

Senso-ji Temple ❼
浅草寺

Stroking the Nade Botokesan Buddha

Popularly known as Asakusa Kannon, this is Tokyo's most sacred and spectacular temple. In AD 628, two fishermen fished a small gold statue of Kannon, the Buddhist goddess of mercy, from the Sumida River. Their master built a shrine to Kannon, then in 645, the holy man Shokai built a temple to her. Its fame, wealth, and size grew until Tokugawa Ieyasu bestowed upon it a large stipend of land. The Yoshiwara pleasure quarter moved nearby in 1657 only increasing its popularity. The temple survived the 1923 earthquake but not World War II bombing. Its main buildings are therefore relatively new, but follow the Edo-era layout. Though the buildings are impressive, it is the people following their daily rituals that make this place so special.

Awashima Hall is dedicated to a deity who looks after women.

The garden of Dembo-in (abbot's residence) is a tranquil stroll garden used as a training center for monks. It is a masterly arrangement of trees, bamboo groves, lawns, and water.

Nade Botokesan Buddha
This delicate statue has been polished smooth by the hands of those hoping for good luck and help with ailments.

Five-Story Pagoda
This replica of the original was constructed in 1973.

★ **Nakamise-dori**
This alley is a treasure trove of traditional wares, including specialists in obi sashes, haircombs, fans, dolls, and kimonos.

Kaminarimon Gate
"Thunder Gate" burned down in 1865 and was not rebuilt until 1960. The guardian statues of Fujin (right) and Raijin (left) have old heads and new bodies.

For more details about individual shops here, see pages 142–5

To Asakusa Station and tourist information office

This hexagonal temple is a rare survivor from the 15th or 16th century.

★ **Main Hall**
Inside the hall (1958) the gold-plated main shrine houses the original Kannon image. Worshipers come to pay their respects by throwing coins and lighting candles.

Yogodo Hall houses eight Buddha statues.

VISITORS' CHECKLIST

Map 4 E2, 4 F2–3.
🛈 by station (03) 3842-5566.
Ⓢ Asakusa stn, Ginza & Toei-Asakusa lines. 🚃 Tobu-Asakusa stn, Tobu-Isesaki line.
Temple ◯ 6am–5pm daily (Oct–Mar: from 6:30am).
Nakamise-dori ◯ 9:30am–7pm daily. 🎏 Sanja Matsuri (3rd Fri–Sun in May), Hagoita-Ichi (Battledore Fair, Dec 17–19).

Asakusa Jinja, built in 1649, is a shrine dedicated to the fishermen who found the Kannon statue.

★ **Main Hall**
Several large paintings hang inside the main hall. The painting of angels with lotus flowers is a 20th-century work by Insho Domoto.

Niten-mon gate was built in 1618 as the entrance to the original Tosho-gu shrine.

Statues donated by a wealthy Edo merchant

Incense Burner
One of the temple's focal points, this incense burner (jokoro) is constantly surrounded by people wafting the smoke over them to keep them healthy.

Benten-yama Shoro belfry stands amid a group of temple buildings. The bell used to ring on the hour in Edo.

Hozo-mon Gate
Built in 1964 of reinforced concrete, this two-story gate has a treasure house upstairs holding a number of 14th-century Chinese sutras.

STAR SIGHTS

★ Nakamise-dori
★ Main Hall

WESTERN TOKYO

Shinjuku and Shibuya, the dual centers of Western Tokyo, three stops apart on the Yamanote Line, started to boom only after the 1923 earthquake. This part of the city is modern Tokyo – all vitality and energy, fast paced, constantly changing, and challenging the more traditional pleasures of Central and Northern Tokyo. Modern architectural landmarks are dotted around, from the Olympic Stadiums of Yoyogi Park to the magnificent twin-towered home for the city government in West Shinjuku. Shibuya, along with neighboring Harajuku and Minami-Aoyama, is the epicenter of both young and haute-couture Japanese fashion. Nightlife is also in diverse and plentiful supply with Roppongi's cosmopolitan clubs, bars, and music venues, and the neon lights and *pachinko* parlors of East Shinjuku. In these overwhelmingly modern surroundings, historical sights are few and far between but include the popular Meiji Shrine and the nearby Sword Museum.

All dressed up in Harajuku

SIGHTS AT A GLANCE

Notable Districts
Akasaka District ⑫
East Shinjuku pp60–61 ①
Harajuku District ⑧
Minami-Aoyama District ⑩
Roppongi District ⑪
Shibuya pp66–7 ⑨
West Shinjuku pp62–3 ②

Shrines
Meiji Shrine ⑥

Museums
Bunka Gakuen Costume Museum ④
Sword Museum ⑤

Stations
Shinjuku Station ③

Parks
Yoyogi Park ⑦

GETTING THERE
Shinjuku, Shibuya, and Harajuku are on the Yamanote Line. The Ginza and Hanzomon subway lines stop in or near Harajuku, Minami-Aoyama, and Akasaka; the Hibiya and Oedo lines serve Roppongi.

KEY

▮	Street-by-Street map pp60–61
▮	Street-by-Street map pp62–3
▮	Street-by-Street map pp66–7
S	Subway station
R	Train station
🚌	Long-distance bus station

0 meters 500

0 yards 500

◁ A selection of entertainment venues, Shinjuku

Street-by-Street: East Shinjuku ❶

東新宿

Façade of a café
in Shinjuku

East Shinjuku is where Tokyo plays. The area has been a nightlife center from Edo times on, when it was the first night stop on the old Tokaido road to Kyoto. Since Shinjuku Station opened in the 19th century, entertainments have been targeted at commuters (mainly men) en route back to the suburbs. Amusements are focused in the tiny bars of Golden Gai and in the red-light district of Kabukicho. Daytime attractions include several art galleries, a tranquil shrine, and some department stores. A late-afternoon stroll as the neon starts to light up both sides of this fascinating, bustling area would be rewarding.

The Koma Theater specializes in Japanese historical melodramas.

Seibu-Shinjuku Station

Movie Houses
This corner of Kabukicho is dominated by cinemas, many showing the latest blockbusters.

← West Shinjuku
(see pp62–3)

Kabukicho
Hostess bars and pachinko parlors (see p67) flourish here alongside cafés and restaurants. In this area of contrasts, prices range from ¥500 for a bowl of noodles to ¥10,000 for a drink.

SAKURA-

YASUKUNI–DORI

Panasonic

ALTA

Studio Alta
Instantly recognizable by its huge TV screen, Studio Alta stands opposite the crossing from Shinjuku Station and is a favorite place for meeting up or just hanging out.

← Shinjuku Station
(see p63)

↓ Yoyogi

Kinokuniya bookstore has one of Tokyo's best selections of foreign books.

KEY

– – – –	Suggested walk route
▬▬▬	Train line

For hotels and restaurants in this region see pp113–16 and pp136–9

Golden Gai

Viewed in the daytime these scruffy alleys look anything but golden. Most of the bars here are just wide enough for a bar, a counter, and a row of stools. Each has a set of regulars – from writers to bikers – and quite a few welcome strangers inside.

LOCATOR MAP
See Tokyo Street Finder Map 1

Hanazono Shrine

Founded in the mid-17th century, this Shinto shrine is a calm and surprising oasis among the concrete towers. In the tree-filled compound are a reconstructed traditional vermilion-and-white building and several Inari fox statues.

0 meters	100
0 yards	100

→ Imperial Palace

KUYAKUSHO-DORI
SHIN-NO-MICHI
YASUKUNI-DORI
MEIJI-DORI
SHINJUKU-DORI

Isetan Department Store

Top Japanese and Western designer boutiques make this stylish store a favorite with Tokyo's affluent young. The food hall in the basement is also worth a visit. On the 8th floor of the Shinkan annex building, the Isetan Art Museum has interesting special exhibitions.

Flags café is a convenient coffee stop opposite Mistsukoshi department store.

West Shinjuku ❷

西新宿

Most of Tokyo's skyscraper office blocks (and some of its most expensive land) are clustered just to the west of Shinjuku Station. About 250,000 people work here each day. Many of the hotels and some office blocks have top-floor restaurants with views of the city. In 1960, the government designated Shinjuku a *fukutoshin* ("secondary heart of the city"); in 1991, when the city government moved into architect Kenzo Tange's massive 48-story Metropolitan Government Offices, many started calling it *shin toshin* (the new capital). Tange's building was dubbed "tax tower" by some, outraged at its US$1 billion cost.

West Shinjuku seen from Tokyo Metropolitan Government Offices

Island Tower

Mitsui Building

Hilton Tokyo

KITA-DORI

GIJIDO-DORI

Sumitomo Building
Inside this block are a shopping center and, at the top, a free observatory.

Dai-Ichi Seimei Building

CHUO-DORI

Century Hyatt Hotel

KOEN -DORI

TOCHO -DORI

FUREAI-DORI

Tokyo Metropolitan Government Offices
This huge complex of two blocks and a semi-circular plaza is unified by the grid-detailing on its façades, recalling both traditional architecture and electronic circuitry. An observatory gives views from Mount Fuji to Tokyo Bay on a clear day.

Shinjuku Central Park

The Washington Hotel has flowing curves (inside and out) and tiny windows in its white façade.

MINAMI-DORI

Keio Plaza Hotel

The NS Building is recognizable by its rainbow-hued elevator shafts. In the 30-story atrium is a 29-m (95-ft) high water-powered clock.

For hotels and restaurants in this region see pp113–16 and pp136–9

LOCATOR MAP
*See Tokyo Street
Finder Map 1*

**Nomura
Building**

**The Yasuda
Kasai Kaijo
Building**, with
its graceful
curving base, is
one of the
area's most
distinctive
buildings.

**Shinjuku
Center Building**

**Shinjuku Station and
East Shinjuku**

**Monolith
Building**
*An imposing
building, as its
name suggests,
this block has a
pleasant courtyard
garden on the
north side.*

**KDD
Building**

0 meters   100

0 yards   100

Shinjuku Station ❸

新宿駅

Map 1 B1–2.

With over two million people
passing through each day,
this is the busiest train station
in the world. As well as being
a major stop on both the JR
and metropolitan subway
systems, Shinjuku Station is
the starting point for trains
and buses into the suburbs.
On the Yamanote and Chuo
line platforms during the
morning rush hour (from
about 7:30 to 9am), staff are
employed to gently but firmly
push those last few commuters onto the train, making
sure the odd body part is not
slammed in the closing doors.

The corridors connecting all
the lines and train networks
are edged with hundreds of
shops and restaurants. It is
easy to lose your way in this
maze of seemingly identical
passages, and it may often be
simpler to find your bearings
at ground level. Look for the
nearest escalator or staircase
up, and then get oriented
once on the street.

Bunka Gakuen
Costume
Museum ❹

文化学園服飾博物館

Map 1 A2. **Tel** (03) 3299-2387.
🚇 *Shinjuku stn, JR, Odakyu, Keio
Shinjuku, Oedo lines.* 🕙 *10am–
4:30pm Mon–Sat.* 🈯

Opened in 1979, the
museum has been
building up its collec-
tion of costumes and
accessories to over
20,000 exhibits that
it holds today.

Clothing and dyed
articles from such
countries and regions
as Africa, the Middle
East, China, and India
are exhibited through-
out the year. Western
attire is represented by
a selection of dresses
typifying fashions of the 18th
to 20th centuries. Among the
permanent items of interest in
the Japanese collection are

modern court dresses, *kosode*
(short-sleeved kimonos), the
lavish costumes worn for
Noh dramas, and bags. The
museum also exhibits the
creations of Japanese haute
couture designers.

**Late 19th-century Western wear,
Bunka Gakuen Costume Museum**

Sword Museum ❺

刀剣博物館

4-25-10 Yoyogi. **Map** 1 A3.
Tel (03) 3379-1386. 🚇 *Sangubashi
stn, Odakyu line.* 🕙 *10am–4:30pm
Tue–Sun.* 🈯

A little out of the way, this
museum is full of fine Japanese swords dating back to
the 12th century. On the
first floor is an interesting
display of the process by
which a sword is produced.

The swords themselves are
exhibited on the second floor,
every detail carefully refined,
even down to the pattern of
burnishing on the blade's
face. There is also a display of
decorated hilts. English explanations trace the history of the
sword, and the processes of
sharpening, handling, and
maintenance. Beautifully
illustrated old Japanese texts
explain the finer points of
sword-making. Among
the ancient samurai
swords are examples
of works by modern
master swordsmiths,
who have kept alive
the tradition of refining
steel from pure iron
sand, painstakingly
manipulating the carbon
content, then hammering,
and cross-welding the steel
for maximum strength.

**Ornate sword
handle**

Minami Shinmon gateway through a wooden *torii*, Meiji Shrine

Meiji Shrine ❻

明治神宮

Map 1 B3. **Tel** (03) 3379-5511.
🚉 Harajuku stn, Yamanote line.
Treasure Museum Annex ⭘
9am–4pm daily (4:30pm Mar–Oct).
Treasure Museum ⭘ 9am–4pm
Sat, Sun, and public hols. 🎫
Meiji-Jingu Gyoen Garden
⭘ daily (times vary). 🎫 🎌 Spring
Festival (May 2–3), Fall Festival
(Nov 1–3). **www**.meijijingu.or.jp

The most important Shinto
shrine in Tokyo, Meiji Jingu
(Imperial shrine) dates from
1920. Emperor Meiji (who
reigned 1868–1912) and his
wife, Empress Shoken, are enshrined here. A focal point for
right-wing militarists during
Japan's colonial expansion
prior to World War II, the
shrine was destroyed by
Allied aerial bombardment in
1945 but rebuilt with private
donations in 1958. During the
New Year holidays it is the
most heavily visited place in
Japan, with over three million
people worshiping here and
buying good-luck charms for
the year ahead.

A wide graveled road
under a huge *torii* (gate)
and shaded by cedars leads
into the shrine grounds. On
the right is an abandoned
entrance to the JR Harajuku
Station. Just beyond is a small
entrance used by the emperor
when he visits by train. Next
on the right is the **Treasure
Museum Annex**. The annex
holds changing exhibitions of
the royal couple's artifacts,
including clothes, lacquerware, and furniture. A left
turn takes you under the

massive **Otorii** (big gate), built
in 1975 of huge logs that came
from a 1,500-year-old Japanese
cypress on Mount Tandai in
Taiwan. A short distance
beyond the gate, on the left, is
the entrance to the **Meiji-jingu
Gyoen Garden**, a favorite of the
Meiji imperial couple. It is said
that Emperor Meiji designed it
himself for his empress. Inside
there is a teahouse over-
looking a pond stocked with
water lilies and carp. To the
right of the pond, a path
leads to the beautiful **Minami-
ike Shobuda** (iris garden),
containing over 150 species.

Past the entrance to the
garden, the road turns to the
right and enters the **main
shrine** area, set in the middle
of a grove of cedars. Another
large wooden *torii* leads to
the Minami Shinmon (outer
gate) through which is a
spacious outer courtyard.
Gracefully curving, the roof
is in the Shinto style of architecture. Through a gateway
to the right is the **Kaguraden**,
a modern hall built for sacred
music and dance.

To reach the **Treasure
Museum**, either return to the
Otorii and turn left, following
the signs, or walk through the
woods to the left of the shrine.
Lining the walls of the single
high-vaulted room of the
Treasure Museum are portraits
of every emperor going back
more than 1,000 years.
Objects on display include the
gorgeous kimonos worn by
Emperor Meiji and Empress
Shoken for court functions.

Yoyogi Park ❼

代々木公園

Map 1 A4, 1 B4. 🚉 Harajuku stn,
Yamanote line.

Kenzo Tange's two **Olympic
Pavilions** (see p15), the landmark structures in Yoyogi
Park, were completed in 1964
for the Tokyo Olympics and
are still used for national
and international sports
competitions. The impressive
curves of the shell-like
structures are achieved by
using steel suspension cables.

For almost three decades
the park filled with a fantastic
array of performers and
bands every Sunday. These
events were stopped by the
authorities in the mid-1990s,
supposedly due to worries
about the rise in criminal
activities. The weekly flea
market on Sundays is worth a
visit. At the entrance to the
park you can see members of
the *zoku* (groups) who used
to perform here, from punks
to hippies and break-dancers.

South of the park, on
Inokashira-dori, **NHK Studio
Park**, run by Japan's leading
broadcaster, offers free tours
of its TV studios.

The main Olympic Stadium in Yoyogi Park

Harajuku District ❽

原宿地区

Map 1 B4, 1 C4. **S** *Meiji-jingumae stn, Chiyoda line.* **R** *Harajuku stn, Yamanote line.* **Ukiyo-e Ota Memorial Museum of Art** **Tel** *(03) 3403-0880.* ☐ *10:30am– 5:30pm Tue–Sun.* ● *27th–end of each month.* 📷

Harajuku Station was the main station for the 1964 Tokyo Olympic village; that concentration of international culture left a great impact on the area, attracting the young and innovative of Tokyo. Today Harajuku remains a fashion center from high-end international stores to bargain boutiques. The neighboring chic and expensive Omote-sando and Minami-Aoyama areas *(see p68)* cater to the more urbane shopper.

Takeshita-dori, a narrow alley between Meiji-dori and Harajuku Station, is the place to find what is hot in teen fashion and culture. Prices range from cheap to outrageous, as do the fashions. Starting from the Harajuku Station end, about 660 ft (200 m) down, a left turn leads up some stairs to **Togo Shrine**, founded for Admiral Togo, the commander who defeated the Russian fleet in the Battle of Tsushima, which took place during the Russo-Japanese War. It was a huge naval victory, the first of an Asian country over a Western one. Admiral Togo remains a hero in Japan, and his shrine has a beautiful garden and pond. A **flea market** is held in the grounds of the shrine on the first, fourth, and fifth Sundays of the month.

Running parallel to, and south of, Takeshita-dori is the more sophisticated **Omotesando**. With its wide, tree-shaded sidewalks and dozens of boutiques showcasing top fashion designers and brands such as Celine, Fendi, and Dior, this

Street performer in Harajuku

is one of the best strolls in Tokyo. More fashion can be found in the **Omotesando Hills** mall complex, designed by renowned architect Tadao Ando. The central atrium is encircled by a spiraling walk-way, which replicates the angle and incline of the outside pavement, creating an effective interior-exterior flow of line and form. Many top brand stores such as Yves Saint Laurent are represented here. The complex's trendy restaurants and cafés provide respite from the intensive shopping experience.

As you walk from Harajuku Station, just before the intersection with Meiji-dori, a small street off to the left leads to the **Ukiyo-e Ota Memorial Museum of Art**, which houses one of the best collections of *ukiyo-e* prints *(see p55)* in Japan. A vivid image of a Kabuki actor portraying an *arogoto* (superhero) by Sharaku and a masterful program of a memorial Kabuki performance by Hiroshige are among many familiar works. There is a small restau-rant and a shop selling prints and other *ukiyo-e* related souvenirs.

Large advertising screens in Harajuku

Just to the left down Meiji-dori is **LaForet**, a fashion mecca, with more than 150 boutiques. Past the pedestrian bridge to the right is the land-mark **Hanae Mori Building**. Designed by Kenzo Tange in 1974, it resembles a stack of glass blocks. Just before it is the **Oriental Bazaar**, many shops full of real and fake antiques and handicrafts *(see p145)*. After checking out the attractions along Omotesando, it is a good idea to walk along the narrow lane that leads off the main street, just before the pedestrian bridge. The lane is lined with a growing number of small stores and boutiques, including those of up-and-coming designers, and extends almost all the way to Shibuya.

A group of teenagers, Harajuku

Street-by-Street: Shibuya 9

渋谷

**Sign for a
pachinko parlor**

Shibuya is the *sakariba* (party town) for Tokyo's youth. It has been so since the 1930s, when façades featured rockets streaking across the sky. Today this is the place to see the latest in fashion, food, music, and gadgets. Shibuya really started to grow after the 1964 Tokyo Olympics, and its continuing expansion has been spurred by the affluent youth of the world's third-biggest economy. The area, which lies to the northwest of Shibuya station and south of Yoyogi Park, is a mix of trendy boutiques, fashionable department stores, and record shops, plus a couple of interesting museums, and the Bunkamura cultural center. Adjoining this area is Dogen-zaka, a jumble of sloping streets and alleyways lined with nightclubs, bars, and love hotels *(see p107)*.

VISITORS' CHECKLIST

S *Shibuya stn, Hanzomon, Ginza & Fukutoshin lines.*
R *Shibuya stn, Yamanote, Tokyu Toyoko, Denentoshi & Keio Inokashira lines.*
Tobacco and Salt Museum
Tel *(03) 3476-2041.*
◯ *10am–5:30pm Tue–Sun.*
● *Tue if Mon is public hol.*
🌐 *www.jti.co.jp/Culture/ museum_e/index.html*

Center Gai
The focus for youth entertainment in Tokyo, Center Gai is lined with shops, pachinko parlors, restaurants, and karaoke bars full of high-school and college-age kids.

Tokyu Hands is a huge store full of housewares and handicrafts.

Bunkamura
A popular site for rock and classical concerts, this cultural center has movies, an art gallery, and a theater.

Dogen-zaka
Named after a bandit who retired here as a monk, this nighttime destination includes old houses, now art galleries.

KEY

- - - Suggested walk route

▬ Train line

This purple clock tower stands in front of the Shibuya Ward Office and is overlooked by Yoyogi Park and the NHK Studios.

The Tobacco and Salt Museum has excellent, well-laid-out exhibits explaining the history of tobacco and salt (both former government monopolies) in Japan.

Yoyogi Park and Olympic stadiums

Harajuku

LOCATOR MAP
See Tokyo Street Finder Map 1

NORTHERN TOKYO

WESTERN TOKYO

CENTRAL TOKYO

K O E N – D O R I

K O E N – D O R I

Tower Records

A popular haunt for music lovers, Tower Records has a good stock of Japanese and international music CDs at reasonable prices.

The Humax Pavilion Building is one of the more fanciful buildings in the area, resembling a cartoon rocket. It houses the Disney Store.

Marui Jam department store is a paradise for clothes – the place for fashionable under 25s.

Statue of Hachiko

A favorite meeting place, this 1934 statue depicts the dog who waited for his master at the station every night for more than a decade after his death. Another popular meeting point nearby is the Statue of Moyai.

Shibuya Station

0 meters 100

0 yards 100

PACHINKO

One of Tokyo's most popular forms of recreation, *pachinko* is similar to pinball, but without the flippers and requiring little skill Players buy some steel balls to feed into the *pachinko* machine, winning more steel balls; these are traded in for a prize (gambling for money is illegal). The prize in turn can be exchanged for money, usually in a small shop nearby. Shibuya and Shinjuku have hundreds of *pachinko* parlors.

A typical *pachinko* machine

The Spiral Building, Minami-Aoyama

Minami-Aoyama District ⑩

南青山地区

Map 1 C4–5, 2 D4–5. **S** *Gaienmae stn, Ginza line.* **Watari Museum of Contemporary Art** *Tel* (03) 3402-3001. ⃝ *11am–7pm Tue–Sun (to 9pm Wed).* 🚫 **Nezu Museum** *Tel* (03) 3400-2536. ⃝ *10am–5pm Tue–Sun.* ⬤ *New Year holidays.* 🚫 **National Children's Castle** *Tel* (03) 3797-5666. ⃝ *12:30–5:30pm Tue–Sun (from 10am Sat, Sun, pub hols, & school vacations).* 🚫 www.kodomono-shiro.or.jp

Favored by artists, writers, and young entrepreneurs, this district lies between the large Aoyama Cemetery and Shibuya. Aoyama-dori, the wide street at its heart, is a center for boutiques and up-scale life. Omotesando crosses it just about in the middle.

On Gaien-Nishi-dori, a fashionable street nicknamed "Killer-dori," is the **Watari Museum of Contemporary Art**. Exhibits are by international and Japanese artists, and change regularly. The bookstore stocks an excellent range of art books.

Back on Omotesando-dori, follow the road southeast away from Omotesando subway station where, on the right, the stunning **Prada Aoyama** fashion store looms into view *(see p14)*. Designed by the dynamic Swiss firm Herzog and de Meuron, the striking building is a six-story chrysalis of diamond-shaped transparent glass that appear to be bubbles, moving as the building is circled. Continue in the same direction to the end of the road, and cross the street for the **Nezu Museum**, which houses Japanese, Chinese, and Korean art and is situated in landscaped gardens containing traditional teahouses. A short walk from here is Kotto-dori, another fashionable street, which is full of antique shops selling scrolls, paintings, and porcelain, among many other items.

This street is one of the hottest in Tokyo, with some notable boutiques, cafés, and shops springing up. Returning to Aoyama-dori, near the Omotesando junction toward Shibuya, the next landmark is the white, geometric **Spiral Building**, which owes its name to the large, spiral ramp inside. Designed by Fumihiko Maki in 1985, and one of the most popular places in Minami-Aoyama, this building is the figurative definition of cool. There is nothing in it that cannot be described as hip and trendy (*torendi* in Japanese), and that includes most of the people seen here. Attractions inside comprise a first-floor exhibition and performance space, the Spiral Hall (on the third floor), also used for exhibitions and performances, an Italian café, a French restaurant, a stationery and housewares boutique, and a beauty salon.

Farther along, the **National Children's Castle** *(see pp10–11)* is marked by a large, moon-faced sculpture by Okamoto Taro. There are many activities for kids here, open to Japanese and non-Japanese speakers alike, including areas for free play with toys, computers, music and art classes, and even a child-friendly hotel.

Roppongi District ⑪

六本木地区

Map 2 E5. **S** *Roppongi stn, Hibiya & Toei-Oedo lines.* **Roppongi Hills** *Tel* (03) 6406-6000. **Mori Art Museum** *Tel* (03) 5777-8600. **National Art Center** *Tel* (03) 6812-9900. **Suntory Museum of Art** *Tel* (03) 3479-8600. ⃝ *10am–6pm Wed–Mon (to 8pm Fri & Sat).*

Roppongi is famed for its hedonistic club scene and is particularly popular with

Nighttime scene in the district of Roppongi

Entrance to the contemporary Mori Art Museum, Roppongi

expats. You can find just about any music you want here – jazz, blues, ska, hip-hop, classic disco, and country-western. This is also the place for big-name international restaurant chains such as the Hard Rock Café, Spago's, and Tony Roma's.

Unveiled in 2003, **Roppongi Hills** aspires to be an all-purpose mini-city. The 54-story Mori Tower forms the focus of the hills. Over 200 shops, restaurants, and bars occupy the complex, which also boasts cinemas, interconnecting walkways, the Grand Hyatt Tokyo *(see p115)*, and the richly imaginative and daring exhibits of the **Mori Art Museum**. Admission to the museum includes access to the **Tokyo City View**, a 52nd-floor observation deck (open later than the museum). *Maman,* the giant, spiny, spider sculpture by Louise Bourgeois outside the main tower, is a major draw.

The **National Art Center** is part of an effort to reinvent Roppongi as something more than just a nightlife zone. The work of renowned architect Kisho Kurokawa, the rippling façade of the building is based on computer-generated rhythmic images inspired by waves and hills. The largest exhibition space in Japan, the art center does not have a permanent collection of its own, but regularly features prominent

Japanese as well as overseas exhibitions. **Almond** (*Amando* in Japanese), at the intersection of Roppongi-dori and Gaien-Higashi-dori, is the main rendezvous spot in Roppongi. The area to the south is where the action is. Clubs come in all shapes and sizes, some just wide enough for a counter and stools. Check the prices of drinks as they vary hugely. West of Almond is the **Square Building**, full of more trendy restaurants and clubs, including the intimate Birdland jazz club.

To the north of Almond lies the complex known as Tokyo Midtown, which houses the **Suntory Museum of Art**. The museum has an unrivaled collection of Edo-era screens, depicting scenes from the Edo court; one particularly fine example is *Namban* (Westerners in Japan). Traditional decorative arts are also well represented here, with ceramics, lacquerware, textiles, and tea utensils. There is also a tea ceremony room, café, and a museum shop.

Akasaka District ⑫

赤坂地区

Ironware kettle in the Suntory Museum of Art

Map 2 E3–4, 2 F3–4. **S** *Akasaka-Mitsuke stn, Ginza & Marunouchi lines; Nagatacho stn, Yurakucho, Namboku & Hanzomon lines.* 🎐 *Sanno Matsuri (Jun 16, Hie Jinja).*

With the Diet Building *(see p43)* and many government offices just to the east,

Akasaka is a favorite place for politicians to socialize. Limousines carry dark-blue-suited men to the many exclusive establishments lining the streets here.

About 656 ft (200 m) along Aoyama-dori from Akasaka Mitsuke Station is the **Toyokawa Inari Shrine** (also called Myogon-ji). With its red lanterns and flags, and dozens of statues of foxes (the messengers of Inari, a Shinto rice deity), this is a pleasant place to linger for a while.

Going back past Akasaka Mitsuke Station and over the moat leads to a large building that some may recognize from the James Bond film *You Only Live Twice*. This is the luxurious **Hotel New Otani** *(see p116)*. On the 17th floor is the revolving Blue Sky restaurant, serving Chinese food and offering stunning views across central Tokyo and the Imperial Palace. In the vast grounds and open to all is a 17th-century Japanese garden.

South of Akasaka-Mitsuke Station is the **Hie Jinja**, a shrine with a history dating back to 830. Shogun Ietsuna moved it here in the 17th century to buffer his castle; the present-day buildings are all modern. Each year in mid-June the Sanno Matsuri is celebrated here with a grand procession of 50 *Mikoshi* (portable shrines) and people in Heian-era costumes *(see pp28–30)*.

A *shinowa* circle, erected for good luck, at Hie Jinja in Akasaka

FARTHER AFIELD

Due to Tokyo's expanding in every conceivable direction, the area around the Imperial Palace is just one among several widely dispersed sights of interest. Seeking them out, though, poses few problems in a city with a superb transport system. The Japan Folk Crafts Museum and the Goto Art Museum are small gems in pleasant surroundings that give an idea of Tokyo life as well as its rich heritage. Ryogoku, home to sumo wrestling, also features the fascinating Edo-Tokyo Museum. The impressive Tomioka

Giant lantern, Gokoku-ji temple

Hachiman-gu shrine in downtown Fukagawa dates from the 17th century. To the northwest, Rikugi-en, near Ikebukuro, is one of the Edo period's last great stroll gardens. The atmospheric Sengaku-ji temple, in the south, reconstructs the final scenes in the story of the 47 *ronin*, a real-life tale of samurai loyalty and revenge. In contrast, Ikebukuro and Ebisu are modern urban centers. Daikanyama, the chic fashion district, and the futuristic man-made island of Odaiba, with its innovative architecture, offer a contemporary experience.

SIGHTS AT A GLANCE

Notable Districts
Daikanyama District ⑫
Downtown Fukagawa ⑧
Ebisu District ⑪
Ikebukuro District ①
Komagome ③
Odaiba ⑨
Ryogoku District ⑦
Shimokitazawa ⑭
Sugamo ②
Zoshigaya ⑥

Temples and Shrines
Gokoku-ji Temple ⑤
Sengaku-ji Temple ⑩

Museums and Galleries
Goto Art Museum ⑮
Japan Folk Crafts Museum ⑬

Scenic Transport Routes
Arakawa Tram Line ④

KEY

	Main sightseeing area
	Expressway
	Main road

0 km　　1.5
0 miles　　1.5

The striking exterior of the Tokyo Metropolitan Theatre, Ikebukuro

Ikebukuro District **1**

池袋地区

S *Ikebukuro stn, Marunouchi, Yurakucho & Fukutoshin lines.*
R *Ikebukuro stn, Yamanote & many other lines.* **Ancient Orient Museum** *Tel (03) 3989-3491.* ☐ *10am–5pm daily.* 🎭 **Tokyo Metropolitan Theatre** *Tel (03) 5391-2111.* 🎭 *for some concerts.*

With the second-busiest train station in Japan (after Shinjuku), Ikebukuro is a designated *fukutoshin* (sub-center) of Tokyo. Devoid of the pretensions of other entertainment districts such as Shinjuku and Shibuya, it is a relaxed place, even when seething with people who are drawn by the area's moderately priced restaurants and bars.

A short walk east of the station lies Ikebukuro's main attraction, **Sunshine City**, a four-block complex whose core building is the iconic **Sunshine 60**, one of Asia's tallest buildings. It is built on top of what was Sugamo Prison, where seven World War II war criminals, including Prime Minister Hideki Tojo, were convicted and hanged. There is a planetarium, aquarium, and 60th-floor observatory here. The often-overlooked **Ancient Orient Museum**, on the 7th floor of

A statue in front of Ikebukuro Station

the Bunka Kaikan Center, is Sunshine City's high-culture component featuring pre-Islamic art from the Middle East and Silk Road. Also located on Sunshine 60-dori, **Toyota Amlux**, a five-floor car showroom with a designer studio and a virtual driving simulator, is worth a look. Over on the west side, visitors can watch craftsmen create ceramic objects, paper, lacquer, knives, and kimonos at the **Japan Traditional Craft Center** (*see p145*). Besides its free art exhibitions on the fifth floor, the nearby **Tokyo Metropolitan Theatre** is famous for its unusually long glass escalator and the world's biggest pipe organ.

Built in 1921, **Jiyu Gakuen Myonichikan** (School of Freedom) is a private school building designed by the famous architect Frank Lloyd Wright in his characteristic geometric style.

Sugamo **2**

巣鴨

S *Sugamo stn, Mita line.*
R *Sugamo stn, Yamanote line.*
Shinsho-ji Temple *Tel (03) 3918-4068.* ☐ *daily.* **Kogan-ji Temple** *Tel (03) 3917-8221.* ☐ *daily.*

Sugamo has two temples of interest. **Shinsho-ji temple**'s courtyard is dominated by a large bronze figure. Worshipped as a protector of children and travelers, it is one of the

six roadside statues cast between 1708 and 1720. Sugamo's best-known temple, **Kogan-ji**, is dedicated to the thorn-removing deity Togenuki Jizo, believed to have curative powers. Street markets outside the temple selling traditional souvenirs and Chinese cures add character to this old quarter.

Komagome **3**

駒込

S *Komagome stn, Namboku line.*
R *Komagome stn, Yamanote line.*
Rikugi-en Garden *Tel (03) 3941-2222.* ☐ *9am–5pm daily.* 🎭
Kyu Furukawa Teien *Tel (03) 3910-0394.* ☐ *9am–5pm daily.*

The celebrated **Rikugi-en Garden** was constructed by Yanagisawa Yoshiyasu, grand chamberlain of the fifth shogun, in seven years, starting in 1695. Yataro Iwasaki, Mitsubishi's founder, oversaw its Meiji-era renovation. The design recreates 88 landscapes in miniature from famous *waka* (31-syllable poems), so the view changes every few steps.

Komagome's other garden of note is the **Kyu Furukawa Teien**. Its main building, a charcoal-grey stone residence designed by British architect Josiah Conder, resembles a small Scottish manor house. The mansion and its English-style rose garden sit on a ridge above steps leading down to a landscaped area, replete with a tea ceremony pavilion and a heart-shaped pond.

Manicured shrubs in the landscaped Rikugi-en garden

For hotels and restaurants in this region see p116 and pp139–41

Minowabashi stop, a terminal of the Toden Arakawa Line

Arakawa Tram Line ❹

荒川都電

S *Edogawabashi stn, Yurakucho line; Otsuka stn, Yamanote line.* **Sumida River trips** (03) 5608-8869.

Back in 1955, 600,000 people a day were riding the dozens of tram lines that crisscrossed the city. Now, the 8-mile (13-km) Arakawa Line is one of only two that remain. The others were eliminated as old-fashioned in the modernization for the 1964 Olympics.

The Arakawa tram line runs from Waseda in the west to Minowabashi in the east and costs ¥160 for each trip, short or long. Near the Waseda end of the line is the quiet stroll garden of **Shin Edogawa**. A short walk from Arakawa Yuenchimae stop is a modest amusement park, **Arakawa Yuen Park**; Sumida River tourboat trips leave from here. Opposite the Arakawa Nanachome stop is **Arakawa Nature Park**.

The line takes in sections of Shinjuku, Toshima, and Arakawa wards, providing easy access to city sights within walking distance of its stations. These include the historically important **Kishimojin** (Pomegranate Temple) in Zoshigaya, and the **Kyu Furukawa Teien** (see p72) in Kita Ward. **Jokan-ji temple**, the last resting place of destitute prostitutes from the old Yoshiwara pleasure quarter, is a short stroll from the line's eastern terminus at Minowabashi.

Gokoku-ji Temple ❺

護国寺

S *Gokoku-ji stn, Yurakucho line.* **Tel** (03) 3941-0764.

Given Gokoku-ji's historical credentials as one of Edo's most important temples, and its survival in the face of earthquakes, fires, and air raids during World War II, the absence of visitors, especially on weekdays, is surprising.

Before entering the spacious grounds of the temple, visitors pass through the arresting **Niomon gate**. The gate takes its name from the statues of two fierce-looking, red-faced Deva kings positioned at either side of the entrance. The statues are meant to ward off malevolent spirits. The right-hand figure's mouth is open, while his compan- ion's is closed. This symbolizes exhalation and inhalation, creation and dissolution; the harmony of opposites encountered in many of Japan's arts.

Seventeenth-century two-story pagoda, Gokoku-ji temple

Stunningly well preserved, the complex's main hall, dating from 1681, with its sweeping copper roof and massive pillars, is a treasure house of Buddhist statuary. Foremost among the deities here are Kannon, the goddess of mercy. Eight celestial

maidens dance across the ceiling in paintings that float over transoms covered with colorful carvings of peonies.

Completing the ensemble of buildings that have been designated Important Cultural Properties are an imposing bell tower and a rare two-tiered pagoda, a popular subject for painters.

Zoshigaya ❻

雑司ヶ谷霊園

S *Higashi-Ikebukuro stn, Yurakucho line.* R *Ikebukuro stn, Yamanote line.*

To the left of Gokoku-ji temple's rear exit at Higashi-Ikebukuro, just beyond the Shuto Expressway underpass, **Zoshigaya Cemetery** is the rest-ing place of several important literary figures, including Japanese novelists such as Soseki Natsume and Kafu Nagai. The Greek-Irish writer Lafcadio Hearn, whose books helped to introduce Japan to the West in the Meiji era, is also buried here. Scenic tree-endowed graveyards such as Zoshigaya can get crowded during the spring cherry-viewing season. Another little-visited spot, the **Zoshigaya Missionary Museum** built in 1907 by an American missionary John Moody McCaleb, is a well-preserved colonial house open to visitors.

Monks praying inside the well-preserved main hall, Gokoku-ji temple

Ryogoku District ❼
両国地区

Map 4 E4–5. **S** *Ryogoku stn, Toei-Oedo line.* **R** *Ryogoku stn, JR Sobu line.* **Sumo Museum** 1-3-28 Yokoami, Sumida-ku. **Tel** *(03) 3622-0366.* ◯ *10am–4:30pm Mon–Fri.* ● *public hols.* **Edo-Tokyo Museum** 1-4-1 Yokoami, Sumida-ku. **Tel** *(03) 3626-9974.* ◯ *9:30am–5:30pm Tue–Sun (7:30pm Sat).* 🎫

Interior of the Fukagawa Edo Museum

On the east bank of the Sumida River, Ryogoku was a great entertainment and commerce center in Edo's Shitamachi. These days it is a quiet place but it still has its most famous residents – sumo wrestlers. Many *beya* (sumo stables) are here, and it is not unusual to see huge young men walking the streets in *yukata* (light cotton kimonos) and *geta* (wooden sandals).

The **National Sumo Stadium** has been here since 1945; the current building dates from 1985. During a tournament *(see p18–19)* many of the wrestlers simply walk from their *beya* just down the street. Inside the stadium is a **Sumo Museum** lined with portraits of all the *yokozuna* (grand champions) dating back to the early 19th century.

Beside the stadium is the huge **Edo-Tokyo Museum**, built to resemble an old style of elevated warehouse. One of Tokyo's most imaginative and interesting museums, it has an exhibition space that is divided into two zones on two floors tracing life in Edo and then Tokyo, as Edo was renamed in 1868. The exhibits, some of

Kabuki actor, Edo-Tokyo Museum

which are interactive, appeal to both adults and children and have explanations in Japanese and English.

The historic route around the museum starts at a traditional arched wooden bridge, a replica of Nihonbashi *(see p42).* There are life-sized reconstructed buildings, including the façade of a Kabuki theater. Marvelous scale-model dioramas, some of which are automated, show everything from the house of a *daimyo* (feudal lord) to a section of Shitamachi. Beside a scale model of Tokyo's first skyscraper is rubble from the 1923 earthquake. There is a rickshaw and Japan's first "light" automobile – a three-seater Subaru with a 360 cc engine. In the media section is a step-by-step example of how *ukiyo-e* wood-block prints *(see p55)* were produced. Models of the boats that once plied the Sumida River give some idea of how important the river was to Edo life. Just up from the

bridge, **Kyu Yasuda Teien**, a tiny Japanese stroll garden replete with traditional stone lanterns, an orange-colored bridge over a carp pond, azalea bushes, and topiary, is located next to the **Earthquake Memorial Park**. The park is dedicated to the victims of the Great Kanto Earthquake, which struck at precisely one minute before noon on September 1, 1923. Today, incense is burnt before the three-story pagoda and memorial hall to mark the catastrophe. The park's Yokami Gallery displays an odd collection of melted metal objects – a broken water pipe, the burnt chassis of a car, and a mass of melted nails.

Downtown Fukagawa ❽
深川

R *Monzen-Nakacho stn, Tozai, Kiyosumi-Shirakawa Oedo & Hanzomon lines.* **Fukagawa Edo Museum** **Tel** *(03) 3630-8625.* ◯ *9:30am–5pm daily.* ● *2nd & 4th Mon.* **Kiyosumi Teien** **Tel** *(03) 3641-5892.* ◯ *9am–5pm daily.*

This area is situated east of the Sumida River and squarely within what was known as Shitamachi, or the "low city" *(see p54).* It took centuries to reclaim the land from Tokyo Bay and the estuary of the Sumida River. To get a good historical grip on the neighborhood, visit the **Fukagawa Edo Museum**. The museum recreates an old area of Fukagawa circa 1840, with 11 original buildings, homes, shops, a theater, a boathouse, a tavern, and a 33-ft (10-m)

Reconstruction of a Kabuki theater in Ryogoku's Edo-Tokyo Museum

For hotels and restaurants in this region see p116 and pp139–41

high fire tower. The interiors of the re-created houses have an authentic atmosphere with fishing nets and workman's clothing casually hung on the walls, and empty shells strewn on the floor of a reproduced clam peddler's home.

Built within the grounds of a large estate in the area of present-day Monzen Nakacho, the **Kiyosumi Teien** is a beautifully landscaped garden in this down-to-earth district of east Tokyo. A wealthy trader, Kinokuniya Bunzaemon, built the large estate and the grounds were later taken over by the Iwasaki family, founders of the Mitsubishi group. The Kiyosumi Teien is a classic Edo-era *kaiyushiki teien*, or "pond walk around garden," with plants that bloom at different times of the year. An exquisite teahouse floats majestically above the water and 55 rare stones, brought from all over Japan by Mitsubishi steamships, are the highlight of this spacious garden.

Nearby, the **Tomioka Hachiman-gu shrine** dates from the 17th century. The current building is a 1968 reconstruction, but its prayer and spirit halls, and towering, copper-tiled roof are very impressive. The shrine is dedicated to eight deities, including the ever-popular Benten, goddess of beauty and the arts. The famed **Flea Market**, the Fukagawa *ennichi*, is another attraction. A lively event, it is held in the shrine grounds on the first two Sundays of the month, from around 8am to sunset.

Crammed balconies of multi-storied apartments

Odaiba �ⓐ

台場

🚉 Yurikamome Line from Shimbashi stn; Rinkai Fukutoshin line to Tokyo Teleport. 🚢 from Hinode Pier 10:10am–7:10pm, every 20–25 mins. **National Museum of Emerging Science and Innovation** *Tel* (03) 3570-9151. 🕐 10am–5pm Wed–Sun. 🏛 **Oedo Onsen Monogatari** *Tel* (03) 5500-1126. 🕐 11am–9am. 🏛

The artificial island of Odaiba across the middle of Tokyo Bay, is both a trendy entertainment zone and an ideal location for cutting edge architecture. Driverless Yurikamome Line trains cross the bay, offering a majestic view of one of the island's most striking constructions, the **Fuji TV Building** *(see p83)*. **Odaiba Marine Park** and its artificial beach lies on the other side of the building. The **Rainbow Bridge** can be seen from the outdoor wooden boulevards, cafés, and eateries of **Decks Tokyo Beach** *(see p83)*.

Statue, Tomioka Hachiman-gu

The futuristic Fuji TV Building with its suspended dome

A short distance from the Telecom Center, the **National Museum of Emerging Science and Innovation (Miraikan)** is dedicated to Japanese high-tech creations. Just across the road from the museum is the **Oedo Onsen Monogatari** (Great Edo Hot-Spring Tales), which combines thermal springs with a historical look at Edo in an attractive theme-park setting. In addition to having a choice of 16 different bathing options, visitors can check out old-style shops and restaurants along the main street and try their hand at traditional games.

Nearby is Tokyo Fashion Town, an enclosed complex of retail shops, boutiques, and cafés. **Palette Town**, a few blocks farther, is home to the giant ferris wheel and the **Mega Web** *(see p82)*, supposedly the world's largest automobile showroom. It also boasts the opulent **Venus Fort** *(see p82)*, a highly original fashion shopping experience. Not far away, the megalithic **Tokyo Big Sight** *(see p82)*, houses a convention center, cafés, and restaurants.

The lively flea market outside Tomioka Hachiman-gu shrine

Sengaku-ji Temple ⑩
泉岳寺

Ⓢ *Sengaku-ji stn, Toei Asakusa line.*
Museum Tel *(03) 3441-5560.*
🕘 *9am–4pm daily.* 📷

This temple is the site of the climax of Japan's favorite tale of loyalty and revenge, retold in the play *Chushingura* and many movies. Lord Asano was sentenced to death by *seppuku* (suicide by disembowelment) for drawing his sword when goaded by Lord Kira. Denied the right to seek revenge, 47 of Asano's samurai, now *ronin* (masterless samurai), plotted in secret. In 1703, they attacked Kira's house and beheaded him, presenting the head to Asano's grave at Sengaku-ji. They in turn were sentenced to *seppuku* and are buried here. Inside the temple gate and up the steps on the right is the well where the samurai washed Kira's head. Farther ahead on the right are the samurai's graves, still tended with flowers. Back at the base of the steps is an interesting **museum** with artifacts from the incident and statues of some of the 47 *ronin*. Overshadowed by the drama, the temple grounds, approached through a small gate with a traditional guard house, merit attention. The temple's original main hall dates from 1612; the current building is a faithful reconstruction. The oldest structure, the Sanmon gate, dates from 1836.

Beer Museum Ebisu, with a Tasting Room for cheap draughts

Ebisu District ⑪
恵比寿地区

Ⓢ *Ebisu stn, Hibiya line.* 🚃 *Ebisu stn, Yamanote line.* **Tokyo Metropolitan Museum of Photography Tel** *(03) 3280-0099.* 🕘 *10am–6pm Tue–Sat (to 8pm Thu & Fri).* 📷 www.syabi.com **Beer Museum Ebisu Tel** *(03) 5423-7255.* 🕘 *11am–7pm Tue–Sun (last adm 1 hr before closing).*

The completion in the mid-1990s of **Ebisu Garden Place**, a commercial and residential center, brought this area to life. The superb **Tokyo Metropolitan Museum of Photography**, to the right of the entrance, has a permanent collection of work by Japanese and foreign photographers, and excellent special exhibitions. In the heart of Ebisu Garden Place are a Mitsukoshi store, boutiques, two cinemas, a theater, and restaurants, including Chateau Restaurant Joël Robuchon, a French restaurant that looks like a 19th-century chateau. The crowded central plaza is a great spot for people-watching. To the left of Mitsukoshi is the small **Beer Museum Ebisu** with exhibits and videos about beer worldwide and in Japan, and free samples.

Daikanyama District ⑫
代官山

🚃 *Daikanyama stn, Tokyu Toyoko line.* **Art Front Gallery Tel** *(03) 3476-4868.* 🕘 *10am–5pm Tue–Sun.* 📷

An important archaeological site, where ancient pit dwellings and well-preserved burial mounds have been discovered, Daikanyama is better known these days as a classy, low-rise neighborhood. It is more popular with the smart set, who come here to explore its trendy boutiques, restaurants, patisseries, and alfresco pavement cafés.

Some big name international fashion brands, such as Jean Paul Gaultier, have outposts here, adding more class and distinction to an already chic district. The area, with its back lanes, shops, and home courtyards full of greenery, makes for a pleasant stroll. Interest in the area first grew when Japanese architect Fumihiki Maki began his ongoing **Hillside Terrace**, an apartment, gallery, and shopping project along leafy Kyu Yamate-dori, in 1969. Buildings

Ebisu Garden Place skyscraper complex, lined with restaurants, shops, and museums

For hotels and restaurants in this region see p116 and pp139–41

Exhibition of flag models by various artists, Japan Folk Crafts Museum

have been added over the decades. The **Art Front Gallery** hosts interesting art exhibitions. Closer to the station **Daikan'yama Address** *(see p147)* and **La Fuente** complexes house boutiques, ritzy restaurants, and trendy cafés.

Japan Folk Crafts Museum 🔵

日本民芸館

4-3-33 Komaba, Meguro-ku. *Tel (03) 3467-4527.* 🚉 *Komaba-Todaimae stn, Keio Inokashira line.* 🕐 *10am–5pm Tue–Sun.* 📷

Known to the Japanese as Mingeikan, this small but excellent museum was founded by art historian Muneyoshi Yanagi. The criteria for inclusion in the museum are that the object should be the work of an anonymous maker, produced for daily use, and representative of the region from which it comes. The museum building, designed by Yanagi and completed in 1931, uses black tiles and white stucco outside.

On display are items ranging from woven baskets to ax sheaths, iron kettles, pottery, and kimonos; together they present a fascinating view of rural life. There are also special themed exhibits, such as 20th-century ceramics or Japanese textiles, and a room dedicated to Korean Yi-dynasty work. A small gift shop sells fine crafts and some books.

Shimokitazawa ⑭

下北沢

🚉 *Shimokitazawa stn, Inokashira & Odakyu lines.* **Honda Theater** *Tel (03) 3468-0030.* 🕐 *daily (times vary according to program).*

The really distinguishing character of this region – more popularly known as Shimokita – is its atmosphere. The seeds of the area's relaxed and well-established bohemian image were sown in the 1960s when a number of small, fringe theaters opened here. Some of these have survived. Underground establishments, such as the famous **Honda Theater**, provide small but convivial spaces for modern, experimental productions.

Back carrier, Japan Folk Crafts Museum

While this youthful, soulful district's north side is a colorful congestion of ethnic restaurants, cafés, fashion boutiques, and music and game stores, the south exit of the station leads to bars and

the best concentrations of live music venues in Tokyo, most hosting an array of eager emerging bands.

This grungy art village, a haphazard mixture of ramshackle, Showa-era buildings, and pop art façades covered in graffiti, is unquestionably one of the city's fashion towns, though it remains light years away from the chic and sophisticated streets of Omotesando or Akasaka. Its numerous shops and stalls offer an eclectic selection.

Goto Art Museum ⑮

五島美術館

3-9-25 Kaminoge, Setagaya-ku. *Tel (03) 3703-0662.* 🚉 *Tokyu Denentoshi line from Shibuya stn to Futako-Tamagawaen, then Tokyu Oimachi line to Kaminoge.* 🕐 *10am–5pm Tue–Sun.* ⬤ *when exhibitions change.* 📷

Set in a pleasant hillside garden, this museum showcases the private collection of the late chairman of the Tokyu Corporation, Keita Goto. Avidly interested in Zen, he was originally attracted to Buddhist calligraphy called *bokuseki*, particularly that of 16th-century priests. Also included are ceramics, paintings, and metalwork mirrors; items are changed several times a year. The museum's most famous works, however, are scenes from 12th-century scrolls of the *Tale of Genji*, painted by Fujiwara Takayoshi, which have been designated National Treasures. They are shown once a year, usually during Golden Week *(see p160)*.

Women in kimonos outside a teahouse at the Goto Art Museum garden

THREE GUIDED WALKS

For all its cosmopolitan sprawl and congestion, Tokyo is a feet-friendly city. Its streets, slopes, temples, shrines, cubbyhole stores, parks and gardens, and architecturally stunning buildings are best experienced on foot. From modern, manmade, sea-facing expanses, and spacious boulevards to the narrow streets of the past, the walks in this book have been designed to maximize time and space by directing you through a concentration of sights, each route presenting different facets of the city's vibrant character. The first walk guides you from the high ground

Bust of missionary Nikolai Kassatkin

of the Yamanote hills, past Shinto and Confucian institutions to the bustling plebian districts of Ochanomizu and Jimbocho. The second walk is a step back in time to the stone courtyards of garden temples, craft shops, and the crumbling tombs of Yanaka, one of the best-preserved older quarters of Tokyo. The final walk introduces useful vantage points from which to take in the monumental scale and novelty of the artificial island of Odaiba. Food and refreshment recommendations are factored into each itinerary as enjoyable stopping-off points.

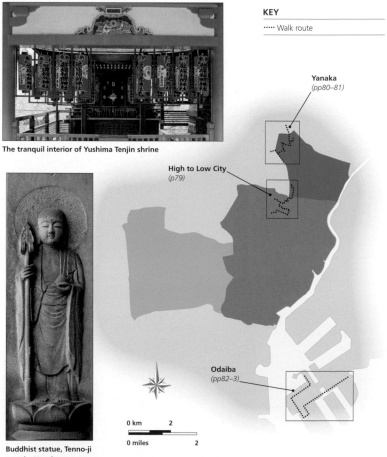

The tranquil interior of Yushima Tenjin shrine

KEY

····· Walk route

Yanaka
(pp80–81)

High to Low City
(p79)

Odaiba
(pp82–3)

0 km　　　2

0 miles　　　2

Buddhist statue, Tenno-ji temple, Yanaka

A 45-Minute Walk from the High to Low City

The walk follows the slopes of the Yamanote, or High City, down to the flat, riverine lands of the Shitamachi, the Low City. Starting from Yushima Tenjin, the great shrine of learning, this route includes Kanda Myojin, one of the foremost places of worship in the city, and a rare Confucian temple sitting on a bluff above the Kanda River. It takes in a Russian Orthodox Cathedral, before ending at the lively streets of Ochanomizu.

The Archeological Museum of Meiji University ⑧

Torii (gate) at the entrance to Kanda Myojin shrine ②

Start at Yushima Tenjin shrine ①, dedicated to a 9th-century scholar deified as Tenjin, the patron of learning. Walk down the gentle slope south of the shrine, crossing Kuramaebashi-dori. A copper-plated *torii* (gate) set at the foot of a slight incline off Hongo-dori announces the entrance to Kanda Myojin shrine ②, the site of the Kanda Matsuri *(see p28)*, one of the city's grandest festivals. Just across the road is the Yushima Seido temple ③, dedicated to the spirit of the Chinese sage Confucius. Shady temple gardens are situated at the base of a bluff above the banks of the Kanda River. Walk down to the river and the stone ramparts of Hijiribashi (The Bridge of the Sages). Pause here to

TIPS FOR WALKERS

Starting point: Yushima Tenjin shrine.
Length: 2.5 km (1.5 miles).
Getting there: The start of this walk is the Yushima metro station on the Chiyoda Line.
Stopping-off points: A tea stop at the entrance to Kanda Myojin shrine; lunch at Kanda Yabu Soba, a local institution.

peer west along the river for a good view of the 19-story Century Tower ⑤, one of Tokyo's impressive office buildings; the twin towers boast innovative air-conditioning strips, and a 19-floor atrium that allows extra light to pour in. Cross the bridge to reach the Russian Orthodox Nikolai Cathedral ⑥, with its deep green onion dome

looming over the Ochanomizu cityscape. It is just a few blocks east from here to Kanda Yabu Soba *(see p132)* ⑦, a legendary buckwheat noodle restaurant just off Shoheibashi-dori. Walk directly west from here to Ochanomizu's main street, Meidai-dori. The Archeological Museum of Meiji University ⑧ appears on the right. It has one of the best collections of ancient objects and artifacts found on digs around Japan. In the same building, check out the university's Criminal Museum ⑨. Casals Hall ⑩ on the left is a smart auditorium designed by world-famous

Japanese architect Arata Isozaki. Turn right at the end of Meidai-dori into Yasukuni-dori and the heart of the famous Kanda-Jimbocho book store district ⑪. The walk ends on this street near Jimbocho subway station.

| 0 meters | 400 |
| 0 yards | 400 |

KEY

••• Walk route

Ⓢ Subway station

🚆 Train station

A 90-Minute Walk in Yanaka

One of the best-preserved old quarters of Tokyo that has survived both the Great Kanto Earthquake of 1923 and the fire bombings of 1945 relatively unscathed, Yanaka is a rare enclave of the old city. Its famous graveyard, with mossy tombs, Buddha stones, and cherry trees, is the resting place of famous literati, actors, and former shoguns. A reclusive retreat for artists, writers, and designers, Yanaka's narrow streets preclude heavy traffic, making it ideal for walking.

The picturesque Kyoji temple housing a wooden hall ④

Start this walk by turning left just after exiting JR Nishi-Nippori Station's south exit. The quiet road here, sitting on a ridge known as the Suwa Plateau, is a good introduction to the old world charms of Yanaka. Follow the sloping road until a row of ginkgo trees and a well-weathered Suwa shrine ① appear on the left. Founded in 1322, the shrine is home to the deity who protects Nippori and Yanaka districts.

Lion sculpture outside Suwa shrine ①

It is just a few steps along to Joko-ji temple ②, known as the "Snow-Viewing Temple." Once a popular spot to watch snowflakes and

TIPS FOR WALKERS

Starting point: Nishi-Nippori station, south exit.
Length: 1.5 miles (2.5 km).
Getting there: Arrive via the JR Yamanote Line train or Chiyoda Line metro.
Stopping-off points: A range of original tea blends at Chaho Kanekichi-en, and Kushiage Hantei, a Japanese restaurant.

compose poetry, it has a rock in the temple garden where the shogun Iemitsu rested while admiring the view. Today only a mass of railway tracks and love hotels can be seen. More interesting are the well-carved stone Buddhas near the temple's entrance, and a bronze figure of Jizo, protector of children, carved in 1691 by a Buddhist priest-artist Kumu-shonin.

Walk past the small road known as Fujimi-zaka or "Fuji-Viewing Slope," a narrow road lined with old red-brick walls. Directly opposite a row of old tenements, the main attraction at Yofuku-ji temple ③ is the Nioman gate. The two guardian statues within the gate were built at the beginning of the 18th century.

Take a left at the end of the road and Kyoji temple ④ comes into view, its zelkova wood gate pitted with bullet holes from an ancient battle. Return to the main road, and continue to the Asakura Choso Museum ⑤, a sculpture gallery dedicated to the work of renowned Japanese sculptor, Fumio Asakura.

Return to the main road, turn left, and continue walking until you see a flight of stone steps descending to a narrow shopping street called the Yanaka Ginza ⑥, selling traditional crafts and foods. Follow the smell of roasting tea to Chaho Kanekichi-en, an old-fashioned teashop near the entrance to the street.

JR Nishi Nippori ⓢ ⓡ

FUJIMI-ZAKA

Return up the stone steps, and continue past Kyoji temple. Turn right up a short flight of steps to enter Yanaka Cemetery ⑦. With its mossy tombstones, leafy walks, wrought iron gates, and worn stone lanterns, Yanaka Cemetery is almost Gothic in character. Head to Tenno-ji temple ⑧, adjoining the cemetery ground. The statue of the Great Buddha of Yanaka, a bronze figure cast in 1691 is the focal point.

Return to the road, bear left and then take the first right, reaching a T-junction at the end. It is easy to miss, but on the right corner, the Gamo residence ⑨ is a fine example

Seventeenth-century bronze statue of Buddha, Tenno-ji temple ⑧

of *dashigeta-zukuri* (projecting girder style) design. Turn left at the T-junction, away from Nishi Nippori Station. Turn right down Sansakizaka and walk to the entrance of Zensho-en temple ⑩. Meditation sessions are held here on Sunday mornings, but the main point of interest is a 20-ft (6-m) high, gold-leaf-covered statue at the rear of the main hall; this is known as the Yanaka Kannon, after the goddess of mercy. Continue down the slope for about 100 meters or so for Daien-ji temple ⑪. Two adjoining halls, one Buddhist and the other Shinto, have fine wooden carvings of dragons, nymphs, and Chinese phoenixes. Across the road from Daien-ji is one of Tokyo's oldest and most exquisite paper arts shops, Isetatsu ⑫. View well-crafted fans, combs, dolls, and colorful chests of drawers. Take the lane next to the shop and walk until you reach a small road. Turn left and then bear right till the T-junction. The Daimyo Clock Museum ⑬ to your right displays a fascinating collection of time-pieces made exclusively for

The ornate exterior of Nezu Shrine ⑭

Japan's feudal lords. Follow the road down to busy Shinobazu-dori. Turn right and walk up to the traffic lights, then turn left for Nezu Shrine ⑭. Enter through the impressive vermilion Zuishin-mon gate, then to a second portal, Karamon gate, with some fine lacquered partitions. You will then reach the main sanctuary, a superb Momo-yama-style structure with vivid carvings. Return to Shinobazu-dori, turn right, and walk a few blocks. Cross Kototoi-dori until you see a unique three-story wooden Meiji-era building that houses the popular Hantei ⑮ *(see p135)*, an atmospheric Japanese-style restaurant. This walk ends near Nezu metro station.

KEY

••• Walk route

S Subway station

R Train station

0 meters 200

0 yards 200

Isetatsu shop, renowned for Edo-style paper with colorful patterns ⑫

A 90-Minute Walk in Odaiba

The post-modernist buildings, art installations, and shopping malls that constitute Odaiba (see p75) seem to hail from another world. Odaiba's sheer audacity, its flamboyant marriage of design, technology, commercialism, and fun, epitomizes Japan's fascination with blending high kitsch into a concoction that is both refined and brashly artificial. In this pleasure quarter for the city savvy, a walk through this island comes with restaurant and café stops to recover from the sheer over-stimulation.

The futuristic Tokyo Big Sight building, an architectural marvel ①

Start the walk at Tokyo Big Sight ①, which is accessed by overhead walkways from Kokusai-Tenjijo Station, or by climbing the steps from the Suijo water bus, Tokyo Big Sight Station. One of Tokyo's prominent architectural marvels, Tokyo Big Sight combines a convention center, exhibition halls, cafés, and restaurants in a pyramidal structure that appears to be upside down. Large atriums and an eighth-floor observation gallery provide superb views of the Tokyo waterfront development and the bay.

Return to the elevated tracks of the Yurikamome Line, following them in the direction of Aomi Station and the Palette Town complex. The gigantic ferris wheel, the Stream of Starlight ②, comes

TIPS FOR WALKERS

Starting point: Kokusai-Tenjijo-Seimon Station on the Yurikamome Line.
Length: 1 mile (2 km).
Stopping-off points:
Recuperate at a table with a view of the goings on at Venus Fort at Thé Chinois Madu. Daiba Little Hong Kong typifies the island's ersatz fun, and the food is good.

into sight on the right. The views from the top are worth the dizzy sensation some passengers may experience as they rise above the picturesque bay. Also in the Palette Town development, Mega Web ③, a state-of-the-art automobile showroom, is run by Toyota. Look out for Toyota City Showcase, with a driving simulator, test-drive area, and a History Garage Museum.

Cross to the next block of Palette Town and enter the unreal world of the Renaissance-themed shopping mall Venus Fort ④, a complex of retail shops and cafés lined with designer boutiques such

The opulent interiors of Venus Fort shopping mall ④

as Jean Paul Gaultier and Vanessa Bruno. Windows have been eliminated for the sake of striking optical illusions, including an artificial overhead sky that permanently re-creates the ambience of twilight. Soak in the scenery, sitting at the authentic Chinese-style teashop, Thé Chinois Madu. Walk to the rear of Palette Town, turn left and move

KEY

• • • Walk route

🚉 Train station

🚉 Monorail

🚢 Riverboat

DAI-SAN DAI
HISTORICAL P.

Daiba

SHIOKAZE
PARK

0 meters   400
0 yards   400

Fune-no
kagakukan

along the Central Promenade, until you reach the 88-ft (27-m) high statue of Flame of Freedom in the form of a golden needle, the work of modern sculptor Marc Coutelier. Turn left here and walk along the West Promenade until the Miraikan ⑤, the National Museum of Emerging Science and Innovation, appears on the right. This museum is dedicated to displays of Japanese high-tech designs, and one of its most popular attractions is the diminutive running robot Asimo. Experimental kits, robots, and interesting space goods are on sale at the gift shop.

Walk from the Miraikan past the Telecom Center to reach Oedo Onsen Monogatari ⑥, a hot-spring theme park that features various kinds of traditional amusements in an old-world atmosphere, in addition to spa facilities. Follow the Yurikamome Line north toward Daiba Station. Ocean-facing Shiokaze Park, a good picnic spot with lots of trees, is on the left. Just beyond the station, the spectacular Fuji TV Building ⑦ (*see p14*)

Rainbow Bridge and the Tokyo skyline ⑪

looms into view. Designed by master Japanese architect Kenzo Tange, the building's two main sections are linked by walkways and a silver sphere containing a restaurant and an observation gallery. Aqua City ⑧, the complex next door, houses countless restaurants, cafés, fashion stores, a video arcade, and a multiplex cinema. Visitors are usually surprised when they glimpse the remarkable replica of New York City's Statue of Liberty ⑨ at the edge of the concourse. Stroll along the outdoor wooden boulevards, cafés, and eateries of Sunset Beach Restaurant Row. This forms the exterior part of Decks Tokyo Beach, a shopping and amusement complex.

The Decks Tokyo Brewery, on the fifth floor, is notable for the Daiba brand micro-beer brewed on the premises. Sega Joyopolis, a virtual reality arcade, occupies the third to fifth floors. Odaiba Marine Park ⑩, a sliver of green abutting a sandy, artificial beach, lies below Decks. Visitors peer over the strip to the graceful lines of the expansive Rainbow Bridge ⑪ (*see p10*), magically illuminated at night. Duck back into the main building of Decks Tokyo Beach. Daiba Little Hong Kong ⑫ up on the sixth and seventh floors consists of several "streets" that simulate a downtown Chinese area. With speakers emitting sounds of feral cats fighting in narrow lanes and the roar of planes descending over washing lines, it is more a romantic throwback to mid-20th-century Hong Kong than the modern skyscraper districts. Chinese dumplings and dim sum at Shi An Gyoza in Little Hong Kong are a treat. The walk ends here. Odaiba Kaihin-koen Station is nearby.

SHUTO EXPRESSWAY NO 11 DAIBA LINE

Kokusai-tenjijo 🚇

🚇 Ariake

ODAIBA KAIHIN PARK

a Seaside Station ⑩

EAST PROMENADE

Odaiba-kaihin-kōen

⑫

SHUTO EXPRESSWAY WANGAN LINE

Kokusai tenjijo seimon 🚇

⑦

🚉 Tokyo-teleport

CENTRAL PROMENADE

③

②

🚆 ①

Tokyo Big Sight Station

④ Aomi

🚆 Palette Town Station

WEST PROMENADE

⑤

🚇 Telecom-center

⑥

The Miraikan, showcasing Japan's high-tech wonders ⑤

BEYOND TOKYO

*S*ome of the country's most famous sights are just a short train *trip away from Tokyo. Foremost among these are the historic temple towns of Nikko, Narita, and Kamakura, and bustling Yokohama, Japan's second-largest city. Hakone is a mountainous hot-spring town and on a clear day, it offers picturesque views of the soaring peak of Mount Fuji – one of the great icons of Japan.*

It takes less time than one would imagine to leave behind the sprawling suburbs, dormitory towns, and industrial fringes of Tokyo to reach breathtaking natural habitats and environs. Fine hiking trails, wildlife, and flora are easily accessed at Chichibu-Tama National Park and the Fuji Five Lakes area, while the volcanic hills and gorges of Hakone and the Izu Peninsula have been hot-spring destinations for foreign visitors since the 19th century.

Yokohama, a cosmopolitan city with a vibrant port area, delightful museums, and a large, atmospheric Chinatown district combines history, ethnicity, and modernity. Yokohama's neighbor Kamakura, sitting snugly between green hills and the Pacific, is a treasurehouse of spectacular Zen temples, tranquil gardens, teahouses, and exquisite craft shops. The origins of the magnificent Tsurugaoka Hachiman-gu shrine date from the 11th century, while the Great Buddha, a splendidly realized bronze statue, has survived from when it was first cast in 1252. To the east of Tokyo, Narita-san, an important temple associated with Fudo, the god of fire, is a place of common worship throughout the year. Located a stone's throw from Narita Airport, this temple provides the chance to see how Japanese observe their faith, right down to having new cars blessed and protective amulets hung on them, in a ritual presided over by robed priests. Just an hour north of the capital, the elaborate shrines, grand gates, and tombs of Nikko, where the first shogun Ieyasu is enshrined, are overshadowed by towering forests of cryptomeria, creating a mood of spiritual grandeur.

A row of Buddhist statues, Nikko, Tochigi prefecture

◁ Snow-capped Mount Fuji with lush green tea fields in the foreground

Exploring Beyond Tokyo

The areas beyond Tokyo offer great geographical and cultural diversity. Bayside Yokohama, a residential zone, sits just above the Miura Peninsula. Ocean-facing Kamakura is an ancient temple city. Narita-san, one of the most important temples in the Kanto area, lies on the flatlands of Chiba beyond the eastern suburbs. The thermally rich and picturesque Izu Peninsula lies to the west. Topographic diversity continues with Hakone and Mount Fuji and the Fuji Five Lakes. At historically rich Nikko, the low slopes of the Ashio-sanchi range span west toward Chichibu-Tama National Park. Nearby Okutama is a favorite weekend hiking area for Tokyoites.

Daibutsu, the Great Buddha of Kamakura

SEE ALSO

• *Where to Stay* p117

• *Where to Eat* p141

SIGHTS AT A GLANCE

Chichibu-Tama National Park ❺	Mount Fuji and the Fuji Five Lakes ❽
Hakone ❻	Narita ❶
Izu Peninsula ❼	Nikko ❿
Kamakura ❹	Shizuoka ❾
Kawagoe ❷	Yokohama ❸

KEY

▬▬	Expressway
▬▬	Major road
▬▬	Main railroad
▬▬	Minor railroad
△	Peak

Kitakata
Fukushima
Iwaki

TOHOKU EXPRESSWAY

🏯🏛🎏🏨 ⑩ NIKKO

Utsunomiya

6

K A N T O

4

Mashiko

Oyama

Mito

Sano
50

122
Koga

17

TOHOKU SHINKANSEN

Tsuchiura

Noda
Saitama
Itako

WAGOE
❷

JOBAN EXPRESSWAY

6

16

HIGASHI KANTO EXPRESSWAY

NARITA LINE

NARITA ❶ 🏯🏛🏨 126

Tokyo
hinji
Chiba

ato
Kawasaki
Togane

🌲🏛🎏 ❸ YOKOHAMA

TATEYAMA EXPRESSWAY

Kimitsu
🎏🏯❹
KAMAKURA

Boso
Peninsula
128

127
Katsuura

cific
cean

Oshima
Island

Tateyama

Landmark modern art steel sculpture
in Minato Mirai 21, Yokohama

0 km   15

0 miles   15

GETTING AROUND

A superb public transport system
provides fast and comfortable access
to these sights. Traffic conditions
make driving less convenient, though
guided tours by coach are an option.
West-bound trains depart from
Shinjuku Station; trains to Nikko run
from Asakusa Station. Other locations
are served by local lines and extended
subways. Hakone, Izu, and the Fuji
areas can be visited as day trips, but
merit an overnight stay.

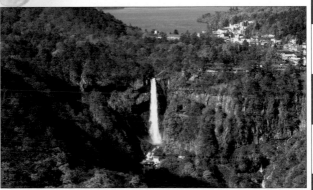

A panoramic view of the Kegon Falls, Nikko National Park

Narita ❶

成田

Chiba prefecture. 🏯 *100,000.*
🚶 🚉 ℹ *in front of JR stn (0476)*
24-3198. **www**.*city.narita.chiba.jp/*
english 🎎 *Setsubun-e (Feb 3).*

A quiet little town, Narita's main attraction is **Narita-san Shinsho-ji**, an Esoteric-Shingon-sect temple founded in 940 and dedicated to Fudo Myo-o, Deity of Immovable Wisdom. Several times daily, the priests burn wooden sticks to symbolize extinguishing of earthly passions. The streets are full of traditional shops for the 12 million temple visitors a year.

Environs
Near Narita are over 1,000 ancient burial mounds (*kofun*); the best are in **Boso Historical Park. The National Museum of Japanese History** offers a good survey of Japan.

🏯 **Boso Historical Park**
15 mins by taxi from Narita stn.
Tel *(0476) 95-3126.* ⬜ *Tue–Sun.*

🏛 **National Museum of Japanese History**
15 mins walk from Sakura stn. **Tel**
(043) 486-0123. ⬜ *Tue–Sun.* 🎫

Kawagoe ❷

川越

Saitama prefecture. 🏯 *322,000.*
🚉 ℹ *at JR stn (049) 222-5556.*
www. *city.kawagoe.saitama.jp*
🎎 *Ashi-odori (Leg-dancing, Apr 14),*
Kawagoe Festival (3rd weekend in Oct).

Nicknamed "Little Edo," Kawagoe preserves the atmosphere of 19th-century Edo (Tokyo) in its *kura*

Yokohama Bay Bridge

buildings. The traditional *kura* structure, with thick clay walls, double doors, and heavy shutters, was used for warehouses and shops.

About 30 *kura* remain, all within a 10-minute walk north of Hon-Kawagoe Station. The **Kura-Zukuri Shiryokan**, formerly a *kura* tobacconist, is now a museum. Nearby, **Toki-no-kane** wooden bell tower was built in 1624 to tell the time and warn of fires. East of the *kura* streets is **Kita-in**, a Tendai-sect temple which includes the only extant rooms from Edo Castle.

At one time, Kawagoe possessed its own castle, which was the dominant structure in the town. Part of that castle remains in the shape of **Honmaru Goten**, the former residence of the feudal lord, which features majestic rooms and elegant reception halls.

🏯 **Kura-Zukuri Shiryokan**
Tel *(049) 225-4287.* ⬜ *Tue–Sun.*
🌑 *4th Fri of month.* 🎫

🏯 **Honmaru Goten**
2-13-1 Kurawa-machi. **Tel** *(049)*
224-6015. ⬜ *9am–5pm Tue–Sun.*

Yokohama ❸

横浜

Kanagawa prefecture. 🏯 *3,690,000.*
🚶 🚉 ℹ *Sangyo Boeki Center Bldg*
(045) 641-4759. **www**.*city.yoko*
hama.jp 🎎 *Chinese New Year (Feb),*
Yokohama Port Festival (May 3).

Japan's second-largest city, Yokohama has been a center for shipping, trade, foreign contact, and modern ideas since the mid-19th century. Formerly a small fishing village on the Tokaido road, it was made a treaty port in 1859; there followed an influx of foreign traders, especially Chinese and British, making it the biggest port in Asia by the early 20th century. The 1923 Kanto Earthquake wiped out 95 percent of the city, killing 40,000 people, then World War II bombing again destroyed half the city. After the war, Yokohama became a base for US soldiers. By the 1970s, it was once again Japan's largest port. The heart of the city is compact and walkable.

Minato Mirai 21, an area of redeveloped docks, has some creative architecture (with high-tech earthquake-proofing) and on weekends comes alive with street performers. Its focal point is the **Landmark Tower**, built in 1993 under US architect Hugh Stubbins and, at 971 ft (296 m), Japan's tallest building. Reached by the world's fastest elevator (at 2,500 ft (750 m) per minute), the 69th-floor public lounge has a spectacular 360-degree view. To the north, Kenzo Tange's **Yokohama Museum**

A row of *kura* buildings in Kawagoe

of Art houses displays of modern art and photography.

In the older, more attractive part of town, the **NYK Maritime Museum** covers the history of shipping, with detailed models. Created on rubble from the 1923 earthquake, **Yamashita Park** is a pleasant promenade overlooking the futuristic Osanbashi Pier; ships, including the restored moored liner **Hikawa Maru**, which cruised between Yokohama and Seattle in 1930–60; and the 2,800-ft (860-m) long **Yokohama Bay Bridge** (1989).

Chinatown, the largest of Japan's three Chinatowns, has around 2,500 Chinese inhabitants, and a mass of restaurants, food shops, Chinese-medicine shops, and fortune-tellers. At its heart is the Chinese **Kantei-byo temple** (1887), dedicated to ancient Chinese hero Kuan-yu, who was worshiped as a god of war but is now popular as a god of business success and prosperity.

Among the many 4,500 tombs in the early 20th-century **Foreigners' Cemetery**

is that of Edmund Morel, the English engineer who helped build Japan's first railroads, with a tombstone shaped like a railroad ticket. The lovely **Sankei-en Garden** belonged to silk-trader Tomitaro Hara (1868–1939). Among the ponds and flowers are 16 architectural treasures, including a three-story pagoda from Kyoto.

> **↑ Landmark Tower**
> *Tel* (045) 222-5015. ☐ *daily.*
>
> **🏛 Yokohama Museum of Art**
> *Tel* (045) 221-0300. ☐ *Fri–Wed.* 📷
>
> **🏛 NYK Maritime Museum**
> *Tel* (045) 221-0280. ☐ *Tue–Sun.* 📷
>
> **Hikawa Maru**
> *Tel* (045) 641-4362. ☐ *daily.* 📷
>
> **⚰ Foreigners' Cemetery**
> *Tel* (045) 622-1311. ☐ *Apr–Nov: Sat, Sun, & public hols.*
>
> **♣ Sankei-en Garden**
> 10 mins by bus from Negishi stn (JR) to Honmoku Sankei-en Mae.
> *Tel* (045) 621-0634. ☐ *daily.* 📷

Environs
Outside the center are two entertaining venues. **Kirin Beer Village**, with tasting tours

of the automated Kirin brewery; and **Shin Yokohama Ramen Museum** *(see p141).* The **Hodogaya Commonwealth Cemetery** (a bus ride from Yokohama, Hodogaya, or Sakuragi-cho stations) contains Allied graves from World War II (including POWs).

> **Kirin Beer Village**
> 🚉 *Namamugi stn, Keihin Kyuko line.*
> *Tel* (045) 503-8250. ☐ *Tue–Sun.*

One of the colorful entrance gates to Yokohama's Chinatown

YOKOHAMA CITY CENTER

Chinatown ⑥
Foreigners' Cemetery ⑨
Hikawa Maru ⑧
Kantei-byo Temple ⑤
Landmark Tower ③
Minato Mirai 21 ①
NYK Maritime Museum ④
Yamashita Park ⑦
Yokohama Museum of Art ②

0 meters 500
0 yards 500

Key to Symbols *see back flap*

Kamakura ❹
鎌倉

An Amida Buddha, Hase-dera temple

A seaside town of temples and wooded hills, Kamakura was Japan's administrative capital from 1185 until 1333. As a legacy, today it has 19 Shinto shrines and 65 Buddhist temples, including two of Japan's oldest Zen monasteries (in Kita Kamakura, *see p92*). Many of the temples and gardens nestle against the hills ringing the town and are linked by three hiking trails. Favored by artists and writers, Kamakura has numerous antique and crafts shops. In cherry-blossom season and on summer weekends it can be swamped by visitors. Some parts are best explored on foot, but there are one-day bus passes and bicycles for rent at Kamakura Station.

The path down the center of Wakamiya-oji, Kamakura's main street

🏯 Hase-dera Temple
🚉 *Hase stn.* ☎ **Tel** *(0467) 22-6300.* ⏰ *daily.* 🌐 www.hasedera.jp
Simple and elegant, Hase-dera is home to a superb 11-faced Kannon, *bodhisattva* of mercy. The Treasure House displays characteristic Muromachi-era carvings of the 33 incarnations of Kannon and a 1421 image of Daikokuten, god of wealth. Beside it is the sutra repository; rotating the sutras is said to earn as much merit as reading them. The 1264 bell is the

town's oldest. Below it is a hall dedicated to Jizo, guardian of children, surrounded by count-less statues to children who have died or been aborted.

🏯 Great Buddha
🚉 *Hase stn.* 🚌 ☎ **Tel** *(0467) 22-0703.* ⏰ *daily.* 🌐
The Great Buddha (Daibutsu) is Kamakura's most famous sight. Cast in 1252, the bronze statue of the Amida Buddha is

44 ft (13.5 m) tall. Having survived tidal waves, fires, earthquakes, and typhoons, it now has shock-absorbers in its base. Its proportions are distorted so that it seems balanced to those in front of it – this use of perspective may show Greek influence (via the Silk Road). The interior is open to visitors.

🏯 Hachimangu Shrine
🚉 *Kamakura stn.* ☎ **Tel** *(0467) 22-0315.* ⏰ *daily.* **Kamakura National Treasure House Museum** ☎ **Tel** *(0467) 22-0753.* ⏰ *Tue–Sun.* 🌐
Hachiman shrines are dedicated to the god of war; this one is also a guardian shrine of the Minamoto (or Genji) clan. Built in 1063 the sea, it was moved here in 1191. The approach runs between two lotus ponds: the Genji Pond has three islands (in Japanese *san* means both three and life) while the Heike Pond, named for a rival clan, has four (*shi* means both four and death). The path leads to the Maiden stage for dances and music. The main shrine above was

SIGHTS AT A GLANCE

The head of the Great Buddha, or *Daibutsu*

YOKOHA
Kita-Kamaku Stati
Toke Tem
Zeni-Arai Benten Shrine ⑤
Sasuke-no Inari Shrine
SHIYAKUSH
Great Buddha Hiking Trail
⑫ **Great Buddha (Daibutsu)**
⑪ **Hase-dera Temple**
Yuigahama Station 🚉
Hase Station 🚉
HIGHW
NATIONAL
Yuigahama Beach
ENOSHIMA

| 0 meters | 500 |
| 0 yards | 500 |

Key to Symbols *see back flap*

The Maiden in front of the main shrine at Hachimangu shrine

reconstructed in 1828 in Edo style. To the east, the **Kamakura National Treasure House Museum** contains a wealth of temple treasures.

🔼 Myohon-Ji Temple
🚉 Kamakura stn. **Tel** (0467) 22-0777. ⬜ daily.
On a hillside of soaring trees, this temple, with its steep, extended roof, is Kamakura's largest of the Nichiren sect. It was established in 1260, in memory of a 1203 massacre.

🔼 Hokoku-ji Temple
🚉 **Tel** (0467) 22-0762. ⬜ daily.
🏞 (for adm to bamboo grove).
The buildings at Hokoku-ji, a Rinzai Zen temple founded in 1334, are modern; its great attraction is its lovely bamboo grove. There is also a pleasant raked gravel and rock garden worth exploring.

fed lake, rocks, and sand; a Zen meditation cave is cut into the cliff. Decorative narcissi also bloom here in January, and Japanese plum trees blossom in February.

🔼 Sugimoto-dera Temple
🚉 **Tel** (0467) 22-3463.
⬜ daily. 🏞
Founded in 734, this is Kamakura's oldest temple and pleasantly informal. The softly thatched hall contains three wooden statues of 11-faced Kannon, protected by ferocious guardian figures at the temple gateway.

🔼 Zuisen-ji Temple
🚉 **Tel** (0467) 22-1191. ⬜ daily. 🏞
This secluded temple is known for its naturalistic garden. Created in 1327 by the monk Muso Soseki, it features a waterfall-

Azalea-lined steps to the thatched hall at Sugimoto-dera temple

Exploring Kita Kamakura

Zen Buddhism came to Japan from China at the end of the 12th century. Its simplicity and accessibility appealed to the ethos of Kamakura samurai warriors as well as to ordinary people. Kita (north) Kamakura, a tranquil area of wooded gullies, includes three of Kamakura's five great Zen temples – Kencho-ji, Engaku-ji, and Jochi-ji (the others are Jomyo-ji and Jufuku-ji). The area is served by its own train station, from which most sights can be reached on foot. Delicate vegetarian food *(see p120)*, which complies with Zen dietary rules, can be tried at Kita Kamakura temples and restaurants.

Statue above Kencho-ji

🏛 Engaku-ji Temple

🚉 *Kita Kamakura stn.* **Tel** *(0467) 22-0478.* ◻ *daily.* 🎫

Deep in trees, the largest of Kamakura's five great Zen temples, Engaku-ji was founded by the Hojo regent Tokimune in 1282. An influential meditation center since the Meiji era, it now runs public courses.

Although much of Engaku-ji was destroyed by the 1923 Kanto Earthquake, 17 of its more than 40 subtemples remain, and careful rebuilding has ensured that it retains its characteristic Zen layout *(see opposite)*. One of its highlights, in Shozoku-in subtemple, is the Shariden. Japan's finest example of Chinese Sung-style Zen architecture, it is open only at New Year but can be seen through a gate at other times. Farther on, the Butsunichian, mausoleum of Engaku-ji's founder, serves *matcha* tea. It was the setting for Kawabata Yasunari's 1949 novel *Senbazuru* (Thousand Cranes).

Stone monuments in the peaceful cemetery at Tokei-ji temple

Bosatsu statue at Kencho-ji

🏛 Tokei-ji Temple

🚉 *Kita Kamakura stn.* **Tel** *(0467) 22-1663.* ◻ *daily.* 🎫

This quiet little temple was set up as a convent in 1285, at a time when only men were allowed to petition for divorce. However, if a woman spent three years here she could divorce her husband. Thus Tokei-ji was nicknamed the "divorce temple." In 1873 the law was changed to allow women to initiate divorce; in 1902 Tokei-ji became a monastery. It is still refuge-like, with gardens stretching back to the wooded hillside.

🏛 Meigetsu-in Temple

🚉 *Kita Kamakura stn.* **Tel** *(0467) 24-3437.* ◻ *daily.* 🎫

Known as the "hydrangea temple," Meigetsu-in is a small Zen temple with attractive gardens. As well as hydrangeas (at their peak in June), there are irises; these bloom in late May, when the rear garden, usually only tantalizingly glimpsed through a round window, is opened to the public.

🏛 Kencho-ji Temple

🚉 *Kita Kamakura stn.* **Tel** *(0467) 22-0981.* ◻ *daily.* 🎫

Kencho-ji is the foremost of Kamakura's five great Zen temples and the oldest Zen training monastery in Japan. Founded in 1253, the temple originally had 7 main buildings and 49 subtemples; many were destroyed in fires, but 10 subtemples remain. Beside the impressive Sanmon gate is the bell, cast in 1255, which has a Zen inscription by the temple's founder. The Buddha Hall contains a Jizo *bodhisattva*, savior of souls of the dead. Behind the hall is the Hatto, where public ceremonies are performed. The Karamon (Chinese gate) leads to the Hojo, used for services. Its rear garden is constructed around a pond supposedly in the shape of the kanji character for heart or mind. To the side of the temple a tree-lined lane leads to subtemples and up steps to Hanso-bo, the temple's shrine.

⛩ Zeni-Arai Benten Shrine

🚉 *Kamakura stn.* **Tel** *(0467) 25-1081.* ◻ *daily.*

This popular shrine is dedicated to Benten, goddess of music, eloquence, and the arts, and one of the "seven lucky gods" of folk religion. Hidden in a niche in the cliffs, it is approached through a small tunnel and a row of *torii* (gates). These lead to a pocket of wafting incense, lucky charms, and a cave spring where visitors wash coins in the hope of doubling their value.

Washing coins at Zeni-Arai Benten shrine

For hotels and restaurants in this region see p117 and p141

The Layout of a Zen Buddhist Temple

Japanese Zen temple layout is typically based on Chinese Sung-dynasty temples. Essentially rectilinear and symmetrical (in contrast to native Japanese asymmetry), Zen temples have the main buildings in a straight line one behind another, on a roughly north-south axis. The main buildings comprise the Sanmon (main gate), Butsuden (Buddha Hall), Hatto lecture hall, sometimes a meditation or study hall, and the abbot's and monks'

Bridge to Jochi-ji temple

quarters. In practice, subtemples often crowd around the main buildings and may obscure the basic layout. The temple compound is entered by a bridge over a pond or stream, symbolically crossing from the earthly world to that of the Buddha. Buildings are natural looking, often of unpainted wood, conducive to emptying the mind of worldly illusions, to facilitate enlightenment. The example below is based on Engaku-ji.

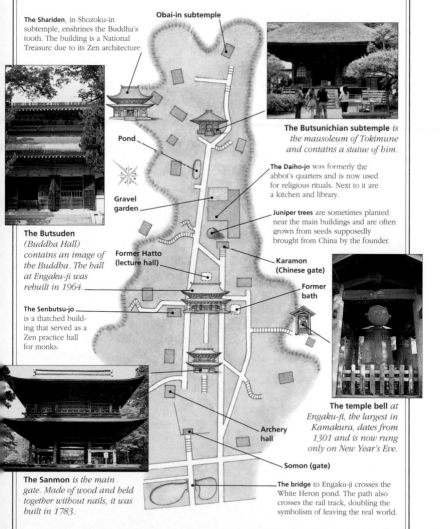

The Shariden, in Shozoku-in subtemple, enshrines the Buddha's tooth. The building is a National Treasure due to its Zen architecture

Obai-in subtemple

Pond

Gravel garden

The Butsunichian subtemple *is the mausoleum of Tokimune and contains a statue of him.*

The Daiho-jo was formerly the abbot's quarters and is now used for religious rituals. Next to it are a kitchen and library.

Juniper trees are sometimes planted near the main buildings and are often grown from seeds supposedly brought from China by the founder.

The Butsuden *(Buddha Hall) contains an image of the Buddha. The hall at Engaku-ji was rebuilt in 1964.*

Former Hatto (lecture hall)

Karamon (Chinese gate)

Former bath

The Senbutsu-jo is a thatched building that served as a Zen practice hall for monks.

The temple bell *at Engaku-ji, the largest in Kamakura, dates from 1301 and is now rung only on New Year's Eve.*

Archery hall

Somon (gate)

The Sanmon *is the main gate. Made of wood and held together without nails, it was built in 1783.*

The bridge to Engaku-ji crosses the White Heron pond. The path also crosses the rail track, doubling the symbolism of leaving the real world.

Chichibu-Tama National Park ❺

秩父多摩国立公園

Tokyo, Saitama, Nagano, and Yamanashi prefectures. 🚶 71,500 (Chichibu city). 🚆 Seibu-Chichibu stn, Seibu-Chichibu line; Chichibu stn, Chichibu line; Okutama or Mitake stns, JR line. 🛈 Chichibu stn (0494) 25-3192. 🎏 Yo Matsuri (Dec 2–3, Chichibu city). **www**.env.go.jp/en/ nature/nps/park/parks/chichibu.html

This remote area of low mountains, rich in traditions and wildlife, stretches from the narrow valleys of Okutama in the south to the basin around Chichibu city in the north. The two parts of the park are separated by mountains, crossed only by a few hiking trails, and are reached by two separate rail networks. Within the park, travel is mostly by bus.

Chichibu was a prime silk-producing region until the early 20th century. Today it is known for its vibrant festivals and its pilgrim route linking 33 Kannon temples. To the north, at **Nagatoro**, the Arakawa River runs past rare crystalline schist rock formations.

In the Okutama area, **Mount Mitake** has good hiking, and an attractive mountaintop shrine village, easily reached by a funicular. Stalactite caves at **Nippara** are worth visiting.

⛰ Nippara Caves
NW of Okutama.
Tel (0428) 83-8491. ⬚ daily. 📷

YOSEGI-ZAIKU MARQUETRY

Originating in the 9th century, this type of marquetry has been a Hakone specialty since the 19th century; today there are about 100 practitioners in the area. Although it looks like inlaid mosaic, *yosegi-zaiku* uses a very different technique.

Craftsman making a *yosegi-zaiku* box

Strips are cut from planks of up to 40 varieties of undyed woods and glued together to form patterned blocks. These are in turn glued into larger blocks, which are then either shaped with a lathe into bowls and boxes, or shaved into cross-sectional sheets, used to coat items such as boxes and purses. The paper-thin sheets are flexible and can be laminated. Some of the most popular creations are "magic" boxes, opened in a sequence of moves to reveal a hidden drawer.

Environs
South of Chichibu-Tama lies **Mount Takao**, (on the Keio train line to Takaosan-guchi). Its slopes have pleasant walks with sweeping views of Tokyo and Mount Fuji.

Hakone ❻

箱根

Kanagawa prefecture. 🚶 14,000. 🚆🛈 698 Yumoto, Hakone (0460) 85-8911. **www**.hakone.or.jp/ english/index.html 🎏 Toriiyaki (Aug 5, Lake Ashi), Daimyo Gyoretsu (Nov 3, Hakone-Yumoto).

Hakone is a hilly hot-spring town whose scattered attractions are both cultural and natural. Popular as a resort since the 9th century, it can be very crowded. The Hakone area extends across the collapsed remains of a huge volcano, which was active until 3,000 to 4,000 years ago, leaving a legacy today of hot springs and steam vents.

Although Hakone can be visited as a long day trip from Tokyo, it is worth an overnight stay. Two- or three-day public transportation passes are available on the Odakyu Line from Shinjuku, Tokyo. A convenient circuit of the main sights starts from the *onsen* (hot spring) town of **Hakone-Yumoto**, taking the Tozan switchback train up the hillside to **Hakone Open-Air Museum**, with its modern sculptures. Continue via funicular to **Hakone Art Museum**, which has an excellent Japanese ceramic collection and garden. Via the funicular and

Crossing the rocky scree and steaming vents of Owaku-dani valley in Hakone

For hotels and restaurants in this region see p117 and p141

A statue of *The Izu Dancer* by a waterfall near Kawazu, Izu Peninsula

then a ropeway over the crest of the hill is the **Owaku-dani** ("valley of great boiling"), an area of sulfurous steam vents.

The ropeway continues to **Lake Ashi**, where replicas of historical Western-style boats run to **Hakone-machi** and **Moto-Hakone**. In clear weather there are breathtaking views of Mount Fuji. At Hakone-machi is an interesting reconstruction of the **Seki-sho Barrier Gate**, a historic checkpoint that used to control the passage of

Yosegi-zaiku box, Hatajuku

people and guns on the Edo-period Tokaido road between Edo (Tokyo) and Kyoto.

From Hakone-machi it is a short walk to Moto-Hakone. In a prominent position on a hilltop overlooking Lake Ashi, **Narukawa Art Museum** exhibits 1,500 artworks by modern Japanese masters, and has spectacular views of the surrounding mountains. Over a pass beyond Moto-Hakone is the **Amazake-chaya** teahouse, and **Hatajuku** village, known for *yosegi-zaiku*, a form of decorative marquetry.

🏛 **Hakone Open-Air Museum**
Tel (0460) 82-1161. ◯ daily. 📷
🏛 **Hakone Art Museum**
Tel (0460) 82-2623. ◯ Fri–Wed. 📷
🏯 **Seki-sho Barrier Gate**
Tel (0460) 83-6635. ◯ daily. 📷
🏛 **Narukawa Art Museum**
Tel (0460) 83-6288. ◯ daily. 📷

Izu Peninsula ❼
伊豆半島

Shizuoka prefecture. 🚆 🛈 *Atami, Ito, and Shuzenji stns.* 🎎 *Daimonji Burning (Jul 22–3, Atagawa), Anjin Festival (Aug 8–10, Ito).*

A picturesque, hilly peninsula with a benign climate, Izu is popular for its numerous hot springs. A place of exile in the Middle Ages, in the early 17th century it was home to the shipwrecked Englishman William Adams, whose story was the basis of the James Clavell novel *Shogun*. **Shimoda**, on the southern tip, became a coaling station for foreign ships in 1854, then opened to US traders. Today Shimoda has little of interest besides pretty gray-and-white walls, reinforced against typhoons with crisscross plasterwork.

Izu's east coast is quite developed, but the west has charming coves and fishing villages, such as **Toi** and **Heda**, offering delicious long-legged crabs and other seafood. The center is also relatively unspoiled, with wooded mountains and rustic hot springs, including **Shuzenji** *onsen* and a chain of villages from **Amagi Yugashima** to **Kawazu**. These latter were the setting for Yasunari Kawabata's short story *The Izu Dancer*, commemorated across Izu. Two-day transportation passes cover parts of the peninsula.

Mount Fuji and the Fuji Five Lakes ❽

See pp96–7.

Shizuoka ❾
静岡

Shizuoka & Yamanashi prefecture. 🏠 713,000. 🚆 🛈 *in JR stn (054) 252-4247.* www.pref.shizuoka.jp 🎎 *Shizuoka Festival (1st w/e Apr).*

Settlement in this area stretches back to AD 200–300. Later a stop on the old Tokaido road, and the retirement home of Tokugawa Ieyasu *(see p101)*, Shizuoka is today a sprawling urban center, the city at greatest risk of a major earthquake in Japan. As a result it is probably the only place that is fully prepared.

The **Toro Ruins** near the port have well-explained reconstructions of ancient buildings and an excellent interactive **museum**. The view from **Nihondaira** plateau, in the east of the city, to Mount Fuji and Izu, is superb. Nearby is **Kunozan Tosho-gu**, one of the three top Tosho-gu shrines.

🏛 **Toro Ruins**
Museum *Tel* (0542) 85-0476. ◯ Tue–Sun. ● last day of month. 📷

Environs

West of Shizuoka, **Kanaya** has one of Japan's largest tea plantations. Fields and processing plants can be visited, and the elegant **Ocha no Sato** museum portrays tea lore. Nearby, the **Oigawa steam railroad** takes you right into the untamed South Alps.

🏛 **Ocha no Sato**
Tel (0547) 46-5588. ◯ daily. ● Tue. 📷

A reconstructed dwelling at the Toro site, Shizuoka

Mount Fuji and the Fuji Five Lakes ❽

富士山と富士五湖

Decorative drain cover in Fuji-Yoshida

At 12,390 ft (3,776 m), Mount Fuji is Japan's highest peak by far, its near-perfect cone floating lilac gray or snow-capped above hilltops and low cloud. Dormant since 1707, the volcano first erupted 8–10,000 years ago. Its upper slopes are loose volcanic ash, devoid of greenery or streams. Before the 20th century, Mount Fuji was considered so sacred that it was climbed only by priests and pilgrims; women were not allowed until 1872. Today pilgrims are greatly out numbered by recreational climbers. The Fuji Five Lakes area, at the foot of the mountain, is a playground for Tokyoites, with sports facilities and amusement parks.

Lake Sai
This is the least spoiled of the Fuji Five Lakes and offers beautiful views of Mount Fuji.

Lake Kawaguchi is the most accessible and commercialized lake.

KEY

🚉	Train station
🚏	Bus stop
ℹ️	Tourist information
⛩️	Shrine
▬▬	Expressway
══	Other road
‑‑	Trail

Lake Motosu is the deepest lake, reaching a depth of 460 ft (140 m).

Lake Shojin is the smallest lake, and good for fishing.

Kawaguchi-ko

LAKE KAWAGUCHI

LAKE SAI

LAKE SHOJIN

LAKE MOTOSU

139

Fugaku Wind Cave

Narusawa Ice Cave

Sea of Trees

The Sea of Trees (Aokigahara Jukai) is a primeval forest famed for being easy to get lost in.

Kawaguchi-ko trail is 5–6 hours up from the 5th stage, and 3 hours down. Another trail, the Yoshida, shares most of its route with this one.

139

5th stage

5th stage

TIPS FOR WALKERS

Planning: *The mountain is open for climbing only in July and August. Trails and huts can be very crowded on weekends.*
Stages: *The trails are divided into 10 stages. Climbers usually start at the 5th stage. To see the sunrise and avoid the midday sun, it is usual to climb by night or start in the afternoon, sleep in a hut at the 7th or 8th stage, and rise very early to finish the climb.*
Conditions: *The climb is hard work as the steep volcanic cinder shifts underfoot like sand. Above the 8th stage, altitude sickness occasionally strikes: if you have a serious head-ache or nausea, descend at once. The summit is much colder than the base.*
What to take: *Sun-protection cream, hat, sweater, raincoat, hiking shoes, flashlight, and emergency drink supplies; a walking stick is useful.*

The top is not a single summit, but a crater rim. A circuit of the rim takes about an hour.

FUJINOMIYA

The Fujinomiya trail is 5 hours up from the 5th stage, and 3 hours 30 minutes down.

Approaching the Crater Rim

At the top, climbers and pilgrims can visit Sengen shrine, 24-hour noodle stalls, a post office, and an office for souvenir stamps.

Sengen Jinja
Many Sengen shrines, including this main one at Fuji-Yoshida, can be found around Fuji. The inner sanctum of Sengen shrines is on the crater rim at the summit. They are dedicated to the deity of the mountain.

OTSUKI AND TOKYO

Fuji-Yoshida, the traditional pilgrim base, has old inns, and waterfalls for ritual cleansing before the climb.

Lake Yamanaka is popular for waterskiing and swimming.

• Oshino

Subashiri trail is 4 hours 30 minutes up from the 5th stage, and 3 hours down.

LAKE YAMANAKA

TOKYO

138

Gotenba

MISHIMA

Tomei Expressway

Gotenba trail is 8 hours up from the 5th stage, and 3 hours down.

0 kilometers   5

0 miles   5

MOUNT FUJI IN ART

Mount Fuji's graceful, almost symmetrical form, its changing appearance at different seasons and times of day, and its dominance over the landscape have made it both a symbol of Japan and a popular subject for artists. The mountain features in various series of 19th-century woodblock prints: Katsushika Hokusai (1760–1849) and Ando Hiroshige (1797–1858) both published series called *Thirty-Six Views of Mount Fuji*, and Hiroshige also depicted Fuji in his *Fifty-Three Stages of the Tokaido* published in 1833–4. It often appears in the background of prints of Edo (Tokyo); it is still sometimes visible among Tokyo's high-rises even today. In other arts, Mount Fuji is echoed in decorative motifs, for instance on kimonos, in wood carvings, and even in the shape of window frames.

One of Hiroshige's *Thirty-Six Views of Mount Fuji*

Beneath the Wave off Kanagawa from Hokusai's *Thirty-Six Views of Mount Fuji*

Nikko ⑩

日光

Over 1,200 years ago, the formidable Buddhist priest Shodo Shonin, on his way to Mount Nantai, crossed the Daiya River and founded the first temple at Nikko. Centuries later, Nikko was a renowned Buddhist-Shinto religious center, and the warlord Tokugawa Ieyasu *(see p101)* chose it for the site of his mausoleum. When his grandson Iemitsu had Ieyasu's shrine-mausoleum Tosho-gu built in 1634, he wanted to impress upon any rivals the wealth and might of the Tokugawa clan. Since then, Nikko, written with characters that mean sunlight, has become a Japanese byword for splendor.

Bato Kannon, with a horse on the headdress, at Rinno-ji temple

NIKKO SIGHTS

NIKKO NATIONAL PARK

↑ TAKINOO SHRINE

Taiyuin-byo Shrine

Hokke-do

Futara-san Shrine

Nikko Botanical Gardens

Route 120

Jogyo-do

Tosho-gu Treasure Hall

Tosho-gu Shrine

Ganman-ga-fuchi Pools

Tosho-gu Museum of Art

Rinno-ji Temple

URUSHI MUSEUM

Daiya River

Route 120

| 0 meters | 250 |
| 0 yards | 250 |

Shinkyo Bridge •

Kanaya Hotel •

Route 119

NIKKO TOWN AND STATIONS ↓

Key to Symbols see back flap

Exploring Nikko Town

Of the two stations in Nikko, the JR station, the oldest in eastern Japan, is a classic. The graceful wooden edifice was built in 1915. Buses to many of Nikko's sights run from here. The half-a-mile- (1-km-) long avenue from the train stations to the Tosho-gu precincts is lined with shops, restaurants, and inns. A good shop for Nikko wood carvings and *geta* (wooden sandals) is Tezuka, on the left halfway up the street. An architectural treat is the venerable 19th-century

Kanaya Hotel *(see p117)*, situated on a rise to the left, just before the Daiya River.

Shinkyo Bridge

☐ *daily.*

This red-lacquered wooden bridge, just to the left of the road bridge, arches over the Daiya River where, legend has it, Shodo Shonin crossed the river on the backs of two huge serpents. The original, built in 1636 for the exclusive use of the shogun and imperial messengers, was destroyed by flood. The current bridge dates from 1907.

🛕 Rinno-ji Temple

☐ *daily.* 📷

The first temple founded at Nikko, by Shodo Shonin in 766, this was originally called Shihonryu-ji. When it became a Tendai-sect temple in the 17th century, it was renamed Rinno-ji. Its **Sanbutsu-do** (Three Buddha Hall) is the largest hall at Nikko. The three gilt images, of Amida Buddha, Senju (thousand-armed) Kannon, and Bato (horse-headed) Kannon, enshrined in the hall correspond to the three mountain deities enshrined at Futara-san shrine. Beyond the hall, the nine-ringed bronze pillar, **Sorinto**, contains 1,000 volumes of

The Shinkyo Bridge spanning the Daiya River

For hotels and restaurants in this region see p117 and p141

sutras (Buddhist scriptures) and is a symbol of world peace. The **Treasure Hall** (Homotsuden) has a large and fascinating array of temple treasures, mainly dating from the Edo period. Behind it is the **Shoyoen**, a lovely landscaped Edo-style 19th-century stroll garden for all seasons. Its path meanders around a large pond, over stone bridges, and past mossy stone lanterns.

The Sanbutsu-do hall at Rinno-ji

🛕 Tosho-gu Shrine
See pp100–1.

♨ Tosho-gu Treasure Hall and Museum of Art
Tel (0288) 54-2558 (Treasure Hall); (0288) 54-0560 (Museum of Art). ⬜ daily. 🎟
In the Treasure Hall are shrine treasures along with armor and swords used by the Tokugawa shoguns. In the Museum of Art is an outstanding collection of early 20th-century painted doors and panels by Taikan Yokoyama and others.

⛰ Hokke-do and Jogyo-do
These two halls belong to Rinno-ji and house Buddhist relics. Linked by a corridor, they are often referred to as the twin halls.

🛕 Futara-san Shrine
⬜ daily. 🎟
Founded by Shodo Shonin in 782, this shrine is dedicated to the gods of the mountains Nantai (male), Nyotai

(female), and Taro, their child. It is actually the main shrine of three; the other two are at Lake Chuzenji and on the summit of Mount Nantai. The bronze *torii* (gate) here is an Important Cultural Property. More interesting is the tall bronze lantern, which was said to take the shape of a monster at night. The gashes in the lantern are from the sword of a samurai.

🛕 Takinoo Shrine
Tel (0288) 21-0765. ⬜ daily.

Shrine interior at Futara-san

A quiet 30-minute uphill walk through the woods via a stone path to the left of Futara-san Shrine, this peaceful, rustic shrine, thought to be dedicated to a female deity, draws women and those looking for love. Toss a stone through the hole in the top of the *torii* (gate) and into the shrine grounds and your wish, they say, will come true.

VISITORS' CHECKLIST

Tochigi prefecture. 🏯 17,000. 🚆 JR and Tobu-Nikko lines. ℹ at Tobu Nikko stn (0288) 54-2496. 🎌 Tosho-gu Grand Festival (May 17–18); Tosho-gu Fall Festival (Oct 17). **www**.city. nikko.lg.jp/fl/index.html

🛕 Taiyuin-byo Shrine
See pp102–3.

🎎 Ganman-ga-fuchi Pools
🚏 to Nishisando bus stop.
Lava flows from an old eruption of Mount Nantai, combines with the limpid waters of the Daiya River to make these unusual scenic pools, a sacred spot to followers of Buddhism. About 70 stone statues of Jizo, the *bodhisattva* of children, line the path by the river. They are known as phantom statues because their numbers always appear to change.

🌸 Nikko Botanical Gardens
🚏 to Rengeishi bus stop. *Tel* (0288) 54-0206. ⬜ Tue–Sun. 🔴 Dec 1– Apr 14. 🎟
Some 3,000 varieties of plants and flowers from Japan and around the world can be seen at these gardens, a branch of the Koishikawa Botanical Gardens of the University of Tokyo. Flora from Nikko National Park are showcased. April to July, when skunk cabbages and irises bloom, is a lovely time to visit.

♨ Urushi Museum
🚏 to Marumi bus stop. *Tel* (0288) 53-6807. ⬜ Mar 20–Nov 20: Mon, Sat, Sun. 🎟
This small museum, which opened in 1998 in wooded Ogurayama Park, showcases the lacquerware arts of Nikko and Japan – *urushi* is Japanese for lacquer. Used in Japan for over 5,000 years, lacquer has reached the height of refinement only in the past 1,000 years. The museum collection also includes examples of lacquerware from China, India, and Egypt.

Painted sliding doors at the Tosho-gu Museum of Art

Nikko: Tosho-gu Shrine

Tokugawa Iemitsu set out to dazzle with this shrine-mausoleum for his grandfather Ieyasu. For two years some 15,000 artisans from all over Japan worked, building, carving, gilting, painting, and lacquering, to create this flowery, gorgeous Momoyama-style complex. Almost anything that can be decorated is. Although designated a shrine in the Meiji period, it retains many of its Buddhist elements, including its unusual pagoda, sutra library, and Niomon gate. The famed *sugi-namiki* (Japanese cedar avenue) leading to the shrine was planted by a 17th-century lord, in lieu of a more opulent offering.

Sleeping Cat Carving
Over an entrance in the east corridor, this tiny, exquisite carving of a sleeping cat is attributed to Hidari Jingoro (Jingoro the Left-handed).

Bell tower

Honden (inner sanctuary)

Haiden (sanctuary)

The Karamon gate is the smallest at Tosho-gu.

The Honji-do's ceiling is painted with the "crying dragon," which echoes resoundingly if you clap your hands beneath it.

Drum tower

The Rinzo contains a sutra library of Buddhist scriptures in a revolving structure.

★ **Yomeimon Gate**
Lavishly decorated with beasts and flowers, this gate has one of its 12 columns carved upside-down, a deliberate imperfection to avoid angering jealous spirits. Statues of imperial ministers occupy the niches.

STAR SIGHTS
★ Yomeimon Gate
★ Pagoda
★ Sacred Stable

Sacred Fountain
The granite basin (1618), for ritual purification, is covered with an ornate Chinese-style roof.

TOKUGAWA IEYASU

Ieyasu (1543–1616) was a
wily strategist and master
politician who founded the
dynasty that would rule Japan
for over 250 years. Born the
son of a minor lord, he spent
his life accumulating power, not
becoming shogun until 1603,
when he was 60. He built his
capital at the swampy village
of Edo (now Tokyo), and his
rule saw the start of the
blooming of Edo culture. He
ensured that after his death,

Ieyasu's treasure tower,
containing his ashes

he would be enshrined as a god and *gongen* (incarnation
of the Buddha). His posthumous name was Tosho-
Daigongen (the great incarnation illuminating the East).

VISITORS' CHECKLIST

Tel (0288) 54-0560. 🚉 🅿 8am–
5pm daily (4pm Nov–Mar).

To Ieyasu's tomb and
treasure tower

The three sacred storehouses
are built according to a
traditional design.

The Niomon (or Omotemon)
gate is guarded by two fear-
some Nio figures, one with an
open mouth to pronounce the
first letter of the Sanskrit
alphabet (ah), the other with
a closed mouth for the
last letter (un).

★ **Pagoda**
*Donated by a daimyo
(feudal lord) in 1650, this
five-story pagoda was
rebuilt in 1818 after a fire.
Each story represents an
element – earth, water,
fire, wind, and
heaven – in
ascending order.*

Ticket office

Granite *torii*
(gate)

Entrance

★ **Sacred Stable**
*A carving of the three wise monkeys
decorates this unpainted wooden
building. A horse given by the
New Zealand government is stabled
here for several hours a day.*

Nikko: Taiyuin-byo Shrine

Completed in 1653, Taiyuin-byo Shrine is the mausoleum of Tokugawa Iemitsu (1604–51), the grandson of Ieyasu *(see p101)* and powerful third shogun, who closed Japan to foreign commerce and isolated it from the world for over 200 years. Tayuin is his posthumous Buddhist name. If Tosho-gu is splendid, Taiyuin-byo is sublime. Set in a grove of Japanese cedars, it has a number of ornate gates ascending to the Haiden (sanctuary) and Honden (inner sanctuary). The shogun's ashes are entombed beyond the sixth and final gate.

The Honden (usually closed to the public) holds a gilded Buddhist altar with a wooden statue of Iemitsu.

The Ai No Ma is a richly decorated connecting chamber.

Kokamon Gate
This striking Ming-dynasty Chinese-style massive gate is beside the picturesque path to Iemitsu's tomb.

★ Haiden
Decorated with lovely carvings of dragons, the Haiden (Hall of Worship) also has some famous 17th-century lion paintings by Kano School painters.

The Karamon gate is adorned with delicate carvings, such as a pair of cranes.

The drum tower leads to Honji-do hall, with a painting of a dragon on its huge ceiling.

Niomon Gate
This marks the main entrance to the shrine. A single Nio warrior god stands guard on each side.

Entrance

STAR SIGHTS

★ Haiden

★ Nitenmon Gate

For hotels and restaurants in this region see p117 and p141

VISITORS' CHECKLIST

Tel (0288) 53-1567. 🎫 🕐 8am–
5pm daily (4pm Nov–Mar).

Bell Tower
*This structure forms a pair
with the drum tower. No
longer used, but the drum
signifies positive/birth, while
the bell negative/death.*

Yashamon Gate
*The third gate is beautifully gilded and
contains four statues of Yasha, a fierce
guardian spirit. It is also known
as Botanmon, or peony gate, after
its detailed peony carvings.*

★ Nitenmon Gate
*Four guardian
statues occupy the
niches here. At the
front are the gods
Komoku and Jikoku,
while at the back are
the green god of wind
and the red god
of thunder.*

Granite Fountain
*On the ceiling above
the basin is a dragon
painting by Kano
Yasunobu, which is
sometimes reflected in
the water below.*

Stone lanterns were
donated over the years by
daimyo (feudal lords).

TRAVELERS' NEEDS

WHERE TO STAY

The choice of accommodations can be truly overwhelming in Tokyo, ranging from five-star skyscraper hotels, well-known foreign brand-name chains, and cozy boutique hotels to *ryokan* (*see p108*), traditional Japanese inns. At higher-end *ryokan*, where you sleep on futons (mattresses), soak in aromatic cedar tubs, and enjoy *kaiseki* (*see p120*) dinners served in private rooms, even a short stay can be a memorable experience. But one thing

Sign for the Palace Hotel, Central Tokyo (*see p112*)

that all opulent establishments, business hotels, and modest, family-run *minshuku* (*see p109*) have in common is a concern for comfort combined with a long tradition of hospitality. Most accommodations are located in the central areas of the city, usually near the main line and metro stations, but if you can forego exquisite service, designer interiors, and spectacular night views, there are cheaper options available on the fringes of the central districts.

HELPFUL ORGANIZATIONS

Designed for overseas visitors, the **Welcome Inn Reservation Center** (WIRC) arranges free bookings through their website for approved traditional inns (*ryokan*), government-run lodges, business hotels, and pensions. JNTO offices (*see p163*) stock the *Directory of Welcome Inns*. There are WIRC counters in the arrivals lobby of Narita Airport, and at Tokyo's TIC (*see p173*).

Many of the traditional inns approved by the WIRC also belong to the **Japanese Inn Group**, which covers about 80 moderately rated *ryokan* that are geared to receiving mainly foreign visitors.

The **Japan City Hotel Association** has online information about member hotels and advance bookings for accommodations in Tokyo

The understated porch of Hotel Seiyo Ginza (*see p111*)

and the areas beyond the capital city. The **Japan Economy Hotel** (JEH) **Group** offers clean, modern rooms at reasonable rates.

BOOKING AND PAYING

Booking accommodations in advance is advisable, especially at times of major public holidays (*see p31*). Reservations made directly need to be confirmed by letter, fax, or email. Rates quoted are often per person, not per room.

Most hotels accept the best-known international credit cards. The bill is usually payable on departure, but business hotels and some others may request advance payment.

There is a basic 5 percent consumption tax on all rooms, rising in the case of higher-end hotels (usually over ¥15,000). A small hotel tax is added in Tokyo hotels for rooms priced above ¥10,000 per person.

DELUXE HOTELS

Top American chains such as the Hilton, Sheraton, Hyatt, Westin, and Four Seasons are well established in Tokyo.

Among Japanese-owned hotels, there is a vast range – staid conservatism; over-the-top opulence; discreet exclusivity; chic minimalism; and quaint eccentricity. In Tokyo "intelligent" hotels are very common; they feature rooms that monitor temperature, have electronic key cards, computerized toilets, a voice-mail message system, mp3 docks, and fast, reliable broadband Internet.

Deluxe hotels often feature popular restaurants and bars, many with spectacular views.

PENSIONS

Western-style pensions are also popular. Located mostly in resort areas, they are rustic and relaxed in style

Fifty-two story Park Tower, Park Hyatt Tokyo (*see p116*)

◁ **Resplendent azalea bushes at Nezu Shrine, Yanaka**

and offer good hearty meals. Generally managed by married couples, they fall somewhere between a *minshuku* and the more service-oriented pamperings of a small hotel.

BUSINESS HOTELS

Many lower- and mid-range hotels in Tokyo fall into the category of business hotels, which are often located within easy reach of stations on the Yamanote Line. As the name suggests, business hotels *(bijinesu hoteru)* cater to budget-conscious business travelers. Anyone can stay, and being generally located in city centers around train stations, they are convenient. Do not expect English to be spoken.

Rooms are Western-style, functional, small, and spotlessly clean. Slippers and a cotton robe are generally supplied. There is no room service, but vending machines offer the ubiquitous "health drinks," beer, and sake. There is often at least one restaurant with a good choice of traditional Japanese or Western-style breakfasts.

CAPSULE HOTELS

Unique to Japan, these custom-built hotels feature encapsulated beds in and out of which guests must slide, since there is no room to sit up, let alone stand. Rattan blinds or curtains can be pulled across for a degree of privacy.

Usually constructed in two tiers, they cater mainly to *"salarymen"* who are too tired or inebriated to make the last train home. Most are clustered around major train stations or nightlife areas. Facilities include a personal TV, radio, alarm call system, and air-conditioning. Smoking is not allowed. Vending machines may be nearby. Baths and sometimes saunas are included in the price.

The size of such hotels varies widely, ranging from 50 capsules to over 600. Some still cater only to men, but women are increasingly encouraged to stay. Expect to pay between ¥3,500–¥5,000 in cash.

LOVE HOTELS

Love hotels are designed for dating couples and married partners living in extended families who may feel that they need some privacy. They are mainly found in entertainment areas and along expressways and highways, much like motels.

Sign showing rates for a Tokyo love hotel

Dual pricing is followed – typically ¥3,500 for a two-hour "rest," and ¥7,000–¥8,000 for an overnight "stay." The most entertaining offer thematic decor as an additional turn-on from a simulated cabin on an ocean liner, vibrating beds, and kitsch cartoon themes.

Entrances to love hotels are screened off by a wall that has a sign listing the room rates – credit cards are not accepted. Privacy is ensured

Sparse interior of a Central Tokyo youth hostel

by a rather anonymous method of payment – couples choose their room from a photo board, and then pay either a cashier who sits behind a screen or at a machine. Guests then receive their change and a key.

Rooms are reasonably spacious, clean, and with a private bath.

YOUTH HOSTELS

Cheap, clean, and open to people of all ages, youth hostels in Tokyo do not usually require membership. The cheapest option for travelers, rates run between ¥2,500–¥4,000. Payment is in cash only. All meals come at an additional cost.

DIRECTORY

Japan City Hotel Association
www.jcha.or.jp/english

Japan Economy Hotel Group
www.kid97.co.jp/~jeh-group/jeh-group.html

Japanese Inn Group
Tel (06) 6225-3611.
Fax (06) 6225-3612.
www.japaneseinngroup.com

Welcome Inn Reservation Center
www.itcj.or.jp

For JNTO offices and website see p163.

Typical capsule hotel, with two tiers of encapsulated beds

Traditional Accommodations

A *ryokan* is a unique fusion of private and communal styles of living. Such Japanese traditions as removing shoes at the right point are important, no matter what the cost of the room, and the most expensive of these traditional inns may demand a high level of etiquette. A family-run *minshuku* – a type of guesthouse – is an even more intimate way to experience the Japanese lifestyle. There are also options that are *ryokan* at heart, but with Western-style touches such as private bathrooms.

Sawanoya *ryokan*, in a quiet neighborhood near Ueno Park

WHAT IS A RYOKAN?

A *ryokan* is a traditional inn, usually associated with older towns, mountain, and hot spring areas. While top-end Tokyo *ryokan* can be relied on to have many of the traditional graces found in their rural counterparts, mid-range *ryokan*, with modern touches and conveniences, can be a little different. Some are set in Edo-period buildings – confections of wood, glass, bamboo, paper screens, and *tatami* matting.

Certain important Japanese customs apply – the biggest difference and greatest surprise for many foreigners is that bathing facilities are traditionally communal, not private. The bathing facilities may be quite elaborate, and when part of an exclusive hot spring resort the establishment is called an *onsen*.

Most *ryokan* place emphasis on the quality of their meals, and the room price often includes breakfast and dinner (as specified in the listings). This can be ideal in quiet areas where few restaurants

are open in the evening, but a constraint elsewhere. Another possible problem, mainly for elderly foreigners, is the Japanese tradition of living at floor level, using legless chairs and beds.

Note that many *ryokan* impose a curfew around 11pm, so check before you step out, or make special arrangements about keys in advance if you plan to stay out late.

ARRIVING AT A RYOKAN

Guests generally check into a *ryokan* in the mid- to late afternoon, to allow plenty of time for bathing and dinner. At larger *ryokan*, there may be a doorman to smooth the way, but in smaller establishments, guests should slide open the front door and politely call *"gomen kudasai"* to announce arrival.

Do not step up into the lobby proper until the *okamisan* (female owner or manager)

appears. This is the signal to remove outdoor shoes and step up into a pair of waiting house slippers *(see p165)*. Then, before entering the guestroom, remove the house slippers and leave them outside the door.

TYPICAL ROOMS

Guestrooms are floored in *tatami* mats. In one corner of the room is an alcove, called *tokonoma*, which may contain a hanging scroll, flowers, or other artifacts. The *tokonoma* is to be respected – no suitcases, ashtrays, or drinks should be left here. There will also be a low table surrounded by cushions *(zabuton)* or folding chairs. On the table top will be a tray, bearing a tea set and possibly *wagashi* sweets *(see p130)*.

Your futon mattress and bedding will be stowed in cupboards when you first enter the room. These will usually be laid out discreetly for you in the evening while you are out of the room.

Ordinarily a room will be further supplied with a TV, airconditioner, and/or heater. There is usually a telephone, although it may not have an international connection. You should also find a small towel in a box or basket, which you can take to the communal bathroom to use as a washcloth. A personal outdoor bath *(rotenburo)* counts as a luxury. A screened-off veranda, with Western-style table and armchairs, is more commonplace. There may be other Western-style touches.

Handle everything in the room with care, and walk only in bare feet or socks on the fragile *tatami*.

Room with *tatami* mats, low table, and *zabuton*, and additional Western-style daybed

Small communal bath and separate low shower for cleansing

WEARING YUKATA

Somewhere in the room will be traditional robes for you to wear, called *yukata*. Most people change into *yukata* for the duration of their stay, since the loose cotton kimonos symbolize relaxation and leisure time. In resort towns and hot springs, they are even worn outside on the streets, together with the high wooden sandals called *geta*. A loose jacket may also be provided. It is best to follow the example of others as to exactly where and when to wear the robes.

Fold *yukata* left-side over right. Right-side over left symbolizes death in Buddhism and can cause upset. Use the *obi* sash provided to secure the gown.

BATHING ARRANGEMENTS

Within the *ryokan* will be at least one communal bath and a toilet block with either Western-style cubicles, Japanese squat toilets, or a choice of the two styles.

In smaller *ryokan* with only one bath, bathing times may differ for men and women. In larger establishments bathing is segregated, with one entrance for men, and another for women *(for symbols see p167)*. Mixed-sex bathing used to be the norm but is very rare these days. The size of the bath and bathroom naturally dictate how many people can bathe at any one time. Check with the *okamisan* if you are unsure about the house rules, which vary between establishments.

In the bathroom, there will be an area for undressing; a low shower or tap area; and the large bath itself. The golden rule to observe is that you must perform ablutions with the shower first and not enter the hot bath until you are clean. The bath itself is intended only for therapeutic relaxation. The same bathwater is used by other guests; thus it is considered extremely bad manners to contaminate the water either with an unwashed body or soap and shampoo.

People wearing *yukata*, the design of which is often specific to each *ryokan*

EATING ARRANGEMENTS

Meals are sometimes served in a dining room, but more often in the room by a maid or the *okamisan*. The more exclusive the establishment, the more likely meals will be served in private.

Meal times are usually set quite early in the evening. Depending on the situation, the *okamisan* may stay for a while, explaining the dishes, demonstrating how they should

be eaten, and to chat. Or she may leave discreetly, returning only to clear the table.

STAYING IN A MINSHUKU

These family-run enterprises open the family home to travelers as and when demand requires. With rates from ¥5,000–¥9,000, this is an economical option as well as a good opportunity to see how regular working people live. The atmosphere is more homely; guests are treated as part of the family at mealtimes and bathtime, and should fold up and stow away their own bedding.

STAYING IN LODGES

People's lodges, or *kokumin-shukusha*, are moderate-rated accommodations within the national parks. Rooms, baths, and toilets are Japanese style. Meals based on local produce are often fresh and of good quality. Room rates are often less than ¥6,000 per person per night (¥8,000 with two meals).

OTHER OPTIONS

There are several other affordable lodging options in Tokyo. Staying at a *shukubo* (on the grounds of a temple) is mostly confined to areas beyond Tokyo; see **Temple Lodging in Japan** for details. The TIC *(see p163)* can provide information on other suitable accommodations in the city such as *onsen* (hot spring resorts), and converted farmhouses.

DIRECTORY

Japan Minshuku Center

Tel 0120-07-6556.

www.minshuku.jp

abc@minshuku.jp

Japan Ryokan Association

Tel (03) 3231-5310.

www.ryokan.or.jp

Temple Lodging in Japan

www.templelodging.com

Choosing a Hotel

The hotels in this guide have been selected across a wide range for their good value, facilities, and location. These listings highlight some of the factors that may influence your choice. Hotels are listed by area, beginning with Central Tokyo. For the location of each hotel in Tokyo refer to the Street Finder, pages 180–89.

PRICE GUIDE
Price categories per night for two people sharing a room, including tax and service charges.
Ⓨ Under ¥8,000
ⓎⓎ ¥8,000–¥15,000
ⓎⓎⓎ ¥15,000–¥25,000
ⓎⓎⓎⓎ ¥25,000–¥35,000
ⓎⓎⓎⓎⓎ Over ¥35,000

CENTRAL TOKYO

Sakura Hotel Ⓨ
2-21-4 Kanda-Jimbocho, Chiyoda-ku **Tel** *(03) 3261-3939* **Fax** *(03) 3264-2777* **Rooms** *43*   **Map** *3 A5*

Ideally located in the center of the Kanda-Jimbocho book quarter *(see p44)*, this small hotel is geared toward accommodating foreign guests. Popular with backpackers (dormitory rooms are also available), the hotel is basic but cozy, and the English-speaking staff helpful. Internet access and a 24-hour café are a bonus. **www.sakura-hotel.co.jp**

Toyoko Inn Tameike Sanno Ⓨ
2-4-14 Nagata-cho, Chiyoda-ku **Tel** *(03) 5510-1045* **Fax** *(03) 5510-1046* **Rooms** *88*   **Map** *2 F4*

A short walk from Tameike Sanno Station, this member of the dependable Toyoko Inn business hotel chain offers a good location between the Imperial Palace and Roppongi. Rooms are very clean and reasonably spacious for this price category. There is free Internet access and breakfast is included. **www.toyoko-inn.com**

Hotel MyStays Ochanomizu ⓎⓎ
2-10-6 Kanda Awajicho, Chiyoda-ku **Tel** *(03) 3258-3911* **Rooms** *124*   **Map** *3 C4*

Situated a 10 minutes walk from JR Ochanomizu Station, this affordable and comfortable upscale business hotel offers all the basic amenities along with the additional benefits of Internet access arranged at check-in. It also houses a handy Family Mart convenience store and a restaurant downstairs. **www.mystays.jp**

New Central Hotel ⓎⓎ
2-7-2 Kanda-Tacho, Chiyoda-ku **Tel** *(03) 3256-2171* **Fax** *(03) 3256-3219* **Rooms** *301*   **Map** *3 C5*

This 12-story Western-style hotel offers easy access to JR Kanda Station and the nearby Akihabara electronics district *(see p45)*. The double rooms are the best value at this reasonably priced accommodation. The highlight is the 24-hour Japanese communal bath. The men's bath is roomier than the women's. **www.pelican.co.jp/centralhotel/index**

Remm Akihabara ⓎⓎ
1-6-5 Kandsakuma-cho, Chiyoda-ku **Tel** *(03) 3254-0606* **Rooms** *260*   **Map** *3 C4*

Located in the center of the action, the Remm Akihabara combines the small rooms typical of a business hotel with the sleek, modern style and designer extras one would find in a more upmarket establishment. In-room amenities include free Wi-Fi and rain showers. **www.hankyu-hotel.com/english/index.html**

Ryokan Ryumeikan Honten ⓎⓎ
3-4 Kanda-Surugadai, Chiyoda-ku **Tel** *(03) 3251-1135* **Fax** *(03) 3251-0270* **Rooms** *12*   **Map** *3 B4*

This modern, Japanese-style *ryokan* just south of the picturesque Nikolai Cathedral *(see p79)* is surrounded by skyscrapers and commercial banks. Relatively spacious and clean, the *ryokan* is curiously located in part of an office block. It has friendly and helpful staff. **www.ryumeikan.co.jp/honten_eng.htm**

Tokyo Green Hotel Korakuen ⓎⓎ
1-1-3 Koraku, Bunkyo-ku **Tel** *(03) 3816-4161* **Fax** *(03) 3818-2406* **Rooms** *135*   **Map** *3 A3*

The Tokyo Green Hotel Korakuen overlooks the Tokyo Dome Sports Stadium and is adjacent to Tokyo Dome City, which houses a hot spring and spa, amusement parks, and multiple shops. This comfortable and spotless hotel provides great value for money. The superb café has a terrace. **www.greenhotel.co.jp**

Courtyard Tokyo Ginza Hotel ⓎⓎⓎ
6-14-10 Ginza, Chuo-ku **Tel** *(03) 3546-0111* **Fax** *(03) 3546-8990* **Rooms** *206*   **Map** *5 B3*

This excellent mid-range hotel close to the Kabuki-za theater is now a popular wedding reception venue. The decent sized, well-furnished rooms are comfortable and equipped with cable TV, minibar, voicemail, and Internet access. The staff is multilingual. **www.tobuhotel.co.jp/ginza**

Diamond Hotel ⓎⓎⓎ
1-10-3 Kojimachi, Chiyoda-ku **Tel** *(03) 3263-2211* **Fax** *(03) 3263-2222* **Rooms** *157*   **Map** *2 F1*

Located in a pleasantly quiet setting, this moderately priced hotel is close to the Hanzomon metro line, the British Embassy, and a few minutes' walk from the Imperial Palace. It is comfortable and boasts a good Chinese restaurant. The multilingual staff is helpful. **www.diamond-hotel.co.jp**

Key to Symbols *see back cover flap*

Ginza Capital Hotel

2-1-4 Tsukiji, Chuo-ku **Tel** (03) 3543-8211 **Fax** (03) 3543-7839 **Rooms** 574 **Map** 5 C3

This well-equipped business hotel in central Tokyo, close to the Tsukiji fish market, is ideally located for both business travel and sightseeing in the city. The annex has women-only rooms. Non-smoking rooms are also available in the main building. The hotel organizes sightseeing bus tours daily. **www.ginza-capital.co.jp**

Ginza Mercure

2-9-4 Ginza, Chuo-ku **Tel** (03) 4335-1111 **Fax** (03) 4335-1222 **Rooms** 208 **Map** 5 2C

This fashionable, boutique hotel is just a stroll away from the popular shopping area of the Ginza. Sound-insulated rooms, stylish decor, and an elegant French restaurant make it popular with business people and shopaholics. Half the rooms are non-smoking. The staff is multilingual. **www.mercureginza.com**

Ginza Nikko Hotel

8-4-21 Ginza, Chuo-ku **Tel** (03) 3571-4911 **Fax** (03) 3571-8379 **Rooms** 112 **Map** 5 B3

An establishment that has been around since the 1960s, this remodelled, reliable, mid-range hotel affiliated with JAL (Japan Airlines) is in a convenient location near Ginza's main department stores, bars, and restaurants. Tsukiji fish market (see p40) makes for a pleasant stroll from this well-appointed hotel. **www.ginza-nikko-hotel.com**

Hill Top Hotel

1-1 Kanda-Surugadai, Chiyoda-ku **Tel** (03) 3293-2311 **Fax** (03) 3233-4567 **Rooms** 75 **Map** 3 B4

This small, Art Deco-style hotel, a favorite of writers such as Yukio Mishima, is located close to Meiji University, the musical instrument store area of Ochanomizu, and the book store mecca of Kanda-Jimbocho (see p44). Oxygen and negative ions are pumped into the rooms to promote a sense of well-being. **www.yamanoue-hotel.co.jp**

Hotel Com's Ginza

8-6-15 Ginza, Chuo-ku **Tel** (03) 3572-4131 **Fax** (03) 3572-4254 **Rooms** 267 **Map** 5 B3

This smart, efficiently run mid-range hotel in the backstreets of Ginza has well-furnished rooms equipped with plasma-screen TVs and broadband access. This is a good location for trips to both Ginza and Shimbashi. Two floors of restaurants cater to all tastes. Guests can enjoy good Szechuan cuisine in the restaurant, Tokagen.

Hotel Ryumeikan Tokyo

1-3-22 Yaesu, Chuo-ku **Tel** (03) 3271-0971 **Fax** (03) 3271-0977 **Rooms** 30 **Map** 5 C1

Set in a terrific location close to the Yaesu exit of Tokyo Station (see p42), this hotel has slightly tatty, Japanese-style rooms. There is a Japanese breakfast on offer – including fish, rice, pickles, and miso soup, which is included in the room rate. Free Internet access, and mobile phone and cycle rental. **www.ryumeikan-tokyo.jp**

Kudan Kaikan

1-6-5 Kudan-minami, Chiyoda-ku **Tel** (03) 3261-5521 **Fax** (03) 3221-7238 **Rooms** 162 **Map** 3 A5

An old stone and brick construction that dates from 1934, this cozy, mid-range hotel, is just a one-minute walk from Kudanshita Station, and the nearby martial arts Nihon Budokan Hall (see p152). The hotel has a famous summer rooftop beer garden. Good views of the Imperial Palace. **www.kudankaikan.or.jp**

Yaesu Fujiya Hotel

2-9-1 Yaesu, Chuo-ku **Tel** (03) 3273-2111 **Fax** (03) 3273-2180 **Rooms** 377 **Map** 5 C2

Part of the well-established Fujiya hotel chain, this medium-range hotel provides good service and larger-than-average rooms that are bright and comfortable. The location near Tokyo Station and Yurakucho is an added advantage. The restaurant options are good for a hotel of this size. **www.yaesufujiya.com/english**

Dai-ichi Hotel Tokyo

1-2-6 Shimbashi, Minato-ku **Tel** (03) 3501-4411 **Fax** (03) 3595-2634 **Rooms** 277 **Map** 5 A5

Part of a huge chain that extends beyond Japan, this hotel has plenty of Western-style amenities and services, including 11 different restaurants and bars, as well as spa and sauna facilities, which make for a good stay. The efficient staff is multilingual. **www.daiichihotel-tokyo.com/english/topframe.htm**

Royal Park Hotel

2-1-1 Nihonbashi-Kakigara-cho, Chuo-ku **Tel** (03) 3667-1111 **Fax** (03) 3667-1115 **Rooms** 406 **Map** 6 E1

In the heart of the business and commercial center, next to the Tokyo City Air Terminal, this well-decked hotel has excellent transportation links. Special features include high-quality Oriental and Western furnishings, a beautiful Japanese garden, and the 20th-floor cocktail bar, Orpheus. **www.rph.co.jp**

Hotel Seiyo Ginza

1-11-2 Ginza, Chuo-ku **Tel** (03) 3535-1111 **Fax** (03) 3535-1110 **Rooms** 77 **Map** 5 C2

This discreet and elegant five-star luxury hotel is within walking distance of the entertainment and shopping centers of the commercial Marunouchi district. Uniquely, each room has its own valet. Noted for its superb Italian restaurant, the hotel also offers kaiseki ryori (see p120) menus, Japan's haute cuisine. **www.seiyo-ginza.com**

Imperial Hotel

1-1-1 Uchisawaicho, Chiyoda-ku **Tel** (03) 3504-1111 **Fax** (03) 3581-9146 **Rooms** 1008 **Map** 5 B2

A deluxe hotel right by Hibiya Station and near Hibiya Park (see p43). The current building replaces architect Frank Lloyd Wright's masterpiece and offers top-notch facilities and services but without a personal touch. Large rooms on the Imperial floor have wide-screen plasma TVs. There are 17 restaurants and bars. **www.imperialhotel.co.jp**

Marunouchi Hotel

Oazo Bldg, 1-6-3 Marunouchi, Chiyoda-ku **Tel** *(03) 3217-1111* **Rooms** *205*   **Map** *5 B1*

This comfortable, tastefully decorated hotel is housed in the Oazo Building facing Tokyo Station. The decor and other features have charming retro touches that add interest to the rooms. The higher floors and bars offer great views over the nearby Imperial Palace and business districts. **www.marunouchi-hotel.co.jp**

Palace Hotel

1-1-1 Marunouchi, Chiyoda-ku **Tel** *(03) 3211-5211* **Fax** *(03) 3211-6987* **Rooms** *290*   **Map** *5 B1*

This well-established luxury hotel boasts spacious rooms and a tranquil ambience, in addition to a superb central location. Guests are treated to sweeping views of the Imperial Palace, moats, and the Otemon gate *(see p43)*. The hotel offers excellent Chinese, French, and Japanese restaurants. **www.palacehotel.co.jp**

Peninsula Hotel Tokyo

1-8-1 Yurakucho, Chiyoda-ku **Tel** *(03) 6270-2888* **Fax** *(03) 6270-2000* **Rooms** *314*   **Map** *5 B2*

Keeping up the high standards of its Hong Kong original, the Peninsula Hotel Tokyo is a destination in itself. Superbly located between the palace grounds and Ginza, the middle and upper rooms of this 24-story tower afford superb views. Among the eating options is a Michelin-starred Chinese restaurant. **www.peninsula.com**

NORTHERN

Hotel New Koyo

2-26-13 Nihonzutsumi **Tel** *(03) 3873-0343* **Fax** *(03) 3873-1358* **Rooms** *76*   **Map** *4 F1*

Popular with backpackers, this may be the cheapest hotel in Tokyo. Located in the day-laborer district of Sanya, Tokyo's Skid Row, the hotel features rooms that are minuscule but spotlessly clean. The management is helpful, and there is even free Internet access. **www.newkoyo.com**

Kikuya Ryokan

2-18-9 Nishi-Asakusa, Taito-ku **Tel** *(03) 3841-4051* *(03) 3841-6404* **Rooms** *6*   **Map** *4 E3*

This slightly shabby concrete building, in a backstreet near Tawaramachi Station, is more comfortable than initial impressions would suggest. With Senso-ji temple *(see pp56–7)* just a stroll away and lots of "Shitamachi" atmosphere in the area, this is a good choice. Western-style breakfast is available.

Ryokan Katsutaro Annex

3-8-4 Yanaka, Taito-ku **Tel** *(03) 3828-2500* *(03) 3821-5400* **Rooms** *17*   **Map** *3 B1*

Just around the corner from the lively Yanaka Ginza street and shops, this hotel has a stylish, modern exterior and crisp and clean Japanese-style *tatami* rooms, each with an attached bathroom. Free coffee and Internet access are available in the lobby. **www.katsutaro.com**

Sakura Ryokan

2-6-2 Iriya, Taito-ku **Tel** *(03) 3876-8118* **Rooms** *18*   **Map** *4 D2*

This hotel is close to the sights of both Asakusa and Ueno *(see pp48–9);* a good location in an area famous for its July morning glory fair. A friendly, English-speaking management runs this cozy place. Half the rooms are Japanese-style, the rest Western. Only some rooms have en-suite bathrooms. **www.sakura-ryokan.com**

Sawanoya Ryokan

2-3-11 Yanaka, Taito-ku **Tel** *(03) 3822-2251* **Fax** *(03) 3822-2252* **Rooms** *12*   **Map** *3 B2*

The Sawanoya has become quite an institution among backpackers and budget travelers over the years. The inn's husband and wife owners are a charming couple, happy to dispense information about this historical locality. Free coffee, tea, and Internet access. No smoking is allowed on the premises. **www.sawanoya.com**

Suzuki Ryokan

7-15-23 Yanaka, Taito-ku **Tel** *(03) 3821-4944* **Rooms** *11*   **Map** *3 C1*

Ideal for exploring the old-world charm of Yanaka, this modest *ryokan* is on the edge of the area's atmospheric graveyard. Run by elderly ladies, the warm welcome more than makes up for the creaky wooden floors and their inability to converse in English. Not all rooms have baths.

Taito Ryokan

2-1-4 Nishi-Asakusa, Taito-ku **Tel** *(03) 3843-2822* **Rooms** *9*   **Map** *4 E3*

Ruinous looking from the outside, the interiors are full of 1940s Asakusa charm. Though there is not enough privacy and the single shower is shared, the friendly, English-speaking staff and affordable rates more than make up for these drawbacks. This old, wooden building is strictly non-smoking. **www.libertyhouse.gr.jp**

Hotel Edoya

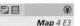

3-20-3 Yushima, Bunkyo-ku **Tel** *(03) 3833-8751* **Fax** *(03) 3833-8759* **Rooms** *49*   **Map** *3 C3*

A very smart looking hotel in the *ryokan* style, it is a short distance from both the Yushima and Ueno areas. Most of the rooms are Japanese-style and come with individual cedar bathtubs – quite a treat. There is also an outdoor bath on the roof, open to both men and women. *Kaiseki* cuisine is available in the restaurant. **www.hoteledoya.com/**

Hotel Lungwood 🗾 🍴 📺 🈴   ¥¥
5-50-5 Higashi Nippori, Arakawa-ku **Tel** *(03) 3803-1234* **Fax** *(03) 3803-2843* **Rooms** *126*   **Map** *3 C1*

Located within walking distance of several subway stations, Hotel Lungwood caters to both the business traveler and the vacationer. There are three restaurants to choose from – including one serving Chinese food and another specializing in Japanese cuisine – and an array of room styles. **www.hotellungwood.com/english.html**

Hotel New Gyominso 🗾 🍴 🈴   ¥¥
2-20-4 Kaminarimon, Taito-ku **Tel** *(03) 3844-5117* **Fax** *(03) 3841-6566* **Rooms** *160*   **Map** *4 F3*

This inexpensive hotel is located close to Asakusa Station, Azuma Bridge, and the famous Kamiya Bar *(see p157)*. The hotel offers both Western- and Japanese-style rooms, in addition to cheaper capsule accommodation. There is a ladies only floor and a Sky Bath that has magnificent views of the Sumida River. **www.gyominso.jp/e/index.html**

Ryokan Shigetsu 🍴 🈴   ¥¥
1-31-11 Asakusa, Taito-ku **Tel** *(03) 3843-2345* **Fax** *(03) 3843-2348* **Rooms** *22*   **Map** *4 E3*

This *ryokan* is a perfect ensemble of Japanese traditional design, with sliding doors, paper screens, and *tatami* mats, all lovingly maintained. Close to Asakusa Park, one of the attractions here is the Japanese-style communal bath on the top floor, affording leisurely views across old Asakusa. Western-style rooms available. **www.shigetsu.com**

Suigetsu Hotel Ogaiso 🗾 🍴 🈴 🈁 🛁   ¥¥
3-3-21 Ikenohata, Taito-ku **Tel** *(03) 3822-4611* **Fax** *(03) 3823-4340* **Rooms** *125*   **Map** *3 C2*

A comfortable, medium-size hotel within walking distance of Nezu Station on the Chiyoda Line. The baths use water from a private hot-spring well, a rarity in the modern city of Tokyo. There are two buildings arranged around a tranquil Japanese garden, one is a traditional *ryokan*. **www.ohgai.co.jp\e\index.html**

Sukeroku No Yado Sadachiyo 🍴 🈴   ¥¥
2-20-1 Asakusa, Taito-ku **Tel** *(03) 3842-6431* **Fax** *(03) 3842-6433* **Rooms** *20*   **Map** *4 E2*

The old world of Edo is successfully re-created in this atmospheric *ryokan* with sumptuously decorated Japanese-style rooms. The traditional baths are made from aromatic cypress and stone. Another highlight is the excellent Japanese food, exquisitely laid out and served. **www.sadachiyo.co.jp**

Ueno First City Hotel 🗾 🍴 🈴 🈁   ¥¥
1-14-8 Ueno, Taito-ku **Tel** *(03) 3831-8215* **Fax** *(03) 3837-8469* **Rooms** *77*   **Map** *3 C3*

This comfortable and efficient hotel, closer to Yushima metro than Ueno, has both Western and Japanese *tatami* rooms, with en suite bathrooms. The relatively small number of rooms and quiet location make this a cozy and comfortable place to stay. All rooms have Internet access. **www.uenocity-hotel.com**

Asakusa View Hotel 🗾 🍴 🈴 🈁   ¥¥¥
3-17-1 Nishi-Asakusa, Taito-ku **Tel** *(03) 3847-1111* **Fax** *(03) 3842-2117* **Rooms** *337*   **Map** *4 E2*

In a perfect location for exploring the Asakusa district, this hotel has spacious rooms that look out over the Sumida River and the rooftops of Senso-ji temple. There are nine restaurants and bars in this hotel. The Karuta Japanese restaurant has a great sushi corner, and tables with lovely garden views. **www.viewhotels.co.jp/asakusa/english**

Hotel Parkside 🗾 🍴 📺 🈴 🈁   ¥¥¥
2-11-18 Ueno, Taito-ku **Tel** *(03) 3836-5711* **Fax** *(03) 3831-6641* **Rooms** *128*   **Map** *3 C3*

This hotel provides good value for this area, especially given the great views over the lotus pond in Ueno Park *(see pp48–9)*. Select rooms on the middle to upper floors for best views. Both Japanese- and Western-style rooms are available. The 10th-floor lounge bar is a romantic spot. **www.parkside.co.jp**

WESTERN TOKYO

Capsule Hotel Fontaine Akasaka 🗾 🍴 🈴   ¥
4-3-5 Akasaka, Minato-ku **Tel** *(03) 3583-6554* **Fax** *(03) 3584-3163* **Rooms** *294*   **Map** *2 E3*

This is one of the few upscale capsule hotels in Tokyo where women are accepted, though only on weekends and national holidays. The luxurious Fontaine Akasaka also features comfortable seating areas, as well as very good bath and sauna facilities. Coin lockers are available but may not be large enough for a big suitcase.

Capsule Land Shibuya 🗾 🍴 🈴   ¥
1-19-14 Dogenzaka, Shibuya-ku **Tel** *(03) 3464-1777* **Fax** *(03) 3464-7771* **Rooms** *158*   **Map** *1 A5*

If you miss the last train, this hotel might be a final resort or a good place to experience capsule life for a night. Units have a small wall bracket TV, and just enough space to stretch out. Other facilities include coin lockers, vending machines, a restaurant, communal bathing, and showers. At present this is for men only. **www.capsule-land.com**

Akasaka Yoko Hotel 🗾 🍴 🈴 🈁   ¥¥
6-14-12 Akasaka, Minato-ku **Tel** *(03) 3586-4050* **Fax** *(03) 3586-5944* **Rooms** *244*   **Map** *2 E4*

This plain, brown, nine-story business hotel with good facilities and helpful staff has some real advantages when it comes to location. Equidistant from Nogi and Hie shrines, the quiet location is within an easy walk of Roppongi's daytime culture venues, international restaurants, and nightlife entertainment. **www.yokohotel.co.jp/english**

Asia Center of Japan Hotel

8-10-32 Akasaka, Minato-ku **Tel** *(03) 3402-6111* **Fax** *(03) 3402-0738* **Rooms** *173*   **Map** *2 E4*

A good value, basic hotel in a location that is good for visiting both Aoyama and Roppongi, this hotel is especially popular with foreign visitors for long stays. The budget priced rooms book up quickly. All rooms are well equipped, but those in the newer wing are a little larger. Free Wi-Fi service. **www.asiacenter.or.jp**

Children's Castle Hotel

5-53-1 Jingumae, Shibuya-ku **Tel** *(03) 3797-5677* **Rooms** *209*   **Map** *1 B5*

Ideal for a family stay, the Castle offers terrific recreational facilities for children. It is also popular with couples and business people. Large windows with good views make up for the slightly small rooms. Note that there is an 11pm curfew. There is also a roof terrace. **www.kodomono-shiro.or.jp/english/hotel**

Hotel Excellent

1-9-5 Ebisu-Nishi, Shibuya-ku **Tel** *(03) 5458-0087* **Rooms** *127*

A moderately priced business hotel in a laidback area just a minute from JR Ebisu Station. The facilities are minimal, with no restaurant or provision for breakfast, but the area has plenty of other eating options. The rooms are clean and pleasant, and free Internet access is available. **www.soeikikaku.co.jp/index.html**

Hotel Sunlite Shinjuku

5-15-8 Shinjuku, Shinjuku-ku **Tel** *(03) 3356-0391* **Fax** *(03) 3356-1223* **Rooms** *197*   **Map** *1 C1*

A budget alternative to Shinjuku's high-end accommodation, this comfortable, well-managed lower mid-range hotel on the east side of the station is ideally located for the shops and Kabukicho nightlife *(see p60)*. The simple rooms are clean, cozy, and comfortable. **www.sunlite.co.jp**

Hotel Sunroute Akasaka

3-21-7 Akasaka, Minato-ku **Tel** *(03) 3589-3610* **Rooms** *91*   **Map** *1 B2*

Part of the Sunroute Hotel Chain, this establishment is located near Akasaka-mitsuke metro station and is a quick taxi ride or 15-minute walk to Roppongi. The hotel has cheerful, well-equipped rooms with Internet access. The Excelsior Café makes up for the absence of a restaurant. **www.sunroute.jp**

Sansuiso Ryokan

2-9-5 Higashi-Gotanda **Tel** *(03) 3441-7475* **Fax** *(03) 3449-1944* **Rooms** *10*

This basic but friendly *ryokan* is just a short distance from JR Gotanda Station. The relaxed and cozy atmosphere with affordable prices makes this place a favorite with long-staying foreigners. The Japanese-style rooms come with private or shared facilities. The doors close at midnight. **www.sansuiso.net/price_e.htm**

Shibuya City Hotel

1-1 Maruyamacho, Shibuya-ku **Tel** *(03) 5489-1010* **Fax** *(03) 5489-1030* **Rooms** *49*   **Map** *1 A5*

This friendly, well-serviced boutique hotel is great value. Just a seven-minute walk from JR Shibuya Station and across the road from Bunkamura, the location is ideal for shopping, arts, and nightlife. The nine-story building has unusually spacious rooms at affordable rates. A friendly and attentive staff. **www.shibuya-city-hotel.com**

Akasaka Excel Hotel Tokyu

2-14-3 Nagatacho, Chiyoda-ku **Tel** *(03) 3580-2311* **Fax** *(03) 3580-6066* **Rooms** *531*   **Map** *2 F3*

Located in an area full of luxury hotels, close to Akasaka and Roppongi, with impeccable service and first-rate facilities, this hotel is a very good deal. Good shops, restaurants and bars, and a mall in the vicinity add to the experience. Select the quieter rooms away from the main road. **www.tokyuhotelsjapan.com**

Ark Tower Hotel

6-1-23 Roppongi, Minato-ku **Tel** *(03) 3404-5111* **Fax** *(03) 3404-5115* **Rooms** *76*   **Map** *2 5E*

Noises rising from the street is the price you pay for this terrific location right in the heart of the upscale Roppongi entertainment district, located between Roppongi Hills and the Tokyo Midtown. Rooms are functional, but even standard singles are furnished with semi-double beds. Good choice of free cable TV. **www.arktower.co.jp**

Creston Hotel

10-8 Kamiyamacho, Shibuya-ku **Tel** *(03) 3481-5800* **Fax** *(03) 3481-5515* **Rooms** *43*   **Map** *1 A5*

Tucked down a quiet backstreet near to NHK and a stroll from Bunkamura, the Creston is an ideal spot for a bit of peace and quiet, although it has a reputation as a hidden getaway for visiting rock stars. Located right in the center of Shibuya *(see pp66–7)*. The staff is bilingual. **www.crestonhotel.co.jp**

Haneda Excel Hotel Tokyu

3-4-2 Haneda Airport, Ota-ku **Tel** *(03) 5756-6000* **Fax** *(03) 5756-6001* **Rooms** *387*   **Map** *1 B1*

If you have an early morning domestic flight, this hotel is a good option as it is on the same floor as the check-in and departure areas of Haneda Airport. With a superior business hotel ambience, the desk is open 24-hours. The staff is bilingual and helpful. Free Internet access. **www.tokyuhotels.co.jp**

Hotel Century Southern Tower

2-2-1 Yoyogi, Shibuya-ku **Tel** *(03) 5354-0111* **Fax** *(03) 5354-0100* **Rooms** *375*   **Map** *1 B1*

Located on Shinjuku's Southern Terrace, and with guest rooms from the 19th floor up, the Hotel Century offers superb views of the area's sights and lights. The rooms cater for a wide range of clients, from single travelers on a limited budget to business executives on expense accounts. **www.southerntower.co.jp/english/index.html**

Hotel Ibis

7-14-4 Roppongi, Minato-ku **Tel** *(03) 3403-4411* **Fax** *(03) 3479-0609* **Rooms** *182*　　　　　**Map** *2 E5*

This stylish hotel in the midst of the Roppongi nightlife scene offers smallish but comfortable rooms. The friendly staff will point you in the direction of the karaoke rooms and the Sabatini restaurant, which claims to re-create the mood of a Roman market. **www.ibis-hotel.com**

Shiba Park Hotel

1-5-10 Shiba-Koen, Minato-ku **Tel** *(03) 3433-4141* **Fax** *(03) 3433-4142* **Rooms** *318*　　　　　**Map** *5 A4*

Set in a quiet, leafy location just 2 minutes walk from Onarimon subway station and the superb Sanmon gate leading to Zojo-ji temple *(see p41)*, this hotel has tastefully decorated rooms. There is a main building and an annexe across the road. The rooms are clean and well equipped, and the bilingual staff very helpful. **www.shibaparkhotel.com**

Shibuya Excel Hotel Tokyu

1-12-2 Dogenzaka, Shibuya-ku **Tel** *(03) 5457-0109* **Fax** *(03) 5457-0309* **Rooms** *407*　　　　　**Map** *1 B5*

Given its location right next to JR Shibuya Station, this is a good deal. Part of the Mark City shopping complex, rooms are surprisingly quiet, but once you step out of the hotel you are in the heart of Shibuya street life. Comfortable, well-equipped rooms; two floors are set aside for women. **www.tokyuhotelsjapan.com**

Shibuya Tobu Hotel

3-1 Udagawacho, Shibuya-ku **Tel** *(03) 3476-0111* **Fax** *(03) 3476-0903* **Rooms** *197*　　　　　**Map** *1 B5*

A business hotel with more space and style than usual. The singles have wide, comfortable, double beds and do not cost much more than standard twins. Although all rooms are double-glazed, try to get a room facing away from the traffic of Koen-dori. There are several restaurants here serving different cuisines. **www.tobuhotel.co.jp/shibuya**

Shibuya Tokyu Inn

1-24-10 Shibuya, Shibuya-ku **Tel** *(03) 3498-0109* **Fax** *(03) 3498-0189* **Rooms** *223*　　　　　**Map** *1 B5*

A stylish hotel close enough to JR Shibuya Station and metro lines for convenience, but far away enough to get a good night's sleep. Double-paned windows block out the street noise. The rooms are spacious, comfortable, and have good facilities, including Internet access. **www.tokyuhotels.co.jp**

Shinjuku Washington Hotel

3-2-9 Nishi-Shinjuku, Shinjuku-ku **Tel** *(03) 3343-3111* **Fax** *(03) 3342-2575* **Rooms** *337*　　　　　**Map** *1 A2*

Just a few minutes' walk from Shinjuku Station, to which it is linked via an underground passage, the Washington Hotel offers great value for this part of town. The choice of restaurants and bars is rather good, rooms are reasonably spacious, and the English-speaking staff are used to dealing with foreign guests. **www.shinjyuku-wh.com/english**

Cerulean Tower Tokyu Hotel

26-1, Sakuragaoka-cho, Shibuya-ku **Tel** *(03) 3476-3000* **Fax** *(03) 3476-3001* **Rooms** *411*

This high-end hotel occupies the 13th–37th floors of the tower, offering spectacular views even from the bathrooms. Zen-like interiors, *kaiseki* restaurants, a Noh theater, and high-speed Internet connections create a modern, highly cultural ambience. The Cerulean Tower is within easy walking distance of Shibuya. **www.ceruleantower-hotel.com**

Keio Plaza Hotel

2-2-1 Nishi-Shinjuku, Shinjuku-ku **Tel** *(03) 3344-0111* **Fax** *(03) 3345-8269* **Rooms** *1,435*　　　　　**Map** *1 A5*

This colossal hotel in the middle of Shinjuku's skyscraper district is an ideal location for exploring the area. The Keio Plaza boasts a spectacular range of restaurants, a tea ceremony room, beauty salon, sauna, shops, and an outdoor, heated Sky Pool, ensuring a comfortable and leisurely stay. **www.keioplaza.co.jp**

Tokyo Prince Hotel

3-3-1 Shibakoen, Minato-ku **Tel** *(03) 3432-1111* **Fax** *(03) 3434-5551* **Rooms** *484*　　　　　**Map** *5 A4*

A large hotel complex surrounded by landscaped gardens and tranquility, it is a short stroll to Zojo-ji temple and the landmark Tokyo Tower *(see p41)*. The rooms are luxurious, with attractive, comfortable furnishings and Internet access. The outdoor swimming pool and beer garden are great summer attractions. **www.princehotels.co.jp**

ANA Intercontinental Tokyo

1-12-23 Akasaka, Minato-ku **Tel** *(03) 3505-1111* **Fax** *(03) 3505-1155* **Rooms** *844*　　　　　**Map** *2 F4*

The flagship hotel of the well-respected ANA airline chain lies within the huge Ark Hills complex in Roppongi, which includes restaurants, shops, cafés, and the Japan Foundation Library. Many rooms have views of either Mount Fuji *(see pp96–7)* or the Imperial Palace. **www.anaintercontinental-tokyo.jp/e/**

Grand Hyatt Tokyo

6-10-3 Roppongi, Minato-ku **Tel** *(03) 4333-1234* **Fax** *(03) 4333-8123* **Rooms** *387*　　　　　**Map** *2 E4*

A spectacular, contemporary design fuses with natural elements, such as stone and hard wood trimmings, in the bedrooms and bathrooms to create a warm, refined mood in the grandest of Tokyo's Hyatt properties. Spa services, a tasty pastry boutique, and a shopping mall add to the interest. **www.tokyo.grand.hyatt.jp**

Grand Prince Hotel New Takanawa

3-13-1 Takanawa, Minato-ku **Tel** *(03) 3442-1111* **Fax** *(03) 3444-1234* **Rooms** *946*

This hotel offers spacious, luxurious rooms with all the modern fixtures and fittings, and views out over extensive manicured landscape gardens. All the rooms have balconies. Although there is not a lot to do at night in the immediate area, JR Shinagawa Station is only a 5 minute walk away. **www.princehotels.co.jp**

Hilton Tokyo

6-6-2 Nishi-Shinjuku, Shinjuku-ku **Tel** *(03) 3344-5111* **Fax** *(03) 3342-6094* **Rooms** *806*   **Map** *1 A1*

Within walking distance of Shinjuku, this branch of the Hilton chain offers an elegant lobby and luxurious guest rooms with all the modern conveniences expected in an establishment of this level. Amenities include tennis courts, a gym, an indoor heated pool for the energetic, shops, restaurants, and bars. **www.hilton.com**

Hotel New Otani Tokyo

4-1 Kioi-cho, Chiyoda-ku **Tel** *(03) 3265-1111* **Fax** *(03) 3221-2619* **Rooms** *1479*   **Map** *2 E3*

This gigantic luxury hotel has labyrinthine corridors, 38 upscale restaurants and bars, boutiques, and gift shops. Former guests include diplomats, noted business leaders, and rock stars. The garden is magnificent. Other New Otani hotels are located throughout Japan. **www.newotani.co.jp**

Hotel Okura Tokyo

2-10-4 Toranomon, Minato-ku **Tel** *(03) 3582-0111* **Fax** *(03) 3582-3707* **Rooms** *857*   **Map** *2 F4*

A popular hotel among the international business community, visiting VIPs, and the discerning and wealthy. The timeless Japanese decor, tearoom, and pristine gardens create a restful mood. The hotel offers an array of cuisines in its many restaurants and bars. Not the most modern hotel, but one that offers superb service. **www.okura.com/tokyo**

Park Hyatt Tokyo

3-7-1-2 Nishi-Shinjuku, Shinjuku-ku **Tel** *(03) 5322-1234* **Fax** *(03) 5322-1288* **Rooms** *177*   **Map** *1 A2*

This is the hotel where the film *Lost in Translation* was shot. It occupies the top 14 floors of this 52-story skyscraper. Well-appointed rooms are finished in natural woods, marble, and fine fabrics, making for a very refined ambience. Sunday brunches at the Park Tower's New York Grill restaurant are legendary. **http://tokyo.park.hyatt.com**

The Ritz-Carlton Tokyo

Tokyo Midtown, 9-7-1 Akasaka, Minato-ku **Tel** *(03) 3423-8000* **Fax** *(03) 3423-8001* **Rooms** *248*   **Map** *2 E4*

With a superb location in the city's tallest building, the Tokyo Midtown in Roppongi, the Ritz-Carlton is a spacious, modern luxury hotel with elegantly appointed rooms that offer dramatic views over the capital. Dining options are first class, and the stylish spa provides a wide range of treatments. **www.ritzcarlton.com/en/tokyo**

Sheraton Miyako Hotel Tokyo

1-1-50 Shirokanedai, Minato-ku **Tel** *(03) 3447-3111* **Fax** *(03) 3447-3133* **Rooms** *495*

Located in a very green and expensive district, this offshoot of the chain's famous Kyoto prototype was designed by the renowned architect Minoru Yamasaki. This is a modern hotel but with carefully executed Japanese aesthetics. Stay here to enjoy lovely gardens and dine at Zen-like restaurants. **www.miyakohotels.ne.jp/tokyo/english**

Westin Hotel Tokyo

1-4-1 Mita, Meguro-ku **Tel** *(03) 5423-7000* **Fax** *(03) 5423-7600* **Rooms** *444*

A grand, European-style hotel, the Westin is part of the Ebisu Garden Place complex *(see p76)*. The lobby has black marble floors and columns, and magnificent flower displays. There are large rooms with faux antique furnishings. Le Spa Parisien offers a European spa experience in 11 treatment rooms. **www.westin-tokyo.co.jp**

FARTHER AFIELD

IKEBUKURO Kimi Ryokan

2-36-8 Ikebukuro, Toshima-ku **Tel** *(03) 3971-3766* **Fax** *(03) 3987-1326* **Rooms** *38*

A very basic *ryokan* with a relaxed atmosphere, the Kimi Ryokan offers great value – an established favorite with long-term foreign visitors. Toilets and showers are shared. The pleasant rooms, traditional bath, and large communal lounge make for a comfortable experience. Choose between Western and *tatami*-mat rooms. **www.kimi-ryokan.jp**

ODAIBA Hotel Nikko Tokyo

1-9-1 Daiba, Minato-ku **Tel** *(03) 5500-5500* **Rooms** *453*

Occupying one of the finest waterfront settings in Tokyo, this hotel is surrounded by picturesque gardens and parks. It is a short stroll away from Palette Town and Aqua City *(see pp82–3)*. Popular with young couples, the hotel has impeccable service, and the setting is romantic, with good night views over Tokyo Bay. **www.hnt.co.jp**

ODAIBA Le Meridien Grand Pacific

2-6-1 Daiiba, Minato-ku **Tel** *(03) 5500-6711* **Fax** *(03) 5500-4507* **Rooms** *884*

Another towering, luxurious hotel opposite Odaiba Station. Although some may think the location is too far out, for others it is a quiet option. Guests can enjoy super bayside views from well-appointed rooms and the hotel's 30th-floor Sky Lounge. The service is excellent. **www.grandpacific.jp/eng**

SHIODOME Conrad Hotel

1-9-1 Higashi-Shimbashi, Minato-ku **Tel** *(03) 6388-8000* **Fax** *(03) 6388-8001* **Rooms** *290*

The views of the serene Hama Detached Palace Garden *(see pp40–41)* from the tastefully understated rooms in this prestigious, sleek, and modern hotel are superb. Guests should indulge in the cedarwood spas, aromatherapy, and other leisure options on offer in this 37-story wonder. **www.conradtokyo.co.jp**

Key to Price Guide *see p110* **Key to Symbols** *see back cover flap*

BEYOND TOKYO

CHICHIBU-TAMA NATIONAL PARK Shukubo Komadori Sanso

155 Mitake-san, Ome-shi **Tel** *(0428) 78-8472* **Rooms** *10*

Dating from 1776, this old pilgrim's mountain lodge on Mount Mitake has all the comforts of a modern *ryokan*. Close to Mitake Shrine *(see p94)*, all the rooms with traditional *tatami* flooring have wonderful views of the mountainside and there are two shared cypress bathtubs. **www.komadori.com**

FUJI FIVE LAKES Inn Fujitomita

3235 Shibokusa, Oshino-mura, Minamitsuru-gun, Yamanashi **Tel** *(0555) 84-3359* **Rooms** *9*

This inn enjoys clear views of breathtaking Mount Fuji *(see pp96–7)* from six of its guest rooms and surrounding gardens. The outside pool, set in a garden, and the natural hot spring add to the leisure options at this relaxing inn. The helpful staff speak English. **www.tim.hi-ho.ne.jp/innfuji**

FUJI-HAKONE Fuji-Hakone Guest House

912 Sengokuhara, Hakone-machi, Kanagawa **Tel** *(0460) 84-6577* **Rooms** *7*

A cozy guesthouse with 24-hour indoor and outdoor hot springs in a lovely setting in the middle of Hakone National Park *(see p94)*. It provides simple but comfortable Japanese rooms, shared baths, and toilets. Located a minute's walk from Senkyoro-mae bus stop No. 4 from Odawara Station. **www.fujihakone.com**

IZU PENINSULA Osawa Onsen

153 Osawa, Matsuzaki-cho, Shizuoka **Tel** *(0558) 43-0121* **Fax** *(0558) 43-0123* **Rooms** *25*

A 17th century former samurai villa in a sleepy village, with beautifully decorated rooms, scenic inner and outer gardens, and cedar *onsen* baths. Western- and Japanese-style bedding is available. The highly rated dinners are served in private rooms. **www.osawaonsen.co.jp**

IZU PENINSULA Shimoda Tokyu Hotel

5-12-1 Shimoda-shi, Shizuoka **Tel** *(0558) 22-2411* **Fax** *(0558) 22-4970* **Rooms** *115*

Built on a cliff 1 mile (2 km) south of Shimoda, this hotel has the full range of hot springs, a sauna, and a swimming pool. Sea views and gardens sloping to the cliff's edge add to the appeal. A minibus picks guests up from Shimoda Station. The outdoor public bath has delightful views across the bay. **www.tokyuhotelsjapan.com**

KAMAKURA Kamakura Hase Youth Hostel

5-11 Sakanoshita, Kamakura-shi **Tel** *(0467) 24-3390* **Rooms** *12*

Nicely situated between the beach, temples, and the Great Buddha, this friendly hostel is just a 5-minute walk from Hase Station. Rooms are Western and Japanese style. Though dinner is not provided, there are facilities to store and heat food. Non-youth hostel members have to pay an extra ¥1,000. **www.jyh.or.jp/english/index.html**

KAMAKURA Kamakura Prince Hotel

1-2-18 Shichirigahama-Higashi, Kanagawa **Tel** *(0467) 32-1111* **Fax** *(0467) 32-9290* **Rooms** *98*

Bright, sea-facing rooms located on a beach in the Shonan area of Sugami Bay create a relaxed resort feel. The curving two-story building, outside pool, and modern Japanese garden blend to form an appealing and original design. Dining options include classic French and Japanese *kaiseki* cuisines. **www.princehotels.co.jp**

NIKKO Turtle Inn Nikko

2-16 Takumi-cho, Tochigi **Tel** *(0288) 53-3168* **Fax** *(0288) 53-3883* **Rooms** *10*

This 'petit inn' is just a 10-minute stroll from the Toshogu Shrine World Heritage sites. The friendly, English-speaking owners will fill you in on local attractions. Fans of Mashiko pottery will appreciate the tableware here, fired in nearby kilns. Guests can choose between Western and Japanese rooms. **www.turtle-nikko.com/turtle/index_en.html**

NIKKO Nikko Kanaya Hotel

1300 Kami-Hatsuishi-machi, Tochigi **Tel** *(0288) 54-0001* **Fax** *(0288) 53-2487* **Rooms** *70*

A classic resort hotel dating from 1873, the Kanaya combines effortless, old-fashioned elegance with superb service. The rooms dating from the Meiji-era to the mid-1950s are equipped with modern amenities. Make reservations during the peak holiday season. **www.kanayahotel.co.jp/nkh/index-e.html**

YOKOHAMA Hotel New Grand

10 Yamashita-cho, Yokohama **Tel** *(045) 681-1841* **Fax** *(045) 681-1895* **Rooms** *249*

This is where General MacArthur had his digs for a short time during the US Occupation of 1945. A luxury European-style hotel, the original building dates from 1927; the tower is an addition from the 1990s. There is a choice of three restaurants, including the very highly rated French Le Normandie. **www.hotel-newgrand.co.jp/english/**

YOKOHAMA Yokohama Royal Park Hotel

2-2-1-3 Minato Mirai, Nishi-ku, Yokohama **Tel** *(045) 221-1111* **Rooms** *603*

A super-luxury hotel within walking distance of the showpiece Minato Mirai port complex. The real appeal here are the unmatched room views of the waterfront and Mount Fuji. Rooms are located on the 52nd–67th floors of the hugely impressive Landmark Tower, the tallest building in Japan. **www.yrph.com/en**

WHERE TO EAT

Tokyo is one of the major gourmet cities of the world, known not only for its sushi and other Japanese delicacies, but also the remarkable variety of foreign cuisines. Humble taverns or grills that have been in business for centuries nestle side by side with gleaming high-rise malls lined with delis and markets serving foods from around the world. The quality of meals at high-end restaurants is matched by their prices, but

A typical selection of Japanese food in a *bento* box

eating out does not have to be exorbitant. There are numerous mid- or low-end diners; noodle shops abound, as do fast-food restaurants (both Western and local); and if pressed for time and money, you can pick up snacks in supermarkets, convenience stores, and mid-range restaurants clustered around train stations. Best of all, wherever you go, standards of service and cleanliness are invariably high. It is hard to get a poor meal in Tokyo.

Savoring a sushi meal at a restaurant in Jingumae

MEALS AND MEAL TIMES

Most *ryokan* (*see p108*) and some hotels serve traditional breakfasts from 7–9am. If your hotel does not serve it, you will easily find a nearby café serving coffee and croissants or Danish pastries. When Japanese eat breakfast out, they usually do so in coffee shops that serve sets called *moningu* (morning), consisting of coffee, toast, a hard-boiled egg, and a small salad. However, breakfast is not a major meal in modern Tokyo.

Tokyo tends to eat lunch early. Typically, lunch runs from 11:30am to 2:30pm, and dinner starts at 5:30 or 6pm. Some upscale restaurants stop serving at 9 or 10pm, while most stay open to around 11 or 11:30pm (later still in areas such as Roppongi) to cater to after-hours office crowd.

RESERVATIONS AND DRESS CODE

Reservations are advisable at top restaurants in Tokyo and essential at the most exclusive Japanese dining places. Elsewhere, you can usually find a table without a reservation, especially if you arrive early in the evening.

Jeans and casual shirts are acceptable in most places, provided they are not torn or dirty. Women may find long, loose clothing advantageous when dining at a place with *zashiki* (low platform) seating. Also be sure to wear clean socks or stockings without holes if seating on *tatami* mats is involved, as you will have to take off your shoes. Avoid wearing strong perfumes or colognes if dining at a *kaiseki* restaurant or participating in a tea ceremony.

SET MENUS (TEISHOKU)

Most restaurants in Tokyo offer fixed-price menus, and these can be especially good value at lunchtime. Usually there will be a number of menu choices. These set menus are called *teishoku*.

Some budget restaurants have window displays with realistic-looking plastic models of their dishes, or menus with photographs. Point to an item if you do not know its name. At many noodle restaurants and basic diners, it may be necessary to buy a ticket at the entrance before you place an order.

PRICES AND PAYING

Tokyo has restaurants to suit all budgets. You can slurp a hearty bowl of noodles for less than ¥500, or spend your entire budget for a week on a single night out on the town. Many upscale restaurants that might charge ¥10,000 or ¥20,000 per head at dinner often have economical lunch menus for ¥3,000 to ¥5,000.

The consumption tax (5 percent) is included in the quoted price, but many Western restaurants add a service charge. At some traditional Japanese eateries, an obligatory starter (*otoshi*) is served to all customers in lieu of a table charge.

At coffee shops and some restaurants, the bill is placed on your table. Just take it to the cashier to pay. At most bars and restaurants you will

Realistic-looking plastic "food" display in restaurant window

be asked to pay your bill at your table. The amount, written on a slip of paper, will generally be presented to you on a small tray. You place your payment (cash or card) on this tray, and your change will be returned on the same tray. Tipping is not expected, and may be refused.

ENTERING A RESTAURANT OR BAR

Traditional restaurants often have *noren* (half-curtains) hanging outside the door. This indicates that they are open for business. Duck past the curtain, slide open the door, and pause at the threshold. If you do not have a reservation, it is common practice to indicate how many people there are in your group by raising the appropriate number of fingers. In some restaurants, you may be asked to remove your shoes. Slippers will, however, be provided for walking around on the wooden floor areas.

Many Japanese restaurants in Tokyo offer Western-style tables and chairs, plus counter seating looking into the open kitchen. They may also have traditional seating, known as *zashiki* with low tables. This involves sitting on thin cushions (*zabuton*) on *tatami* mats. Shoes and slippers are never worn on *tatami* mats. Women are expected to sit with their legs underneath them, *seiza*-style or to the side, mermaid-style; men usually sit cross-legged. It is ill-mannered to stretch your legs out under a low table. Special chairs with backs but no legs are often provided, or there may be leg-wells set under the tables, a plus for most visitors.

The counter is often the preferred place to sit, especially in sushi and tempura restaurants, as it gives prime views of the chefs skillfully preparing the food. Increasingly, smoking is discouraged at seats close to the kitchen.

Lunchbox counter in shopping mall

FOOD CUSTOMS, ETIQUETTE & TABOOS

Most restaurants offer guests *oshibori*, small damp towels, often hot, after they are seated for a meal. These are used to wipe hands (not the face and neck), and then left on the table top for dabbing fingers and spills, rather than being placed in the lap. Never blow your nose into the *oshibori* or even a handkerchief in public.

Japanese say, "*itadakimass*" ("I humbly receive") before eating; on leaving, it is customary to say "*gochiso-sama desh'ta*" ("it was a feast"). Calling "*sumimasen*" (excuse me!) is the standard method of attracting the waiter's attention.

Japanese drinking etiquette requires that you pour for the other person and vice versa. When on the receiving end, you pick up your glass, supporting the bottom with the other hand. When a toast (*kampai*) is made, beer and whiskey glasses should be clinked; with sake, cups are raised in a salute.

Japanese meals comprise numerous courses, each served in separate bowls or plates. In formal situations, each person will have his own individual vessels; more informally, you serve yourself from shared bowls in the middle of the table. Instead of eating directly from communal bowls, you first transfer a few bite-sized portions onto a small plate in front of you, using the serving chopsticks, if provided.

It is quite acceptable to pick up small bowls (such as rice bowls) and hold them half way to the mouth. Soup is slurped directly from the bowl, but any solid morsels should be picked out with chopsticks (*hashi*). If a morsel proves too difficult to handle, you can hold a chopstick in each hand and make a sawing motion to cut it.

Do not use chopsticks to spear food, or to push it straight from the bowl into the mouth (as commonly done in China). Gesturing and pointing with your chopsticks are also impolite. When not using them, lay your chopsticks on your chopstick-rest (*hashi-oki*) if provided, or place them across the lowest dish, keeping them uncrossed and parallel with your side of the table.

Chopsticks should never be stuck upright into bowls of rice or other food; and food should never be passed from one set of chopsticks to another. These are associated with funerary customs and are taboo at the dinner table.

Sitting *seiza*-style on *zabuton* cushions

Types of Restaurants and Bars

Tokyo has restaurants to suit every taste and budget, from hole-in-the-wall noodle stands to havens of refinement serving formal *kaiseki* banquets, not to mention the fine French, Italian, and Chinese cuisine. Most Japanese restaurants tend to specialize in specific genres, such as sushi, sukiyaki, tempura, or even in individual ingredients such as tofu and *fugu* (blowfish).

Re-created traditional warehouse *(kura)*, Gonpachi restaurant, Ginza

KAISEKI RYORI

Japan's traditional haute cuisine, *kaiseki ryori* is derived from the food served to accompany tea ceremonies, developed in Kyoto some 500 years ago. A typical banquet comprises numerous small courses, each exquisitely arranged, served in a prescribed order, and with careful reference to the season. Typically, *kaiseki* meals are served with great formality in elegant restaurants (sometimes known as *ryoriya*) or at *ryotei*, discreet establishments with courtyard gardens and spare but elegant private rooms.

KYO-RYORI AND KAPPO

Traditional cuisine prepared in the Kyoto style is often known as *Kyo-ryori*. Although the procession of dishes follows the established *kaiseki* pattern, the atmosphere is less formal. Meals feature typical Kyoto ingredients such as *fu* (wheat gluten) and *yuba* (soy-milk skin). Smaller places, with often no more than a single counter and where you do not have to order full-course meals, are often called *kappo*.

SHOJIN RYORI

The tradition of vegetarian cuisine known as *shojin ryori* developed along with Zen Buddhism in the 12th century. Meals can range from elaborate banquets similar to *kaiseki* (and just as expensive) but without using any fish, meat, or eggs to modern versions served in contemporary settings. Although Kyoto is better known for its *shojin ryori*, there are several fine specialist restaurants in Tokyo, as well as around the Zen temples in Kamakura.

IZAKAYA AND DINING BARS

Izakaya are down-to-earth places where you eat as you drink (rather than vice versa), ordering a few dishes at a time. At their most basic, these are budget taverns, identified by raucous, smoke-filled interiors, and battered red lanterns by the front door. Others are more refined, and may serve food of considerable quality. Many have large platters of pre-cooked items on their counter tops to pick from. A similar genre, now common in Tokyo, is the "dining bar." The approach is similar to an *izakaya* but with plenty of French and Italian influences.

SUSHI RESTAURANTS

Restaurants specializing in sushi *(see pp128-9)* vary greatly in style, from low-priced *kaiten-zushi* shops, where the sushi comes to you on a conveyor belt, to astronomically expensive places where everything, from the fish to the ginger, is of optimum freshness and quality. As a general rule, if there are no prices listed anywhere, it will be expensive.

While sitting at the counter, diners normally order servings of *nigiri-zushi* (hand-pressed sushi). If seated at a table or a *zashiki* (low platform), diners tend to have combos of *nigiri-zushi*, served on a platter or slab of polished wood.

Counter seating looking into the open kitchen, sushi restaurant, Ginza

Specialty *dengaku* restaurant

SPECIALTY RESTAURANTS

Tempura, sukiyaki, teppanyaki, and *tonkatsu* are generally served at restaurants that focus on each particular genre. Other areas of specialization worth investigating include *yakitori* (charcoal-grilled skewers of chicken), *unagi* (eel, grilled to delectable perfection), *nabe* (winter hotpots cooked at the table), and *dengaku* (skewered food, such as grilled tofu). *Fugu* restaurants serve up the delight of the adventurous gourmet, the poisonous blowfish.

VEGETARIAN FOOD

Although traditional Japanese cuisine includes plenty of vegetables and high-protein soyfoods such as tofu and

THE TANUKI

In Japanese folklore badgers are celebrated as lovable buffoons or drunken rascals. This is one of the reasons why the ceramic likeness of the *tanuki* is often found at the entrance of *iza-kaya* and other drinking places.

natto (fermented soybeans), it is not a vegetarian's paradise, as most dishes are cooked in fish-based *dashi* stock. However, *shojin ryori* restaurants use kelp and mushroom stock instead. Tokyo has a growing number of macrobiotic and natural foods eateries. Indian restaurants also offer good vegetarian options.

NOODLE RESTAURANTS

Japanese noodles come in two forms – brown buckwheat *soba*, a favorite in Tokyo since Edo times, and white *udon*, made from wheat flour. These are served cold with a dip or in a hot, savory soup. *Ramen* is a Japanese variant on Chinese noodles, usually served with a meaty broth. Late-night *ramen* counters are cheap, ubiquitous, and enduringly popular.

A cozy noodle bar with compact outdoor seating, Shinjuku

OTHER ASIAN RESTAURANTS

Chinese and Korean food is hugely popular in Tokyo. *Yakiniku* (Korean-style barbecue with plenty of red meat) diners are found throughout the city, with the most authentic found in Korea Town, north of Shinjuku. Good Thai, Vietnamese, and Mongolian restaurants are also available throughout the city.

WESTERN RESTAURANTS

Yoshoku are Western cuisine restaurants, some of which serve Japanese versions of Western dishes, such as *omu-raisu* (omelet rice) and hamburger steak. Tokyo boasts French and Italian cuisine to rival the finest in Europe and North America. There are also numerous budget bistros and trattorias of remarkable authenticity. Spanish food is catching on fast, while German, Belgian, and Portuguese restaurants can be easily found. The British Isles are well represented by many pubs of varying quality. However servings, especially of wine, tend to be skimpy.

FOOD HALLS AND MARKET STALLS

The food halls, located in the basements of most upmarket department stores are an essential stop for anyone with an interest in food. Colorful delicatessen-type stalls display a huge range of food both cooked and packaged. On the same floor, there may be small counter-style restaurants serving sushi, tempura, or a variety of noodles. Most department stores have restaurants on the top floor that serve substantial meals. You may also be offered free samples, with no obligation to buy.

Food markets have artful displays and stalls offering snacks and presentation boxes of sweets, tea, rice crackers, and fruit.

FAST FOOD AND CONVENIENCE STORES

There are a number of fast-food chains, serving burgers, fried chicken, and the like. Many have familiar names (McDonald's, Kentucky), albeit with Japanese variations. Local clones such as Mosburger offer innovative twists, such as serving burgers between rice patties, with shreds of cooked burdock.

Convenience stores offer a good selection of *bento* boxes *(see p127)*, *onigiri* (rice balls), and snacks.

Reading the Menu

General vocabulary likely to be useful when eating out is given in the *Phrase Book* on pages 204–8. Individual ingredients are also listed there. A selection of some of the most popular dishes and styles of cooking are listed in this glossary, including Japanese script to help you read menus in Japanese. Further details about some of the dishes follow on pages 124–9.

DONBURI: RICE-BOWL DISHES

Katsudon
カツどん
Rice bowl topped with a breaded, deep-fried pork cutlet and semi-cooked egg.

Nikudon
肉どん
Rice bowl with beef, tofu, and gelatinous noodles.

Oyakodon
親子どん
Rice bowl with chicken, onions, and runny, semi-cooked egg.

Tamagodon
卵どん
Rice bowl topped with a semi-cooked egg.

Tendon
天どん
Rice bowl that has one or two shrimp tempura and sauce.

Unadon
鰻どん
Rice bowl with grilled eel.

OTHER RICE DISHES

Kamameshi
釜飯／かまめし
Rice and tidbits steamed in a clay or metal pot with a wooden lid. Served in the container it was steamed in.

Kare raisu
カレーライス
"Curry rice", Can be *ebi-kare* (shrimp curry), *katsu-kare* (with deep-fried pork cutlet), etc.

Makunouchi bento
幕の内弁当
Classic *bento (see p127)*.

Ocha-zuke
お茶漬け
Rice in a bowl with a piece of grilled salmon, pickled plum, etc., over which tea is poured.

Omu-raisu
オムライス
Thin omelet wrapped around rice mixed with tomato sauce and chicken or pork bits.

Onigiri
おにぎり
Two or three triangular chunks of rice wrapped with strips of dried seaweed *(nori)*.

Unaju
鰻重
Grilled eel served over rice in a lacquered, lidded box.

Yaki-onigiri
焼おにぎり
Variation of *onigiri*, without seaweed, grilled over a flame.

Three pieces of *onigiri*

Zosui
雑炊
Rice soup made with the leftover stock of a one-pot *(nabemono)* meal.

NOODLE DISHES

Kitsune soba/udon
きつねそば／うどん
Soba or *udon* noodles in flavored *dashi* broth with pieces of fried tofu.

Nabe yaki udon
鍋焼うどん
Udon noodles simmered in a lidded ceramic pot *(donabe)* with a flavored *dashi* broth, perhaps with shrimp tempura, shiitake mushroom, and egg. Popular in winter.

Ramen
ラーメン
Chinese-style noodles in a broth. Usually there are some thin slices of roast pork on top, along with sliced leeks, seaweed, and a slice of fish-paste roll.

Reimen (Hiyashi chuka)
冷麺（冷やし中華）
Chinese noodles topped with strips of ham or roast pork, cucumbers, and cabbage. Dressed with a vinegar and sesame oil sauce. Popular summer dish.

Somen
そうめん
Very thin white noodles, usually served in ice water. A summer dish.

Tamago-toji soba/udon
卵とじそば／うどん
Soba or *udon* in a flavored *dashi* broth into which an egg has been dropped and stirred to cook gently.

Tempura soba/udon
天ぷらそば／うどん
Soba or *udon* in a flavored *dashi* broth with one or two pieces of shrimp tempura.

Yakisoba
焼そば
Soft Chinese noodles sautéed on a griddle with vegetables and some form of meat or fish.

Zarusoba
ざるそば
Soba noodles served cold on a bamboo rack. Variation: *ten-zarusoba* has shrimp and vegetable tempura next to noodles.

RICE CRACKERS AND NIBBLES

Crackers *(senbei* or *osenbei)* are sold in supermarkets. Beautifully made and presented, they are also sold at station gift counters and stalls at the popular tourist attractions.

Rice crackers with *nori* seaweed

Chocolate-coated "Pocky" sticks

Mixed rice crackers

Prawn crackers

Rice crackers shaped like persimmon seeds

Pea and soy-bean crackers

DISHES PREPARED AT THE TABLE

Mizutaki/Chirinabe
水焚き／ちり鍋
Nabemono (one-pot meal) of vegetables, tofu, and chicken *(mizutaki)* or fish *(chirinabe)*.

Okonomiyaki
お好み焼
Thick pancake-shaped mix of cabbage, egg, shrimp, squid, or pork cooked on a griddle.

Shabu-shabu
しゃぶしゃぶ
Nabemono (hot pot) with thinly sliced beef and vegetables cooked in a metal pan.

Table condiments: seven-spice *(shichimi)* powder, jar of soy sauce, and ground chili pepper *(ichimi)*

Sukiyaki
すき焼き
High-quality pan-cooked beef or chicken and vegetables.

Teppanyaki
鉄板焼
Meat and/or shrimp or squid and vegetables grilled on a griddle in front of the diner.

Udon-suki
うどんすき
Udon noodles, chicken, and sometimes clams or shrimp simmered in a soup.

SUSHI

Chirashi-zushi
ちらし寿司／鮨
"Scattered" sushi *(see p128)*.

Nigiri-zushi
握り寿司／鮨
"Fingers" of sushi *(see p128)*.

Maki-zushi
巻寿司／鮨
"Rolled" sushi *(see p129)*.

SET MEAL

Teishoku
定食
A set meal *(see p118)*, with rice, soup, some vegetables, salad, a main meat dish, and pickles.

MENU CATEGORIES

Aemono
和え物
Dressed salad dishes.

Agemono
揚げ物
Deep-fried foods.

Nimono
煮物
Simmered foods.

Sashimi (Otsukuri)
刺身（お造り）
Raw fish *(see p129)*.

Sunomono
酢の物
Vinegared dishes.

Yakimono
焼き物
Grilled foods.

À LA CARTE

Agedashi-dofu
揚げだし豆腐
Deep-fried tofu (bean curd) in a stock.

Chikuzen-ni
筑前煮
Vegetables and bits of chicken simmered together.

Eda-mame
枝豆
Soybeans steamed in the pod. Popular summer snack.

Hiya-yakko/Yudofu
冷やっこ／湯豆腐
Cold/simmered tofu.

Kinpira
きんぴら
Sautéed burdock and carrot strips seasoned with sauces.

Natto
納豆
Fermented soybeans.

Niku-jaga
肉じゃが
Beef or pork simmered with potatoes and other ingredients.

Oden
おでん
Hot pot with white radish, boiled egg, and fish cake in soy broth.

Ohitashi
おひたし
Boiled spinach or other green leafy vegetable with sauce.

Shio-yaki
塩焼
Fish sprinked with salt and grilled over a flame or charcoal.

Tamago-yaki
卵焼
Rolled omelet.

Tonkatsu
豚カツ／トンカツ
Breaded, fried pork cutlet.

Grilled eel *(unagi)* basted in a sweet sauce, a *yakimono* dish

Tori no kara-age
鶏の空揚げ
Deep-fried chicken.

Tsukemono no moriawase
漬物の盛り合わせ
Combination of pickles.

Yakitori
焼鶏／やきとり
Marinated chicken grilled on skewers.

Yakiniku
焼肉
Korean-style beef barbecue.

CHINESE-STYLE DISHES

Gyoza
餃子／ギョウザ
Fried dumplings.

Harumaki
春巻
Spring roll.

Shumai
焼売／シュウマイ
Small, pork dumplings crimped at the top and steamed.

Yakimeshi/chahan
焼めし／チャーハン
Fried rice.

IZAKAYA SNACKS

Cucumber and sea-weed

Dried squid

Onion and bonito

At *izakaya (see p120)* establishments, which are tavern-like places serving food rather than restaurants, dishes such as dried strips of squid and pickles complement the beer, *shochu* and other drinks *(see pp130–31)*.

The Flavors of Japan

More so than in most developed countries, where the produce of the entire world is available in supermarkets all year round, Japan is a country in which local and seasonal produce is still highly valued. The traditional cuisine of Tokyo reflects its waterfront location and its easy access to the fertile plains inland. Tokyo is also the focus of the nation's food distribution network, especially through the busy stalls of its central wholesale market in Tsukiji *(see p40)*. The city also boasts numerous restaurants serving the specialties of other regions of Japan. Its modern cuisine reflects influences from all around the world.

Ramen noodles

Chef at work, using chopsticks to arrange exquisite dishes

EDO CUISINE

In the early 17th century, Tokyo, then known as Edo, became the administrative capital of Japan after the powerful Tokugawa family moved there. With them arrived thousands of rich landowning samurai and wealthy merchants. This led to the development of Edo cuisine, a fusion of dishes from diverse parts of the country, that is today the most commonly recognized form of Japanese food.

The story of the ascendancy of Edo cuisine is also that of the decline in dominance of typically delicate flavors from Western Japan. *Soba* (buckwheat noodles) has been a popular food among Edo residents since the late 17th century and is renowned as one of the true tastes of Edo cuisine. As more people from the north of Japan moved to Edo, *udon* noodles, which were popular in the south, were replaced by *soba* noodles. *Soba* is most commonly eaten in the same simple way that it was eaten in the past: in a *zaru* (a small bamboo sieve). The weaker soy sauce of Western Japan

Shiitake mushrooms · Eggplants (aubergines) · *Daikon* radish · *Nori* (seaweed) · Sweet potato · *Enoki* mushroom · Bean sprouts
Selection of vegetables that feature in Japanese cuisine

TRADITIONAL JAPANESE SPECIALTIES

A typical banquet, such as might be served at a *ryotei* (upscale restaurant), may have up to 20 courses. Much is made of seasonal ingredients, with decorative flourishes also chosen to reflect the time of year. *Kaiseki* is a traditional style of cuisine in which a dozen or more dishes are served to each person, categorized according to cooking method, not ingredients. Sake *(see p131)* is the usual accompaniment. Vegetarian cusine, called *shojin ryori*, uses protein-rich tofu rather than meat or fish. It was developed by Zen Buddhists and is now found in many restaurants located in or near the precincts of Zen temples. The Japanese have also elevated tea snacks to an art form – delicate and pretty *wagashi* are usually made from sweet bean paste.

Bonito tuna flakes

Unadon, *featuring grilled eel over a bed of rice, is popular as it is thought to have great health benefits.*

Tuna being laid out for sale at Tokyo's Tsukiji Fish Market *(see p40)*

Chilly Hokkaido in Northern Japan boasts warming hotpots. Osaka and Hiroshima in Western Japan vie over their respective recipes for *okonomiyaki* pancakes *(see p135)*. On the island of Shikoku, Kochi is famous for *katsuo* (skipjack tuna); on the island of Kyushu, Kumamoto is renowned for horsemeat sashimi, while Kagoshima washes its seafood down with copious *shochu* liquor *(see p131)*. The southern islands of Okinawa boast a pork-rich cuisine.

also became less favored when people in Edo adopted a stronger tasting sauce. Even grilled eel, which is thought to be a typical part of Edo cuisine, was originally a dish from Kyoto, but it is the Edo method of cooking the eel and preparing the sauce that we know today. Other foods which feature strongly in Edo cuisine are sushi, tempura, and oden *(see p123)*.

REGIONAL CUISINE

As the nation's capital, Tokyo has continued to draw its population from all corners of the country. This has had a significant impact on the way the city eats. There are numerous restaurants serving regional cuisines, and it is quite possible to sample the specialties of every corner of Japan without leaving the city. The cuisine of Kyoto is esteemed for its refinement and exquisite arrangements, especially *kaiseki* and temple cuisine *(see p120)*, featuring tofu and other products based on soybeans. Areas along the Sea of Japan are renowned for their seafood.

Omoide Yokacho, a lane of restaurants in Shinjuku, Tokyo

KOBE BEEF

One significant contribution that the Japanese have given to meat connoisseurs across the world is Kobe beef. The black *wagyu* cows of Hyogo prefecture, of which Kobe is the capital, are bred and reared using strictly guarded and time-honoured traditions to make some of the highest-quality beef in the world. Although similar cows are raised in America and Australia, the meat is not considered to be genuine if it is not from Hyogo, which makes authentic Kobe beef an expensive delicacy. Kobe beef is an extremely tender meat, and it is identifiable by the striations of fat that run through it. It is used in a range of Japanese dishes – it can be eaten raw as sashimi, cooked as teppanyaki or, as is popular nowadays, served simply as a big hearty steak or even a luxurious burger.

Tempura, *originally a Portuguese dish, is lightly battered deep-fried vegetables or seafood.*

Okonomiyaki *is a thick, pancake-shaped mix of egg and other ingredients, cooked on a griddle.*

Yakiudon *are thick noodles fried with seafood, seaweed, shiitake mushrooms, tuna flakes, and bean sprouts.*

The Japanese Meal

Along with the indispensable rice and miso soup (made from fermented soy bean paste), a Japanese meal usually consists of a variety of smaller dishes which are designed to complement each other. Plain ingredients are often given strong flavors, such as a bowl of rice topped off with an *umeboshi* (sour plum) or pickled ginger, or tofu that has been marinated in a strong, vinegary sauce. Two liquid ingredients central to most Japanese dishes are *dashi*, a light stock made from giant kelp *(konbu)* and dried skipjack tuna shavings, and Japanese soy sauce *(shoyu)*.

Firm tofu

Japanese family enjoying breakfast together

THE JAPANESE BREAKFAST

One of the many attractions of staying in the home of a Japanese family, or in a traditional Japanese hotel, is sampling the Japanese breakfast. Like most other Japanese meals, it consists of different dishes served separately. At its heart is a bowl of rice and some miso soup. It is polite for the rice to be placed to the left and the soup to the right of the sitter. Not only is it common for there to be variations in miso soup from region to region, individual families tend to have their own idiosyncratic method of producing this most Japanese of soups.

The basic rice and soup are accompanied by a range of side dishes, of which the most common is a portion of grilled fish, often salted salmon or mackerel. Other dishes may include dried seaweed, omelet, and a small portion of pickles.

Natto is a dish made out of fermented soy beans and it is a much-loved breakfast dish among health-conscious Japanese. Usually eaten with rice, it is famous not only for being extremely healthy, but also for its obnoxious smell.

Miso soup   *Nori* (seaweed)   Grilled salmon

Pickled eggplant (aubergine)   *Umeboshi* (pickled plums)   Rice   Pickled *daikon* radish   Tofu

Some of the ingredients for a typical Japanese breakfast

PREPARATION AND PORTIONS

A fastidiousness about detail characterizes both the preparation and presentation of Japanese food. Good presentation is vital to a Japanese restaurant's success, but it is not only the highly expensive, multi-course *kaiseki* meals that display this quality; even the cheapest food has a touch of the meticulous about it. This attention to culinary aesthetics naturally favors portions that are small and served individually to maximize the impact that they have on both taste and sight. Vegetables are cooked to remain crisp and retain their colors and, even when fried, food is not allowed to become greasy – the oil is heated high enough to seal the food instantly. The serving of small portions also has health benefits, and it should come as no surprise that obesity is much less of a problem here than in Western developed countries. Nowhere else in the world is healthy eating so attractive, varied, or delicious.

Small portions of a number of complementary dishes

The Bento Box

A *bento* is a take-home meal in a compartmentalized box – office workers buy them for lunch, schoolchildren eat from them at their desk, and business travelers have them with a beer on the bullet train. In its neat, individual compartments there will invariably be a large portion of rice, a main serving of meat or fish, pieces of omelet, some vegetables, and a selection of pickles. But part of the charm of the *bento* is that anything goes. It is not uncommon to open a *bento* and find a small octopus or a tiny whole fish gazing up at you, or even something that completely defies identification.

Slivers of pickled ginger

Pickled daikon radish • Tempura • *Tamagoyaki* (omelet) • *Sake* (salmon) • *Hijiki* (seaweed)

Rice with black sesame • *Umeboshi* (pickled plums) • *Nishime* (simmered vegetables)

Typical selection of food to be found in a *bento* box

IN THE BENTO BOX

Agedofu Fried tofu.

Chikuwa Tubular steamed fishcakes.

Furikake Variety of condiments to add extra flavor, including *nori* (seaweed) flakes and toasted sesame seeds.

Jako Miniature whole dried fish.

Kabocha Squash, often served simmered.

Konnyaku Gelatinous paste made from Devil's Tongue (similar to sweet potato).

Korokke Croquettes filled with potato and meat.

Kurage Jellyfish.

Maguro sashimi Tuna sashimi.

Negi Salad onion, used for flavoring and garnish.

Onigiri Triangles of rice with various fillings.

Saba sashimi Mackerel sashimi.

Takenoko Bamboo shoots.

Tonkatsu Deep-fried breaded pork.

Tsukemono Pickled vegetables.

Umeboshi Pickled apricot.

Unagi Grilled eel in black bean sauce.

Yakiniku Miniature meatballs.

Japanese student eating lunch from a *bento* box

Sushi and Sashimi

Newcomers to Japan are most often both fascinated and intimidated by these native dishes. The term "sushi" applies to a variety of dishes (usually written with the suffix "*-zushi*") in which cold, lightly sweetened, and vinegared sushi rice is topped or wrapped up with raw fish or other items such as pickles, cooked fish, and meat. Sliced fillets of raw fish served without rice are called sashimi. Even those visitors used to Japanese restaurants abroad may be surprised at how ubiquitous such foods are in Japan. Fresh fish is always used, and the vinegar in sushi rice is a preservative.

Shiso leaf, garnish for sashimi

Sushi bar counter and sushi chefs with years of training

Nigiri-zushi

Here, thin slices of raw fish are laid over molded fingers of sushi rice with a thin layer of wasabi (green horseradish) in between. Using chopsticks or fingers, pick up a piece, dip the fish lightly in soy sauce, and consume in one mouthful.

Shredded daikon radish

Hirame (halibut)

Ebi (shrimp)

Hotate (scallop)

Wasabi (Japanese horseradish)

Gari (ginger), eaten separately

Hokkigai (type of clam)

Suzuki (sea bass)

Kazunoko (salted herring roe)

Toro (belly flesh of a tuna)

Aji (horse mackerel)

Maguro (tuna)

Shimesaba (salted, vinegared mackerel)

Ika (squid)

Tamagoyaki (sweetened egg omelet), a popular non-fish item often accompanying sushi and sashimi

Denbu, flakes of shrimp and whitefish that have been boiled, then dried and seasoned

Chirashi-zushi

The "scattered" style of sushi involves a colorful combination of toppings arranged artfully with a deep bed of cold sushi rice. Slices of raw fish, fish roe, chunks of omelet, and other raw or cooked vegetables are placed on top of the rice (as shown).

Kazunoko (salted herring roe)

Ebi (shrimp)

Aji (horse mackerel)

Uni (the ovaries of a sea urchin), a highly prized delicacy in Japan

Ikura (salmon roe)

Gari (ginger)

Slice of *kamaboko*, a type of steamed fish-paste roll with pink-dyed rim

Thin slice of *ika* (squid)

Maki-zushi

"Rolled" sushi is becoming increasingly familiar outside Japan – the California roll, for instance, is a version using avocado and other non-Japanese ingredients. For maki-zushi the sushi rice is combined with slivers of fish, pickles, or other morsels, and rolled up in a sheet of toasted seaweed (nori).

Temaki-zushi is rolled by hand into a large cone shape.

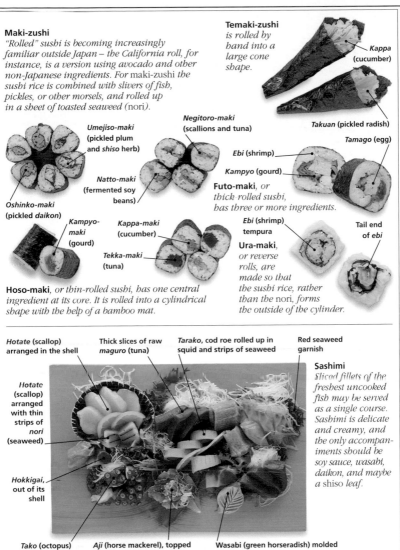

Kappa (cucumber)

Umejiso-maki (pickled plum and *shiso* herb)

Negitoro-maki (scallions and tuna)

Takuan (pickled radish)

Tamago (egg)

Ebi (shrimp)

Natto-maki (fermented soy beans)

Kampyo (gourd)

Futo-maki, or thick-rolled sushi, has three or more ingredients.

Oshinko-maki (pickled *daikon*)

Kampyo-maki (gourd)

Kappa-maki (cucumber)

Ebi (shrimp) tempura

Tail end of *ebi*

Tekka-maki (tuna)

Ura-maki, or reverse rolls, are made so that the sushi rice, rather than the nori, forms the outside of the cylinder.

Hoso-maki, or thin-rolled sushi, has one central ingredient at its core. It is rolled into a cylindrical shape with the help of a bamboo mat.

Hotate (scallop) arranged in the shell

Thick slices of raw *maguro* (tuna)

Tarako, cod roe rolled up in squid and strips of seaweed

Red seaweed garnish

Hotate (scallop) arranged with thin strips of *nori* (seaweed)

Sashimi

Sliced fillets of the freshest uncooked fish may be served as a single course. Sashimi is delicate and creamy, and the only accompaniments should be soy sauce, wasabi, daikon, and maybe a shiso leaf.

Hokkigai, out of its shell

Tako (octopus)

Aji (horse mackerel), topped with finely sliced scallions

Wasabi (green horseradish) molded into the shape of a *shiso* leaf

---

Fish display at Kochi street market

POPULAR FISH IN JAPAN

Of the 3,000 or so varieties of fish eaten in Japan, the most common, available year-round, are *maguro* (tuna), *tai* (sea bream), *haze* (gobies), *buri* (yellowtail), *saba* (mackerel), crustaceans such as *ebi* (shrimp) and *kani* (crab), and fish that are usually salted such as *sake* (salmon) and *tara* (cod). Spring is the start of the season for the river fish *ayu* (sweetfish), traditionally caught by trained cormorants. *Katsuo* (skipjack tuna) is available in spring and summer, *unagi* (eel) in midsummer, *sanma* (saury) in the fall. Winter is the time for *dojo* (loach), *anko* (angler fish), and *fugu* (globefish), prized for its delicate flavor but also feared for deadly toxins in its liver and ovaries.

What to Drink in Tokyo

Tea ceremony

Green tea and sake (rice wine) are the traditional drinks of Japan. Both have ancient histories, and the appreciation of each has been elevated to connoisseurship. The tea ceremony is the ultimate expression of tea appreciation, a social ritual imbued with Buddhist ideals. Sake has long associations with Shinto – the fox god Inari presides over sake – and many Shinto festivals still involve the drink as a central theme. Other Japanese drinks include *shochu* spirit and "health" drinks.

Picking green tea in May, when leaves are at their most tender

TYPES OF TEA

Green tea leaves are divided into three main grades – *gyokuro*, which are the most tender, protected leaves that come out in May; *sencha*, which are tender leaves picked in May or June; and *bancha*, which are large leaves left until August. Leaves are sterilized with steam and then dried. *Bancha* is often roasted or mixed with other ingredients such as brown rice to form robust teas. Other teas are available; of foreign ones the Japanese especially enjoy imported fine English teas.

Basic green tea *is sold loose or in tea bags.*

Mugicha *is a tea brewed from roasted barley.*

Hojicha *is roasted bancha, a coarse tea.*

Genmaicha *is brown rice (genmai) and bancha.*

Sencha *is a popular medium- to high-grade tea.*

Gyokuro *is a delicate high-grade tea.*

Powdered matcha *is used in tea ceremonies.*

SOFT DRINKS

With names that conjure up disturbing images for English-speaking foreigners, Calpis and Pocari Sweat are among the most popular Japanese brands of canned soft drinks. Some are marketed as energy and vitamin boosters. Vending machines *(see p143)* stock them alongside canned green tea and coffee, and a wide range of fruit juices.

Chawan, a wide-brimmed cup without handles

Kyusu (teapot)

Wagashi (sweets)

Tea leaves, *usually loose, are placed in a teapot. Bancha is brewed with boiling water, but sencha and gyokuro should be brewed with boiled water that has been allowed to cool slightly first. The brewing tea should then stand for about a minute.*

SAKE (RICE LIQUOR)

Sake is made from rice and water, which are fermented together then pasteurized to create a superb alcoholic wine-like beverage. Many connoisseurs judge sake on the five qualities of sweetness, sourness, pungency, bitterness, and astringency. Sake may be drunk warm, but the finer types should be lightly chilled to retain the subtle flavors. Unlike wine, sake is rarely expected to improve in the bottle. Store it in a cool, dry place for no more than a few months.

Everyday *hon-jozo* type by Gekkeikan   Fine *ginjo* type by Nihonsakari   Finer *dai-ginjo* by Tsukasa Botan

Taruzake (cask sake) *is matured in wooden casks made of cypress. Casks are often presented to Shinto shrines as offerings. The brewer's logo is displayed prominently.*

The finest grade of sake, dai-ginjo, *is made from the hardest core of the rice – more than 50 percent of each grain is shaved away. For the* ginjo *type about 40 percent is shaved; for* hon-jozo, *the average sake, about 30 percent. Some are brewed with added alcohol; those without are called* junmai, *"pure rice."*

A classic serving set *consists of a ceramic bottle* (tokkuri) *and matching cups* (sakazuki). *The bottle can be placed in hot water to warm the sake to about 122°F (50°C).*

Sake breweries *traditionally hang a ball of cedar leaves* (sakabayashi) *and sometimes a sacred rope* (shimenawa) *over their entrance.*

OTHER ALCOHOLIC DRINKS

Japan has several beers that have become well known around the world. Suntory whiskey is also sold abroad, popular with those who prefer a milder whiskey. Less well known abroad, *shochu* is a name for a group of Japanese spirits made from barley or other grains, or potatoes.

The alcohol content of *shochu* varies from 40 to 90 proof. The distilled spirit is often mixed with hot water or used as a base for cocktails, but it is also drunk neat, either heated or on the rocks. In addition, it is used to make bottled fruit liqueurs such as *umeshu*, which is made with whole Japanese apricots.

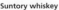

Suntory whiskey   **Sapporo beer**   **Asahi beer**   **Barley *shochu***   **Rice *shochu***

Choosing a Restaurant

The restaurants in this guide have been selected across a wide range for their exceptional food, good value, and interesting location. Restaurants are listed by area, and within these by price, both for central Tokyo and surrounding areas. For the location of each restaurant in Tokyo refer to the Street Finder, pages 180–89.

PRICE GUIDE
Price categories are for an average size dinner for one. Lunchtime menus are often cheaper.

(¥) Under ¥2,000
(¥)(¥) ¥2,000–¥5,000
(¥)(¥)(¥) ¥5,000–¥10,000
(¥)(¥)(¥)(¥) Over ¥10,000

CENTRAL TOKYO

Aroyna Tabeta   (¥)
3-7-11 Marunouchi, Chiyoda-ku **Tel** *(03) 5219-6099*   **Map** 5 B2

In the shadow of the Tokyo International Forum building (*see p43*), this cozy little diner under the train tracks provides an extensive array of full-flavored Thai street food. The Thai cooks pull no punches with their seasonings. The set meals, available at any time of the day, are great value for money.

Kanda Yabu Soba   (¥)
2-10 Kanda-Awajicho, Chiyoda-ku **Tel** *(03) 3251-0287*   **Map** 3 C4

A squat building set in its own quiet garden houses a restaurant that is refined yet informal. For locals, it is just the neighborhood noodle joint, albeit one with a century of history. House specials include *anago-nanban* (hot noodles in soup with slices of conger eel) and tempura *seiro* (cold noodles with deep-fried prawns).

Meal Muji   (¥)
Infoce Yurakucho 2F, 3-8-3 Marunouchi, Chiyoda-ku **Tel** *(03) 5208-8241*   **Map** 5 B2

A casual, self-service, Western-style cafétéria in the spacious, light-filled mezzanine of Muji's flagship Ginza store. Its wholesome and inexpensive menu draws lots of students and families. The almost-Scandinavian simplicity of the Muji decor comes as a welcome contrast to the rest of Ginza.

Yakitori Bars   (¥)
Under the JR tracks in Yurakucho to the east of Harumi-dori   **Map** 5 B2

Cramped, smoky, and always convivial, these grills under the railroad arches are a throwback to what Tokyo used to be like before it was cleaned up. Huddle with the afterhours salarymen for *yakitori* (skewers of grilled chicken) and grilled innards at the stalls. Wash it down with sake or beer. Open from late afternoon till around midnight.

Bangkok Kitchen   (¥)(¥)
Ginza Corridor, 8-2 Ginza, Chuo-ku **Tel** *(03) 5537-3886*   **Map** 5 B3

Authentic Thai cuisine much as you would find in the heart of Bangkok, transported to Ginza with very little lost in translation. They use all the right spices and herbs in their fiery curries, soups, and yam salads. The lighting is rather too bright, but the service is fast and always with a smile. There are other locations throughout the city.

Bar de España Pero   (¥)(¥)
6-3-12 Ginza, Chuo-ku **Tel** *(03) 5537-6091*   **Map** 5 B2

The look is that of an archetypal Spanish tapas bar, with Iberico hams hanging from the ceiling, excellent hot and cold tapas, and a good range of sherries and Riojas – all to a flamenco backbeat. Dining at the rooftop lounge is preferable during the heat of the summer.

Coca Restaurant   (¥)(¥)
2-1-11 Yurakucho, Chiyoda-ku **Tel** *(03) 3507-5489*   **Map** 5 B2

The most accessible of all the Coca outlets in the city, this branch is geared just as much to dining solo. The specialty here is Thai-style *sukiyaki*, an exotic Southeast-Asian take on Japanese *shabu-shabu* (*see p123*). Diners can watch their food cook in front of them in a bubbling casserole. Dips are rich and spicy.

Daiwa-zushi   (¥)(¥)
Chuo Shijo Bldg No. 6, 5-2-1 Tsukiji, Chuo-ku **Tel** *(03) 3547-6807*   **Map** 5 C3

Of the many hole-in-the-wall counters inside Tsukiji Market (*see p40*), Daiwa-zushi has the longest queue, no matter what time in the morning you arrive. The seating is cramped, but the set meal is the ultimate breakfast, featuring the freshest sushi. A daytime eatery, it closes soon after midday.

Dhaba India   (¥)(¥)
Sagami Bldg 1F, 2-7-9 Yaesu, Chuo-ku **Tel** *(03) 3272-7160*   **Map** 5 C2

Nowhere in Tokyo serves up spicy South Indian cuisine better than this Indian restaurant. Top-value *thali* (platter) meals; curries rich in coconut, tamarind, and chili; *sambhar* (lentil purée) and *rasam* (peppery soup) on the side; and the finest *dosas* (savory pancakes) in the city straight from the griddle. There are plenty of vegetarian options.

Key to Symbols *see back cover flap*

Edogin

4-5-1 Tsukiji, Chuo-ku **Tel** *(03) 3543-4401*   **Map** 5 C3

This large, no-frills sushi emporium close to Tsukiji Market is known for the generous cuts of seafood that dwarf the rice underneath. Needless to say the fish is super-fresh – indeed it may be netted from the giant tank in the center of the room, prepared, and dispatched to your table still visibly twitching.

Kanda Shinpachi

Shin-Marunouchi Bldg 5F, 1-5-1 Marunouchi, Chiyoda-ku **Tel** *(03) 3287-3688*   **Map** 5 B1

Featuring fresh seafood shipped straight from Japanese seaports and a cellar with dozens of varieties of premium sake, Kanda Shinpachi offers a superior take on traditional Tokyo *izakaya (see p120)* values. It is a small place, with many loyal customers, so reservations are at a premium.

Khyber

1-14-6 Ginza, Chuo-ku **Tel** *(03) 5159-7610*   **Map** 5 C2

Tokyo's first tandoor specialist positions itself several notches above the standard curry houses. The chefs (all from the Indian subcontinent) do not stint on the spices as they turn out delectable *seekh* kebabs (skewered meat), tandoori-cooked vegetables, spicy fish tikkas (cutlets), and several chicken dishes to accompany great oven breads.

Saikabo

Coredo Nihonbashi Bldg 4F, 1-4-1 Nihonbashi, Chuo-ku **Tel** *(03) 5204-0108*   **Map** 5 C1

Set in an attractive modern setting, this restaurant serves Korean cuisine such as *bulgogi* (grilled) beef, *jjigae* (spicy seafood and tofu) stews, and excellent *chijimi* (savory) pancakes. In deference to local palates, none of the preparations are too spicy, but if you like your chili they provide plenty of their trademark *kimchi* (fermented vegetables).

Shin Hinomoto

2-4-4 Yurakucho, Chiyoda-ku **Tel** *(03) 3214-8021*   **Map** 5 B2

The cramped seating, boisterous laughter, and cigarette smoke here make for a convivial dining experience. This old-school *izakaya (see p120)* under the railroad tracks in Yurakucho is typical in every way except one – the master of the house is British. This accounts for the English menu and the non-Japanese faces among the customers.

Soba Sasuga

Riken Bldg B1, 1-19-12 Ginza, Chuo-ku **Tel** *(03) 3567-0012*   **Map** 5 C2

Soba noodles *(see p122)*, hand-chopped with craftsmen's expertise, are the specialty of this stylish basement eatery. At lunchtime that is about all they serve. In the evening however, it transforms into a sophisticated *izakaya*, serving both sake and wine, with a delicate range of side dishes.

Sushi Zanmai

4-11-9 Tsukiji, Chuo-ku **Tel** *(03) 3541-1117*   **Map** 5 C3

Bright and brash, Sushi Zanmai is not a place for a leisurely sushi dinner. But it is accessible, affordable, and, unlike the other market shops, open around the clock. Just ask for one of the set meals, or point at whatever you fancy. There is unlimited green tea to wash it all down. Good value for money.

Azumitei

Ginza Inzu 1 Bldg 2F, 3-1 Ginza Nishi, Chuo-ku **Tel** *(03) 5524-7890*   **Map** 5 B2

Azumitei serves meals of *sukiyaki* and *shabu-shabu (see p123)* from Japanese *wagyu* beef. However, it is the interior that makes it special – tables are set in private bowers formed from huge sake barrels, linked by flagstone paths. This is not what you expect to find inside a mundane mall underneath an expressway.

Bird Land

Tsukamoto Sozan Bldg B1F, 4-2-15 Ginza, Chuo-ku **Tel** *(03) 5250-1081*   **Map** 5 B2

Yakitori (see p123), usually considered a fast-food option, is raised to the level of high craftsmanship at this unpretentious but ever-popular grill. The premium free-range chicken is served in many ways, both raw and cooked. Start with liver pâté and do not miss the *sansho-yaki* grilled chicken. It all goes just as well with wine as with sake.

Botan

1-15 Kanda-Sudacho, Chiyoda-ku **Tel** *(03) 3251-0577*   **Map** 3 C5

This charming, old-world restaurant serves only one item – chicken *sukiyaki (see p123)*, cooked in a sweet-savory sauce over charcoal braziers. Install yourself at a low table (*tatami* rooms only) and choose what to drink; the kimono-clad waitresses take care of everything else.

Isegen

1-11-1 Kanda-Sudacho, Chiyoda-ku **Tel** *(03) 3251-1229*   **Map** 3 C4

Isegen's specialty is *anko nabe*, cuts of anglerfish cooked in bubbling hotpots at the table in traditional Edo style. It is not refined dining but is warming and hearty, and the venerable timber building is wonderful. Be aware that *anko* is only in season April to September, and you cannot reserve a table. Get there early or be ready to wait.

Maimon

Ginza Corridor, 8-3 Ginza, Chuo-ku **Tel** *(03) 3569-7733*   **Map** 5 B3

The oyster bar is the first thing you see as you enter this gleaming designer restaurant. Run by the same group that operates the uber-chic Japanese Megu restaurant in New York, the menu features a range of grilled tidbits and more elaborate fusion dishes.

Omatsuya   ⊛⊛⊛
5-6-13 Ginza, Chuo-ku **Tel** *(03) 3571-7053*   **Map** *5 B3*

The interior of this restaurant looks quaintly rustic, but the quality of meals and service are as refined as one would expect from a Ginza address. Omatsuya serves the food and sake of the mountainous Yamagata prefecture. Each table has its own grill, where guests cook their seafood, river fish, or prime Yonezawa beef.

Rangetsu   ⊛⊛⊛
3-5-8 Ginza, Chuo-ku **Tel** *(03) 3567-1021*   **Map** *5 B2*

A Ginza institution, Rangetsu has been offering its distinctive Japanese cuisine for over half a century. Full-course *kaiseki* meals are served by demure waitresses in kimonos. Highlights include *sukiyaki* and *shabu-shabu* prepared from top-grade, finely marbled beef from Japanese cattle. Other appetizing seafood dishes are also served.

Salt   ⊛⊛⊛
Shin-Marunouchi Bldg 6F, 1-5-1 Marunouchi, Chiyoda-ku **Tel** *(03) 5288-7828*   **Map** *5 B1*

A perfect place for business lunches or romantic dinners, where celebrity chef Luke Mangan brings his innovative Australian cooking to Tokyo. Lots of eclectic flourishes – including green-tea-smoked scampi, quail tempura, lamb in *ras el hanout* spices – and a good cellar of Australian wines are on offer.

Shunju Tsugihagi   ⊛⊛⊛
Nihon Life Bldg B1F, 1-1-1 Yurakucho, Chiyoda-ku **Tel** *(03) 3595-0511*   **Map** *5 B2*

Shunju Tsugihagi epitomizes modern, seasonally based Japanese dining, blending flavors and inspiration from Europe and Asia, both in its food and decor. It is a rambling warren of interconnected alcoves, each with its own design motifs. Whether you want sushi, grilled meat, or home-made tofu, this eclecticism works brilliantly.

Viron   ⊛⊛⊛
Tokyo Bldg 1F, 2-7-3 Marunouchi, Chiyoda-ku **Tel** *(03) 5220-7288*   **Map** *5 B2*

The interior of Viron is a faithful replica of a Parisian brasserie and so is the cuisine. Cassoulet, *choucroute*, confit of goose, or *pot au feu* – it is all hearty bourgeois cuisine, but cooked with a precision and quality only found in Japan. Those in a hurry can stand at the zinc bar or order a sandwich from the bakery.

Daigo   ⊛⊛⊛⊛
Forest Tower 2F, 2-3-1, Atago, Minato-ku **Tel** *(03) 3431-0811*   **Map** *5 A4*

Tokyo's preeminent *shojin ryori* (vegetarian temple, *see p120*) restaurant is as refined as any *kaiseiki* establishment. There is no menu – diners need to specify a price range when they reserve a table. Dining is in private rooms, served by matrons in kimonos who bring in a succession of courses as simple, beautiful, and uplifting as Zen brush paintings.

Kanetanaka-an   ⊛⊛⊛⊛
Kanetanaka Bldg 2F, 7-6-16 Ginza, Chuo-ku **Tel** *(03) 3289-8822*   **Map** *5 B3*

One of Tokyo's most exclusive restaurants, Kanetanaka-an caters to politicians and captains of industry. This Ginza branch is not as well regarded, but the *kaiseki* banquets are just as refined. A limited number of simpler *kaiseki bento* (*see p127*) lunches are also offered each day on a first-come first-served basis.

Les Saisons   ⊛⊛⊛⊛
Imperial Hotel 2F, 1-1-1 Uchisaiwai-cho, Chiyoda-ku **Tel** *(03) 3539-8087*   **Map** *5 B2*

Les Saisons's reputation for high-end dining has been bolstered by the arrival of reputed chef Thierry Voisin. His culinary flair and superb cooking technique is complemented by the seamless service and luxurious decor. This is heavyweight haute cuisine that can match the best in France.

Ten-Ichi   ⊛⊛⊛⊛
6-6-5 Ginza, Chuo-ku **Tel** *(03) 3571-1949*   **Map** *5 B3*

One of the finest tempura (vegetables and seafood) restaurants in the city, Ten-Ichi's flagship outlet in Ginza has a plush traditional feel and offers impeccable service. A popular restaurant, it plays host to visiting celebrities and politicians. Full-course banquets showcase the full gamut of delicacies, along with a range of side dishes.

NORTHERN TOKYO

Nezu-no-Jinpachi   ⊛
2-26-4 Nezu, Bunkyo-ku **Tel** *(03) 5685-1387*   **Map** *3 C3*

It is easy to miss the entrance to this modest *izakaya* (pub, *see p120*) in the alleys of Nezu. If there is no room at the small counter, guests will be shown to the *tatami* room at the back, which has the intimate feel of someone's living room. The menu (in English) includes various home-made snacks to go with sake or beer.

Otafuku   ⊛
1-6-2 Senzoku, Taito-ku **Tel** *(03) 3871-2521*   **Map** *4 E2*

Oden – chunks of fish cake, vegetables, tofu, and eggs, slow-simmered in a savory broth – has been the *raison d'etre* of this neighborhood diner since the early 20th century. This is nibbling food to accompany a flask or two of good sake, of which Otafuku boasts a fine selection.

Key to Price Guide *see p132* **Key to Symbols** *see back cover flap*

Sometaro

2-2-2 Nishi-Asakusa, Taito-ku **Tel** *(03) 3844-9502*   **Map** *4 E3*

Round off a day exploring the Asakusa backstreets with a light meal of *okonomiyaki* pancakes, which guests prepare themselves on a hot plate set into the table. This can be hot work in midsummer. Sitting in this vine-covered old-world shack, one feels a century away from the glitter of downtown Tokyo.

Hantei

2-12-15 Nezu, Bunkyo-ku **Tel** *(03) 3828-1440*   **Map** *3 B2*

This handsome century-old wooden townhouse serves only one thing – *kushiage*. Morsels of fish, meat, and vegetables are skewered, breaded, and deep-fried, then eaten with a savory dip. There is no need to order (just specify beer or sake). The staff bring course after course till they are told to stop. Arrive early as they do not take reservations.

Hatsuogawa

2-8-4 Kaminarimon, Taito-ku **Tel** *(03) 3844-2723*   **Map** *4 E3*

Broiled *unagi* (eel) is considered one of the specialties of old Tokyo. Entering this atmospheric little diner with its bric-a-brac-cluttered interior is like stepping back in time. The *unagi* is served as *kabayaki* (on rice) or *unaju* (separately) – either way it comes slathered in soy sauce and is delectable. The eel liver soup is superb.

Ikenohata Yabu Soba

3-44-7 Yushima, Bunkyo-ku **Tel** *(03) 3831-8977*   **Map** *3 C3*

This branch may not be as atmospheric as its namesake in Kanda (the parent restaurant), but the noodles – cold in summer and hot in winter – are predictably satisfying at this simple *soba* restaurant to the south of Ueno Park (*see pp48–9*). Tempura and a good range of side dishes are also on offer.

Kuremutsu

3-22-9 Nishi Ogi Minami, Suginami-ku **Tel** *(03) 3333-2284*   **Map** *4 F2*

With its low gables, antique furnishings, and polished wooden floors, Kuremutsu has a centuries old feel about it. Seafood is the specialty here, along with tidbits to accompany the sake. The prices are reasonable, and there is a very good selection of *shochu* (Japanese distilled beverage).

Mugitoro

2-2-4 Kaminarimon, Taito-ku **Tel** *(03) 3842-1066*   **Map** *4 F3*

Close to the ferry jetty in Asakusa, this traditionally styled upscale restaurant is a popular lunch spot. It serves a wide range of simple, satisfying meals, many featuring its trademark rice cooked with barley, served with bowls of grated yam. There are plenty of other options too, ranging from simple lunches to full evening meals.

Sasanoyuki

2-15-10 Negishi, Taito-ku **Tel** *(03) 3873-1145*   **Map** *4 D1*

A humble place in a nondescript part of town, Sasanoyuki "Snow on Bamboo" has specialized in tofu cuisine for more than 300 years, preparing the humble bean curd in numerous guises. Aficionados come from far and wide for its multi-course meals. However, few of the dishes are strictly vegetarian.

Vin Chou

2-2-13 Nishi-Asakusa, Taito-ku **Tel** *(03) 3845-4430*   **Map** *4 E3*

Part bistro, part *izakaya*, Vin Chou proves that imported French fowl (duck, guinea fowl, and quail) is just as delicious as local chicken when given the *yakitori* (skewer) treatment; and that it all goes just as well with wine as with sake or *shochu*. The home-made sausages are not to be missed, nor is the crème brulée.

Yoshiba

2-14-5 Yokoami, Sumida-ku **Tel** *(03) 3623-4480*   **Map** *4 E4*

A converted sumo stable is the perfect place to sample *chanko-nabe*, the substantial stew of meat, fish, and vegetables reputed to give the giant wrestlers their strength and girth. Diners sit at tables around the periphery of the clay practice ring, while their meal cooks in front of them. This is simple but warming winter fare.

Bon

1-2-11 Ryusen, Taito-ku **Tel** *(03) 3872-0375*   **Map** *4 C1*

Housed in a charming old Japanese house, this restaurant serves traditional vegetarian temple cuisine executed with understated simplicity and a devotion to seasonal flavors. The multi-course set meals are a succession of miniature edible landscapes. The utensils are of hand-crafted lacquer, wood, and ceramic. Reservations are required.

Nakase

1-39-13 Asakasa, Taito-ku **Tel** *(03) 3841-4015*   **Map** *4 E2*

An Asakusa institution for over a century, Nakase fries its tempura in sesame oil, giving it a rich, aromatic flavor. The multi-course dinners are substantial meals. For lunch, the most popular choice is *tendon* – a bowl of white rice topped with a single large tempura mixture of shrimp and vegetables.

Nezu Club

2-30-2 Nezu, Bunkyo-ku **Tel** *(03) 3828-4004*   **Map** *3 B2*

Tucked away in the backstreets of old-time Nezu, this relaxed, atmospheric restaurant is the perfect place to round off a day wandering around the historic neighborhood. Chef Etsuko Yamada prepares simple, creative meals with the elegance of *kaiseki* and the hands-on personal touch of home cooking.

WESTERN TOKYO

Angkor Wat

1-38-13 Yoyogi, Shibuya-ku **Tel** *(03) 3370-3019* **Map** *1 B2*

This is the place to savor authentic Cambodian home cooking with the complete flavors of a Phnom Penh street stall. The house specialties reflect Thai, Chinese, and Vietnamese influences – spicy salads, chicken curries, vegetable spring rolls, and robust noodle dishes. If you are not sure what to order, just ask the cheerful waitresses.

Heirokuzushi

5-8-5 Jingumae, Shibuya-ku **Tel** *(03) 3498-3968* **Map** *1 C4*

This perennially popular *kaitenzushi* (conveyor belt sushi) restaurant in a prime location on Omotesando is one of the best and most established. Just grab whatever you want as the array of food goes past, or you can order dishes from the chef. Each portion comes in a color-coded tray – pink is cheapest and gold the most expensive.

Nataraj

Sanwa-Aoyama Bldg B1, 2-22-19 Minami-Aoyama, Minato-ku **Tel** *(03) 5474-0510* **Map** *1 D4*

A welcome change of pace and cultures in the heart of busy Tokyo, this tranquil basement restaurant serves a full range of classy vegetarian Indian cuisine. Spice levels are restrained in deference both to local palates and the yogic teachings of its founder.

Natural Harmony Angolo

3-38-12 Jingumae, Shibuya-ku **Tel** *(03) 3405-8393* **Map** *1 C4*

No artificial additives, no smoking, no cellphones – good, honest home cooking using organic produce characterizes this restaurant. The cuisine is mostly Japanese, but with a few Western dishes. While the food is not purely vegetarian, there are plenty of meat- and fish-free options. Organic beer is on offer.

Yakitori Yokocho

1 Nishi-Shinjuku, Shinjuku-ku **Map** *1 B1*

"Yakitori Alley" is a warren of hole-in-the-wall bars and eateries that occupies an entire block by the northeast exit of Shinjuku Station. Not all of them are salubrious, but most are welcoming. Unchanged since it opened in the 1950s, this is one of the last vestiges of blue-collar city life.

Bosphorus Hassan

Dai-Ichi Tamaya Bldg 2F, 3-6-11 Shinjuku, Shinjuku-ku **Tel** *(03) 3354-7947* **Map** *1 B1*

One of the first and still among the best of Tokyo's Turkish restaurants, Bosphorus Hassan offers an extensive range of mezes, flavorful kebabs, authentic Turkish bread, and plenty of Anatolian beer, wine, and raki. A couple of times a week, the restaurant hosts belly dancing performances.

Butagumi

2-24-9 Nishi-Azabu, Minato-ku **Tel** *(03) 5466-6775* **Map** *2 D5*

This small, free-standing house has been beautifully converted to create Tokyo's finest *tonkatsu* (deep-fried, breaded pork cutlet) restaurant. Only premium pork, from contract farmers around Japan (plus Iberico black hogs), is used here. The cutlets are delectable and the presentation impeccable, with absolutely no use of cooking oil.

Chinese Café Eight

Court Annex 2F, 3-2-13 Nishi-Azabu, Minato-ku **Tel** *(03) 5414-5708* **Map** *2 E5*

Located opposite the Grand Hyatt Tokyo *(see p115)*, this Chinese restaurant is one of Tokyo's best bargains. House specialties include *jiaozi* dumplings, stir-fried dishes, and a whole Peking duck large enough for three or four people. Open round the clock, the café is also well known for the erotic artwork displayed and thus not for the prudish.

Gempin Fugu

Hodaka Bldg 2-5F, 4-12-12 Roppongi, Minato-ku **Tel** *(03) 5775-5029* **Map** *2 E5*

The spotlit giant fish displayed on the roof of this restaurant tells what is in store here – *fugu* (blow fish). Its flesh is potentially lethal, but the licensed chefs carefully remove all the toxins. Not that flavorful when eaten as sashimi, it goes nicely in *nabe* hotpots *(fugu-chiri)*. Visit the tanks filled with live fish on the second floor.

Gonpachi

1-13-11 Nishi-Azabu, Minato-ku **Tel** *(03) 5771-0170* **Map** *2 D5*

Located inside an Edo-style building, the fabulous faux-medieval dining room at Gonpachi serves cheerful *izakaya* (pub) cuisine – *yakitori* chicken, *soba* noodles, simple seafood, tofu, and vegetables accompanied by beer, sake, or *shochu*. Film buffs come here to see the decor that inspired the sets for the movie *Kill Bill*.

Jap Cho Ok

Alteka Belte Plaza B1, 4-1-15 Minami-Aoyama, Minato-ku **Tel** *(03) 5410-3408* **Map** *2 D4*

The striking interior of this casual but sophisticated restaurant evokes the calm of a mountain monastery. The large and diverse menu of Jap Cho Ok (House of Weeds) proves that there is more to Korean cuisine than just barbecue beef and kimchi, and it includes a variety of seafood and vegetarian dishes.

Key to Price Guide *see p132* **Key to Symbols** *see back cover flap*

Kurosawa

2-7-9 Nagata-cho, Chiyoda-ku **Tel** *(03) 3580-9638* **Map** *2 F3*

The great Japanese film director Akira Kurosawa loved *soba* noodles, hence the inspiration for this restaurant which replicates a house in his movie *Yojimbo*. A casual dining room on the ground floor serves fresh, hand-cut noodles. Private rooms upstairs serve full meals, focusing on pork *shabu-shabu* and *nabe* hotpots.

Kuu

Shinjuku Sumitomo Bldg 50F, 2-6-1 Nishi-Shinjuku, Shinjuku-ku **Tel** *(03) 3344-6457* **Map** *1 A1*

A high-rise dining spot, Kuu offers a brilliant view of the city of Tokyo while serving reasonably priced charcoal-grilled seafood, free-range chicken, and seasonal vegetables. It also has a good selection of sake, taking the traditional *izakaya* (pub) into the 21st century. The dishes are simple but outstanding thanks to the fine ingredients.

Maisen

4-8-5 Jingumae, Shibuya-ku **Tel** *(03) 3470-0071* **Map** *1 C4*

The attraction at this famous restaurant is *tonkatsu* – deep-fried pork cutlets with a crisp, breaded coating and soft, juicy meat inside. This is served with grated cabbage and slathered in Worcestershire sauce. Various grades of pork are used; choose between lean and fatty. The set meals are a popular choice, featuring a range of side dishes.

Ninja

Akasaka Tokyu Plaza 1F, 2-14-3 Nagatacho, Chiyoda-ku **Tel** *(03) 5157-3936* **Map** *2 F3*

An informal restaurant, Ninja is a fun place to take kids. It is located in a basement decked out to evoke an ancient Japanese castle, and the waiters dress as ninjas, black-clad spies trained in martial arts. The menu features light *izakaya* dishes, such as sushi rolls, other seafood specialties, and salads.

Pintokona

Hollywood Plaza B2, 6-4-1 Roppongi, Minato-ku **Tel** *(03) 5771-1133* **Map** *2 E5*

A *kaiten* (conveyor-belt) sushi counter with a difference – you do not just wait to see what comes past, but can also order from the menu. A small range of non-sushi items is also on offer. It is classier (and a bit more expensive) than other conveyor-belt sushi joints, as expected in the affluent Roppongi Hills.

Reikyo

House Ikeda 101, 1-14-18 Tomigaya, Shibuya-ku **Tel** *(03) 3485-3052* **Map** *1 B5*

Popular as much for its atmosphere as for the quality of its food, this bustling little restaurant has been serving up stir-fries and other Taiwanese dishes for decades. The imported sausages, served steamed and sliced, go perfectly with a glass or two of warmed, sticky Shaoxing rice wine.

Rice Terrace

2-7-9 Nishi-Azabu, Minato-ku **Tel** *3498-6271* **Map** *2 D5*

With a look less overtly "ethnic" than other Thai eateries, this bistro-sized place in the back streets of Nishi-Azabu serves up sophisticated and flavorsome Thai cuisine. In hot weather, the two outside tables are popular as the small upstairs dining room can get stuffy. The location is a bit hard to find, but it is worth tracking down.

Roti Brasserie

Tokyo Midtown Garden Terrace 1F, 9-7-4 Akasaka, Minato-ku **Tel** *(03) 5413-3655* **Map** *2 E5*

Set inside Tokyo Midtown, this elegant, brasserie-style diner serves a varied menu of modern American cooking, including pasta, rotisserie chicken, fresh lobster, and burgers (the spicy Cajun catfish burger is a novelty). Roti Brasserie is also a wine bar, with a good cellar of New World wines and a choice of imported ales on tap.

Teyandei

2-20-1 Nishi-Azabu, Minato-ku **Tel** *(03) 3407-8127* **Map** *2 D5*

A local favorite, Teyandei is situated in an old house on a residential street in Nishi-Azabu. The menu of modern Japanese gourmet charcoal-grilled fare provides large portions at reasonable prices. There are several charming private rooms and a bar with an excellent selection of sakes. A great off-the-beaten-track alternative.

Tsunahachi

3-31-8 Shinjuku, Shinjuku-ku **Tel** *(03) 3352-1012* **Map** *1 B1*

Tempura was originally street food, and Tsunahachi keeps it much simpler than at other gourmet tempura restaurants. It is housed in a rambling, wooden building that has somehow survived in the Shinjuku back streets. Though the interior seems a little dated, the tempura is superb and very reasonably priced.

Vietnam Alice

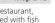

Belle Vie Akasaka 2F, 3-1-6 Akasaka, Minato-ku **Tel** *(03) 3588-5020* **Map** *2 F3*

Waitresses dressed in *ao dai* (Vietnamese national dress) flit through the Neo-Colonial interior of this restaurant, serving noodles and delicate dim sum-like snacks (ask for the Spring Roll Basket), authentically seasoned with fish sauce and coriander. This is an ideal place for a light meal in the sweltering summer heat in Tokyo.

Wa Café Yusoshi

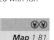

Lumine 1, 6F, 1-1-5 Nishi Shinjuku, Shinjuku-ku **Tel** *(03) 5321-7233* **Map** *1 B1*

The menu changes periodically at this stylish Shinjuku favorite, but it always offers a fresh twist on Japanese classics. Popular entrées may include cod-roe cream croquettes or California rolls. The *kabocha* pumpkin coconut cake and glazed sweet potatoes with ice cream make for great dessert options.

Beacon

1-2-5 Shibuya, Shibuya-ku **Tel** *(03) 6418-0077*   **Map** *1 B5*

Plush but understated decor and attention to detail make this a good place for entertaining clients or just unwinding at the end of the day. For those wanting a change from Japanese fare, this "urban chop house" is the place to go for charcoal-grilled, prime, grain-fed beef, free-range chicken, or wild Scottish salmon. A great brunch spot.

Bincho

Marina Bldg 2F, 3-10-5 Roppongi, Minato-ku **Tel** *(03) 5474-0755*   **Map** *2 E5*

A rare oasis of calm so close to the Roppongi Crossing, this genteel *yakitori* house has as its focal point the charcoal grill in the center of the room, where top-quality chicken is cooked to perfection over premium Bincho charcoal. The traditional sake and an appetizing range of side dishes are also on offer.

Brasserie Paul Bocuse Le Musée

National Arts Center 3F, 7-22-2 Roppongi, Minato-ku **Tel** *(03) 5770-8161*   **Map** *2 D5*

The French master chef's first overseas restaurant is worth a visit, if only for its remarkable setting in the dazzling concrete and glass building of the National Arts Center. The cuisine is simple and light. The fixed price lunches are hugely popular, so it is best to go for a late lunch after the crowds subside.

Fonda de la Madrugada

Villa Bianca B1, 2-33-12 Jingumae, Shibuya-ku **Tel** *(03) 5410-6288*   **Map** *1 C4*

Bordering on kitsch but promising great fun, this rambling restaurant is located three flights below street level in the central courtyard of a transplanted hacienda. Mariachi singers serenade guests as they sip margaritas or Dos Equis lager, and dine on first-class Mexican food.

Fukuzushi

5-7-8 Roppongi, Minato-ku **Tel** *(03) 3402-4116*   **Map** *2 E5*

This elegant sushi restaurant is a Roppongi institution and feels worlds away from the high-decibel clamor of the neon world nearby. Fukuzushi is stylish but casual, with none of the snobbery found at many traditional Tokyo sushi counters. This is a good place for visitors not fluent in the argot of the sushi shop.

Hassan

6-1-20 Roppongi, Minato-ku **Tel** *(03) 3403-8333*   **Map** *2 E5*

Hassan's satisfying all-you-can-eat meals shatter the myth that *sukiyaki* and *shabu-shabu* can be procured only at exorbitant Ginza prices. Wafer-thin slices of marbled beef are served in quantities to challenge the heartiest of appetites. The decor is classic Japanese – all wooden beams and paper *shoji* screens.

Inakaya

4-10-11 Roppongi, Minato-ku **Tel** *(03) 5775-1012*   **Map** *2 E5*

Diners sit around a market array of vegetables, beef, and seafood, watching as chefs in *happi* (traditional coats) grill food and hand it over on long paddles. Just point to whatever you want to eat. This is a place for snacking with sake or beer, rather than filling the stomach, and it is boisterous, theatrical, and fun.

Mikawa

Roppongi Hills Residence B 3F, 6-12-2 Roppongi, Minato-ku **Tel** *(03) 3423-8100*   **Map** *2 E5*

The unnamed gilt façade of this tempura house may look gaudy, but inside it is serene and traditional. Mikawa prepares classic tempura from the succinct menu with utter precision, using seafood that used to be netted in Tokyo Bay, but which now comes from farther afield. The lunch menu is particularly good value.

Nodaiwa

1-5-4 Higashi-Azabu, Minato-ku **Tel** *(03) 3583-7852*   **Map** *2 F5*

Housed in a beautifully converted ancient storehouse, Nodaiwa is one of Tokyo's finest *unagi* (eel) restaurants, elevating this humble fish to gourmet status. Broiled over charcoal, daubed with a sweet-savory sauce, and served over rice, the *unagi* is delicious. Light meals are served on the ground floor; full-course meals upstairs.

Sushi Ouchi

2-8-4 Shibuya, Shibuya-ku **Tel** *(03) 3407-3543*   **Map** *1 C5*

The chef at this restaurant, Hisashi Ouchi, does not use commercial seasonings and cultivated fish; he uses free-range eggs and organic soy sauce for his preparations. The dining room is as relaxed as a coffee shop. The range of sushi is not as extensive as at some restaurants, but the quality is excellent. Highly recommended.

Union Square Café

B1F Tokyo Midtown Garden Terrace, 9-7-4 Akasaka, Minato-ku **Tel** *(03) 5413-7780*   **Map** *2 E4*

The Union Square Café's ethos of international cuisine, notably premium burgers and quality Italianesque food, translates perfectly from New York to Tokyo Midtown. The waiters are informal but helpful, and the outdoor tables are always in great demand. There is a small bar area for those dining solo or in a hurry.

Yuan

Shinjuku Park Tower B1, 3-7-1 Nishi-Shinjuku, Shinjuku-ku **Tel** *(03) 5322-6427*   **Map** *1 A2*

The decor at Yuan blends *kaiseki*, farmhouse, and urban sensibilities. You can sit at the massive wooden counter, sip sake, and nibble on seasonal delicacies or take a low table in the main restaurant for inventive multi-course meals of fish, wild herbs, mushrooms, and premium Kobe beef *shabu-shabu*.

Key to Price Guide *see p132* **Key to Symbols** *see back cover flap*

Zakuro

Nihon Jitensha Kaikan B1, 1-9-15 Akasaka, Minato-ku **Tel** *(03) 3582-2661* **Map** *2 F4*

This long-established restaurant in front of the US embassy serves traditional Japanese cuisine with refinement and decorum. Full-course evening meals feature high-quality beef served as *shabu-shabu*, *sukiyaki*, and *teppanyaki*, in addition to various seasonal specialties. The lunchtime menu is particularly good value.

Gesshinkyo

4-24-12 Jingumae, Shibuya-ku **Tel** *(03) 3796-6575* **Map** *1 C4*

The interior of Gesshinkyo looks as traditional as a tea ceremony hut, but chef Tonio Tanahashi's unorthodox vegetarian Buddhist cuisine is quite unlike anything you would find in a temple. His handmade *goma-dofu* (savory sesame tofu) is delicious. He serves just one set hearty meal each day. Reservations are essential.

Heichinro

Sanno Park Tower 27F, 2-11-1 Nagatacho, Chiyoda-ku **Tel** *(03) 3593-7322* **Map** *2 F4*

Superlative nouvelle Hong Kong cuisine prepared by chefs from the former crown colony and matched by the bold, contemporary decor and dramatic cityscape from the 27th-floor picture windows. Start and finish the evening with drinks in the suave "hidden" cocktail bar.

Kozue

Park Hyatt Hotel 40F, 3-7-1-2 Nishi-Shinjuku, Shinjuku-ku **Tel** *(03) 5323-3460* **Map** *1 A2*

Traditional *kaiseki* meets the 21st century at Kozue, high up in the Park Hyatt Hotel *(see p116)*. Inventive, multi-course meals feature seasonal seafood and premium Kobe beef. From this ultra-modern, high-ceilinged restaurant, you can catch glimpses of Mount Fuji *(see pp96–7)* in the distance on clear days.

New York Grill

Park Hyatt Hotel 52F, 3-7-1-2 Nishi-Shinjuku, Shinjuku-ku **Tel** *(03) 5323-3458* **Map** *1 A2*

In the soaring, glass-fronted apex of the Park Hyatt Hotel *(see p116)*, splurge on modern American food at its finest – superb seafood, juicy steaks, and robust rotisserie fare. The lavish Sunday brunches are terrific value and hugely popular with Tokyo's expat population. It is worth getting dressed up for dinner here.

Oak Door

Grand Hyatt Hotel 6F, 6-10-3 Roppongi, Minato-ku **Tel** *(03) 4333-8784* **Map** *2 E5*

This luxurious restaurant is the place to relish the best steaks in town, prepared and cooked to juicy perfection. There is a lovely terrace in summer and an extensive range of international wines. A romantic spot, as nighttime sees well-heeled couples gazing at each other over candlelit tables.

Roku Roku

Grand Hyatt Hotel 6F, 6-10-3 Roppongi, Minato-ku **Tel** *(03) 4333-8788* **Map** *2 E5*

Seafood is the core of the menu at this sleek, modern restaurant inside the Grand Hyatt Tokyo *(see p115)*. A range of fish dishes, both cooked and raw, are on offer here. The sushi is superb. Whether seated at the sushi counter or in the main dining room, you can choose from the à la carte menu or impressive set meals.

Tofuya Ukai

4-4-13 Shiba Koen, Minato-ku **Tel** *(03) 3436-1028* **Map** *2 F5*

With its beautifully landscaped garden, carp ponds, and traditional architecture, Tofuya Ukai resembles a feudal mansion. One of the city's must-visit dining destinations, this first-class restaurant serves traditional Japanese cuisine. As the name suggests, tofu plays a central role in the complex *kaiseki* meals.

Yamanoue

Tokyo Midtown Garden Terrace 3F, 9-7-4 Akasaka, Minato-ku **Tel** *(03) 5413-3577* **Map** *2 E4*

After half a century at the Hilltop Hotel in Kanda, the owners of this prestigious tempura house were coaxed into setting up a branch in the far more glamorous setting of Tokyo Midtown. The attention to service and quality have not changed, but the view is certainly better here. Reservations recommended.

FARTHER AFIELD

AZABU-JUBAN Banreki-ryukodo
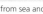

2-33-5 Higashi-Azabu, Minato-ku **Tel** *(03) 3505-5686*

Rustic sophistication meets contemporary *kaiseki* at this designer dining bar. Many seasonal delicacies from sea and mountain are served on dishes of hand-crafted lacquer and ceramic. The main dining area is a single massive wooden counter; the downstairs seating is more discreet. A lighter menu is served after 10pm. Reservations required.

EBISU Afuri

117 Bldg 1F, 1-1-7 Ebisu, Shibuya-ku **Tel** *(03) 5795-0750*

The Ebisu district has numerous *ramen* eateries. This one stands out from the pack, both in its appearance – concrete minimalist – and its subtle flavors, especially its *yuzu*- (citrus-) flavored soup. Buy a ticket from the machine by the entrance (there are pictures to guide you) and then wait till a seat is free at the long counter.

EBISU Ebisu 18-ban

2-3-13 Ebisu-Minami, Shibuya-ku **Tel** *(03) 3794-1894*

A combination of Japanese *izakaya* food and Spanish tapas is served at this convivial late night bar. If you cannot get a seat at the counter that runs around the central kitchen area, then prop yourself up at one of the large barrels by the door. *Shochu*, wine, and sherries are the drinks of choice, depending on which genre of food is ordered.

EBISU Delizioso Italia

Rupinas Ebisu Bldg 1F, 4-27-17 Ebisu, Shibuya-ku **Tel** *(03) 3440-5510*

An intimate trattoria with a casual, rustic look and doors that open onto a quiet side street. Parma hams hang over the counter; a wood-fired pizza oven glows in the kitchen. The pasta is good and so are the grill platters. There is a fine selection of grappa to close the meal. Prices are reasonable for this quality.

EBISU Ebisu Imaiya Sohonten

1-7-11 Ebisu-Nishi, Shibuya-ku **Tel** *(03) 5456-0255*

Akita Prefecture, on the northern Sea of Japan coast, is famous for its local Hinai chicken. Here, the chicken is grilled as *yakitori* or served in delectable *nabe* hotpots featuring a good mix of vegetables and rice dumplings. There is a fine selection of sake too. English-language menus make this a visitor-friendly place.

EBISU Cardenas Charcoal Grill

1-12-14 Ebisu-Nishi, Shibuya-ku **Tel** *(03) 5428-0779*

Sleek, spacious, and stylish, CCG is a big favorite with the expat population, thanks to its cutting-edge cuisine – plentiful fresh produce, seafood, and steaks prepared on the grill, and a good cellar of Californian wines. With its high ceiling and mezzanine bar, it is easy to forget that it is two floors below street level.

HIROO Cicada

5-2-40 Minami-Azabu, Minato-ku **Tel** *(03) 5447-5522*

Cicada's Spanish-accented pan-Mediterranean tapas cuisine is the best of its kind in Tokyo. The excellent ambitious cooking of American chef David Chiddo, great ambience, well-stocked bar, and warm, inviting no-smoking dining room explain this restaurant's popularity with locals and expats alike.

IKEBUKURO Chion Shokudo

Miyakawa Bldg B1, 1-24-1 Ikebukuro, Toshima-ku **Tel** *(03) 5951-8288*

Mandarin, not Japanese, is the lingua franca at this no-frills basement eatery run by and for the mainland Chinese community. With a menu including chili-laden *huoguo* hotpots, fiery stir-fries, and spicy stews, this is the best Sichuan street food in the city, and the prices are unbeatable too.

IKEBUKURO Chugoku Chakan
1-22-8 Nishi-Ikebukuro, Toshima-ku **Tel** *(03) 3985-5183*

Ikebukuro has more authentic Chinese food than Yokohama's Chinatown, thanks to its sizeable population of visiting Chinese students and businessmen. Chugoku Chakan serves Taiwan-style dim sum, prepared in-house and served to order (not from a trolley). Their all-you-can-eat specials are great value.

IKEBUKURO Sasashu
2-2-2 Ikebukuro, Toshima-ku **Tel** *(03) 3971-9363*

With its fine range of lesser-known regional brews and a strong food menu, this upscale sake pub is one of the best in the area. The specials of the day vary according to the season, but the duck dishes are always worth ordering. Even though this area is well off the beaten tourist track, locals are quite used to foreigners dropping in.

KAGURAZAKA Café-Crêperie Le Bretagne
1F Comfort Kagurazaka 4-2, Kagurazaka, Shinjuku-ku **Tel** *(03) 3235-3001*

This friendly and atmospheric restaurant is an authentic slice of Brittany within the colorful entertainment area of Kagurazaka. The specialty of this café is its superb *galettes* (buckwheat crêpes), with various ingredients, both sweet and savory, prepared by French chefs and washed down with the excellent cider of that region. Closed Mon.

KAGURAZAKA Stefano
Terui Bldg 1F, 6-47 Kagurazaka, Shinjuku-ku **Tel** *(03) 5228-7515*

Chef Stefano Fastro presents the flavors of his native Veneto region here. He is especially strong on meat dishes and his *gnocchi* (dumplings made of starched potato, semolina, or flour) are among the best in town. It is a small, creative restaurant with Chef Fastro and one sous-chef, which means the service is excellent.

NAKA-MEGURO Kuro-Hitsuji
1-11-6 Kami-Meguro, Meguro-ku **Tel** *(03) 5457-2255*

Kuro-Hitsuji specializes in the Japanese version of Mongolian barbecue known as "Genghis Khan" – slices of mutton and vegetables cooked over a dome-shaped cast-iron griddle. It is very smoky but great fun, and priced to please the students and young families who come here. Do not wear your best clothes.

NAKA-MEGURO Higashiyama

1-21-25 Higashiyama, Meguro-ku **Tel** *(03) 5720-1300*

Designer-casual, modern Japanese food in a setting to match on the fringes of the hip enclave of Naka-Meguro. Sit at the counter and watch the chefs in the open kitchen or settle down at tables in the spacious dining room. The easiest approach is to order one of the set meals, which change with the seasons.

Key to Price Guide *see p132* **Key to Symbols** *see back cover flap*

ODAIBA Icho

Hotel Nikko Tokyo 3F, 1-9-1 Daiba, Minato-ku **Tel** *(03) 5500-5715*

Ensconced in JAL's flagship hotel, Icho specializes in teppanyaki. Light morsels of seafood, vegetables, and Kobe beef are cooked to perfection on a heated metal plate right in front of diners. If visitors get bored with watching the chef work, they can gaze out over the spectacular Odaiba waterfront and the Rainbow Bridge *(see p83)*.

SHIBUYA Sora no Niwa

4-17 Sakuragaoka-cho, Shibuya-ku **Tel** *(03) 5728-5191*

This youthful dining bar with a gorgeous interior serves tofu, *yuba* (the protein-rich skin that forms on hot soy milk), and other traditional soy-based foods in a hip, modern context. Several dishes are vegetarian. Do not miss the *hiki-age yuba*, cooked right by your table. The food is light on the stomach and the wallet.

SHIMO-KITAZAWA Bio Ojiyan Café

5-35-25 Daita, Setagaya-ku **Tel** *(03) 5486-6997*

Bio Ojiyan serves mainly rice porridge (*kayu*) in a sun-filled dining room. Also on the menu is an interesting selection of organic dishes. The cozy, casual decor features pieces by local artists on the stone walls, and the clientele consists mostly of local bohemian types.

TENNOZU T.Y. Harbor Brewery

2-1-3 Higashi-Shinagawa, Shinagawa-ku **Tel** *(03) 5479-4555*

This converted dockland warehouse is home to Tokyo's first and best brew-pub. Sip ale in the brewery bar, or adjourn to the spacious restaurant next door for creative modern American fare. The canalside tables are always in demand on hot summer nights. More exclusive still is Waterline, the floating bar moored close by.

BEYOND TOKYO

FUJI FIVE LAKES Mama-no-mori

Heiya 2470, Yamanakako Mura, Yamanashi, 401-0502 **Tel** *(0555) 62-0346*

This is a classic, old thatched-roof restaurant, sitting on the north side of Yamanaka Lake, offering good food (*kaiseki ryori*) and gorgeous views of picturesque Mount Fuji on a clear day. The restaurant is named after a beloved mother figure of the community who started this restaurant.

HAKONE The Fujiya

Fujiya Hotel, 359 Miyanoshita, Kanagawa, 250-0404 **Tel** *(0460) 82-2211*

Excellent French fare is served in Hakone's oldest and grandest hotel. The bright dining room is from "an age gone by," complete with crisp, white tablecloths and attentive, bow-tied staff. There are good views and the menu includes such classic dishes as *Tournedos Rossini* (filet mignon on a crouton, topped with foie gras). Reservations required.

IZU PENINSULA Fujiichi

7-6 Shizumi-cho, Ito, Shizuoka, 414-0002 **Tel** *(0557) 37-4705*

Fujiichi is located right on the waterfront, next to the fish market. Well-loved by locals, this simple, second-story restaurant serves great fresh food at very reasonable prices. There are fantastic views of the harbor. Diners can choose either the excellent *teishoku* (set menu) or from the more expansive (and expensive) à la carte menu.

KAMAKURA Nakamura-an

1-7-6 Komachi, Kamakura, Kanagawa **Tel** *(0467) 25-3500*

Hearty, honest, hand-made *soba* noodles, rolled and chopped as guests watch. There is always a line outside at lunchtime, since it is just as popular with the locals as the visitors. The specialty is chilled *soba* with shrimp tempura; ask for *ten-seiro* or just point to the plastic models in the window.

NIKKO Kanaya Hotel

1300 Kami-Hatsuishi-machi, Nikko, Tochigi **Tel** *(0288) 54-0001*

The historic Kanaya, one of the oldest Western-style hotels in Japan, is one of the main sights of Nikko – especially its stately wood-clad dining room. The Continental cuisine is good but not outstanding, but they make the best breakfast in town. Failing that, stop by for coffee in the adjoining lounge.

YOKOHAMA Shin-Yokohama Ramen Museum

2-14-21 Shin-Yokohama, Kohoku-ku, Yokohama, Kanagawa **Tel** *(045) 471-0503*

The ground floor has displays on the history and Chinese origins of Japan's favorite home-grown fast food – *ramen* noodles. But the fun part is in the cavernous basement, where half a dozen stalls offer *ramen* styles from all over Japan in a movie-set re-creation of Tokyo *circa* 1960.

YOKOHAMA Tung Fat (Dohatsu Honkan)

148 Yamashita-cho, Naka-ku, Yokohama, Kanagawa **Tel** *(045) 681-7273*

One of the longest-serving Chinese restaurants in Yokohama, Tung Fat is still one of the most popular restaurants. Plenty of Cantonese specials, including good wind-dried duck, home-made sausages, and noodles, are available. It is easy to find as it stands on the central street of Chinatown.

SHOPPING IN TOKYO

Tokyo is often described as the "warehouse of the world," and it is possible to procure anything under the sun here, from handcrafted boxwood combs to robot pets. The constant innovation and commercial ingenuity that characterize the city have resulted in a rash of mini shopping cities such as Tokyo Midtown and Omotesando

Decorative cat, a goodwill charm

Hills; high-tech convenience stores and high-end fashion towns such as Harajuku and Ginza; and Akihabara, an almost exotic electronic market. The world's highest concentration of vending machines per capita is also visible at every turn. And, compared with other global cities, the prices are not as outrageous as presumed.

PRICES AND SALES TAX

The Japanese yen continues to be regarded as a stable currency. Cash is by far the easiest method to pay for most goods. International credit cards are still unpopular in smaller shops. VISA, American Express, Diners Club, and MasterCard are the most widely accepted.

In department stores and boutiques, and in inner-city areas, prices are nearly always marked in Arabic numerals. In local shops and supermarkets, and in areas where non-Japanese are few and far between, prices may be written only in kanji characters.

All purchasable items and services are subject to a consumption tax of five percent. The price displayed should by law include the tax, although in practice this may not be the case.

TAX-FREE SHOPPING

Tokyo's tax-free shops offer a good range of domestic and imported brand items without the five percent sales tax added elsewhere. The best authorized outlets are the **Tokyo International Arcade**, near the Imperial Hotel *(see p111)* and **Laox** *(see p45)* for electronic goods.

In some shops, particularly department stores *(depatos)*, you may have to pay the full price for an item, then obtain a refund and customs document from a tax-exemption counter. This document is retained by customs when you leave Tokyo. Most major department stores offer tax exemption, but usually on

Youth entertainment area in Shibuya

goods over the value of ¥10,000. One advantage of shopping at department stores is that they usually have tax-exemption counters with English-speaking staff. The counters will issue a customs document, which they will attach to your passport for presentation when you depart. Large electronic stores in Akihabara *(see p45)*, such as **Yodobashi Camera** and Laox provide this service.

SHOPPING ZONES

Tokyo has many shopping zones identified by the popular goods they display. **Akihabara** *(see p45)* is the world's largest and most up-to-date electronic and camera center. **Aoyama/Omotesando** *(see p68 & p65)* is known for its high fashion in the city. Visit **Asakusa** for traditional Japanese souvenirs, foods, toys, and pop culture trinkets. **Daikanyama Address Dixsept** *(see pp146–7)* has several reputed boutiques, catering to the young and trend conscious. High-end department stores and art galleries make their home in **Ginza** *(see pp38–9)*.

Harajuku *(see p65)*, a fun street-oriented clothing, accessories, and cuddly toy district, caters to high-teens shoppers on small budgets. **Jimbocho** *(see p44)* is Tokyo's oldest book center. **Shibuya** *(see pp66–7)* with its department stores and fashion buildings, is one of the city's most diverse shopping zones. **Shinjuku**, to the west side of the station, is all electronics and software; the east side has department stores and multipurpose shopping complexes.

DEPARTMENT STORES

Many stores are owned by railroad companies, so that passengers coming off from their platforms are fed through passages bulging with advertising and display goods. Apart from selling a vast variety of top-range items, department stores, like convenience stores, also sell tickets for concerts and exhibitions. Roofs are often set aside as children's attraction parks, mini-golf ranges, and beer gardens. One early innovator was **Mitsukoshi**, perhaps Tokyo's most famous store. The great flagship stores such as **Takashimaya** and **Isetan** follow a similar layout, with delectable foods in the basement, a wide range of Western and Japanese restaurants on the top floor, and every conceivable type of goods between. Some stores are known for certain commodities – **Matsuya** for top fashion brands and for Japanese crafts, quality souvenirs, and furnishings; **Matsuzakaya** for its textiles, kimonos, and food basement; **Tokyu Hands** for household goods, and **Wako** for watches and jewelry.

MULTI-PURPOSE COMPLEXES

Roppongi Hills *(see p69)*, with its high-end shopping options, a prestigious art gallery, observation lounge, cinemas, and live events, was the first of several multi-purpose complexes. The **Marunouchi Building** in the Tokyo Station area has turned into a skyscraper shopping, restaurant, and office space. Shiodome, another shopping, office, and residential nexus, seems to grow exponentially with each visit. The shopping centerpiece of this millennium complex, **Caretta Shiodome**, attracts a young office crowd intent on keeping up with the latest in clothing. **Omotesando Hills** *(see p65)* features many Japanese and overseas designer stores. **Tokyo Midtown** houses several fashion and lifestyle outlets.

Automatic vending machine

MARKETS

Food markets provide an insight into the Japanese enthusiasm for food and cooking. The basement food floor of a major department store is a good place to start. A whole street of highly visible plastic food and kitchenware suppliers along **Kappabashi-dori** *(see p54)* creates the mood of a lively market place along this well patronized street. The ultimate market experience is **Tsukiji Fish Market** *(see p40)*; the area to the east is full of small restaurants and shops with pungent crates of wasabi (horseradish) and dried fish hanging from storefronts.

CONVENIENCE STORES AND VENDING MACHINES

Convenience stores (*konbini*) are easy to spot. They have catchy names such as 7-Eleven and AM-PM. Many people depend on these stores for more than just foods, toiletries, and magazines. they also book concert tickets and use ATMs and photocopiers. The quality of *konbini* food is surprisingly high and fresh. Among the popular take-out food items are boxed lunches, steamed buns, and cup noodles. Beverages include soft drinks, hot coffee, beer, and sake. Stores are often open 24/7. A Tokyo fixture since 1926, besides drinks and snacks, vending machines dispense batteries, flowers, eggs, underwear, disposable cameras, and even oxygen.

ARCADES AND MALLS

Many arcades and malls date from the postwar period and, being generally located in downtown areas, are old-fashioned in style and appearance. Along the approach to Senso-ji temple *(see pp56–7)* is an arcade of shops selling a mixture of tourist souvenirs, traditional crafts, snacks, and kitsch pop culture items.

Fuji-Torii antique shop displaying Japanese pottery, Omotesando

ANTIQUE STORES AND FLEA MARKETS

Flea markets, a Sunday-only institution, are often held in the grounds of old shrines, adding extra interest. These are attractive to professionals and to those just looking to pick up a bargain. The antique market in the basement of the **International Antique House** along Ometsando-dori may be a little gloomy, but the glassware, swords, and antique jewelry brighten up the setting. Five minutes' walk along the same side of the road in the direction of Harajuku, the **Oriental Bazaar** has genuine and replica antique furniture, pottery, and a good deal more. Nearby **Fuji-Torii** is known for the quality of its antiques, woodblock prints, *tansu* chests, scrolls, and lacquerware craft.

The market at **Tomioka-Hachimangu shrine**, held on the first two Sundays of the month, is a lively event. **Togo Shrine** holds a similar, though smaller, event in the heart of Harajuku every first and fourth Sunday. Closer to the center, the market at **Hanazono Shrine**, near Shinjuku's legendary watering hole Golden Gai *(see p61)*, is open every Sunday.

Beautiful glass building of Prada store, Aoyama

An elegant display of jewelry in Omotesando

COSMETICS, JEWELRY, AND ACCESSORIES

Mikimoto sells its pearls and jewelry in opulent surroundings. For a selection of silver and jewelry, visit Mori Silver in the **Oriental Bazaar** and **Takane Jewelry**. Nakamise-dori at Senso-ji temple *(see pp56–7)* is the place to find Japan's traditional jewelry. **Matsuzakaya** sells *kanzashi*, (hairpins) plus other jewelry, and nearby **Ginkado** sells *kanzashi*, costume swords, and fans. Next door is **Bunsendo**, also selling fans. The last maker of handmade wooden combs is **Jusanya** in Ueno. The red, stucco façade of the **Shiseido Building** in Ginza is complemented by the Shiseido Cosmetics Garden in Omotesando. For "cute" culture accessories, **Takeshita-dori** *(see p65)* is hard to beat.

TRADITONAL ARTS AND CRAFTS

Maruzen in Nihonbashi is an excellent source of traditional arts and crafts including ceramics, woodcraft, and lacquerware, as is **Takumi** in Ginza. **Itoya**, also in Ginza, is packed with crafts, especially fine *washi* (Japanese paper). **Kuroeya**, at Senso-ji temple, has been selling *washi* since the mid-19th century and stocks everything from modern stationery to traditional kites. The **Japan Folk Crafts Museum** *(see p77)* has a small, high-quality selection.

Ironware kettle, Japan Traditional Craft Center

The **Japan Traditional Craft Center** in Ikebukuro is an excellent place for purchasing affordable traditional crafts.

CONTEMPORARY ART AND DESIGN

The Spiral Garden in Minami-Aoyama's Spiral Building *(see p68)* usually has something interesting by Japanese artists.

In Ginza, you can find works by Japanese artists at **Galleria Grafica**, **Plus Minus Gallery**, and **Yoseido Gallery**. **Ginza Graphic Gallery** exhibits both Japanese and foreign works. The **Karakuri Museum** in Shibuya displays and sells artworks based on optical illusions. Located in the Tokyo Opera City building *(see p183)* in Shinjuku, the **NTT Inter-communication Center** features exhibits and installations using the latest technology. In the same building is the **Tokyo Opera City Gallery**, which displays Japanese painting, and graphic art. Contemporary prints can be found at the **Tolman Collection** near Tokyo Tower. For ceramics, try **Koransha** in Ginza. Good sources of modern houseware are the department stores **Tokyu Hands** and **Matsuya**. For cutting-edge interior design, head to **Axis** in Roppongi, a complex of galleries selling kitchenware, ceramics, furniture, and more. Shibuya's **Loft** has several floors of contemporary novelty housewares, jewelry, accessories, and toys.

BOOKS, MUSIC, AND MANGA

Isseido, an Art Deco Jimbocho institution, keeps used and rare books. The biggest stock of secondhand English titles though, can be found at **Good Day Books** in Ebisu. Another specialty store, **Crayon House** in Omotesando, caters exclusively to children. The younger of the two Shinjuku **Kinokuniya** stores has the best selections of titles in Tokyo. **Maruzen** has a good choice of titles in its Marunouchi shop. **Tower Records** boasts an up-to-date collection of books. **Cisco**, also in Shibuya, rates highly among Tokyo's young and savvy. For used CDs and vinyl, the Shinjuku branch of the **Disk Union** chain has the best stock. Manga fans will love **Mandarake** in the Shibuya Beam building for its second-hand magazines and related products. **Sekaido** in Shinjuku has a good range of manga.

Boxed sweets decorated with characters in a Kabuki play

SPECIALTY SHOPS

Head to **Sanbido** for religious statues and beautiful dolls; **Nishijima Umbrellas** has traditional umbrellas, while **Tokiwado** has *kaminari okoshi* crackers. **Nakatsuka** sells candies and sweet crackers, and **Kappabashi-dori** *(see p54)* is the place for kitchenware and plastic food. **Puppet House** is a shop, gallery, and workshop. **Isetatsu** specializes in *chiyogami* designs taken from textiles worn by samurai; and **Sagemonoya** sells antique *netsuke*, small, ornate accessories designed to hang from kimono belts.

DIRECTORY

DEPARTMENT STORES

Isetan
3-14-1 Shinjuku. **Map** 1 B1. **Tel** (03) 3352-1111.

Matsuya
3-6-1 Ginza. **Map** 5 C2. **Tel** (03) 3567-1211.

Matsuzakaya
6-10-1 Ginza. **Map** 5 B2. **Tel** (03) 3572-1111.

Mitsukoshi
1-4-1 Nihonbashi Muromachi. **Map** 5 C1. **Tel** (03) 3241-3311.

Takashimaya
5-24-2 Sendagaya. **Map** 1 B2. **Tel** (03) 5361-1111.

Tokyu Hands
12-18 Udagawacho, Shibuya. **Map** 1 B5. **Tel** (03) 5489-5111.

Wako
4-5-11 Ginza. **Tel** (03) 3562-2111.

MULTI-PURPOSE COMPLEXES

Caretta Shiodome
1-8-2 Higashi-Shimbashi. **Map** 5 B3. **Tel** (03) 6218-2100.

Marunouchi Building
2-4-1 Marunouchi. **Map** 5 B1. **Tel** (03) 5218-5100.

Omotesando Hills
4-12-10 Jingumae, Omotesando. **Map** 1 C4. **Tel** (03) 3497-0310.

Tokyo Midtown
9-7-1 Akasaka. **Map** 2 E3. **Tel** (03) 3475-3100.

ANTIQUE STORES AND FLEA MARKETS

Fuji-Torii
6-1-10 Jingumae. **Map** 1 C4. **Tel** (03) 3400-2777.

International Antique House
Hanae Mori Bldg B1, 3-6-1 Kita Aoyama. **Map** 1 C4. **Tel** (03) 3407-2675.

Oriental Bazaar
5-9-13 Jingumae. **Map** 1 B4. **Tel** (03) 3400-3933.

Togo Shrine Market
1-5-3 Jingumae. **Map** 1 B4. **Tel** (03) 3425-7965.

Tomioka-Hachimangu Shrine Market
1-20-3 Tomioka. **Map** 6 E2. **Tel** (0276) 38-3417.

COSMETICS, JEWELRY, AND ACCESSORIES

Bunsendo
1-30-1 Asakusa. **Map** 4 F3. **Tel** (03) 3841-0088.

Ginkado
1-30-1 Asakusa. **Map** 4 F3. **Tel** (03) 3841-8540.

Jusanya
2-12-21 Ueno. **Tel** (03) 3831-3238.

Matsuzakaya
See Department Stores.

Mikimoto
4-5-5 Ginza. **Map** 5 B3. **Tel** (03) 3535-4611.

Oriental Bazaar
See Antique Stores and Flea Markets.

Shiseido Building
7-8-10 Ginza. **Map** 5 B3. **Tel** (03) 3571-7731.

Takane Jewelry
1-7-23 Uchisaiwaicho. **Map** 5 A3. **Tel** (03) 3591-2764.

TRADITIONAL ARTS AND CRAFTS

Itoya
2-7-15 Ginza. **Map** 5 C2. **Tel** (03) 3561-8311.

Japan Folk Crafts Museum
4-3-33 Komaba. **Tel** (03) 3467-4527.

Japan Traditional Craft Center
Metropolitan Plaza Bldg 1-2F, 1-11-1 Nishi-Ikebukuro. **Tel** (03) 5954-6066.

Kuroeya
1-2-6 Nihonbashi. **Tel** (03) 3272-0948.

Maruzen
Oazo Bldg, 1-6-4 Marunouchi. **Map** 5 C1. **Tel** (03) 5288-8881.

Takumi
8-4-2 Ginza. **Map** 5 B3. **Tel** (03) 3571-2017.

CONTEMPORARY ART AND DESIGN

Axis
5-17-1 Roppongi. **Map** 2 E5. **Tel** (03) 3587-2781.

Galleria Grafica
Ginza S2 Bldg, 6-13-4 Ginza. **Map** 5 B3. **Tel** (03) 5550-1335.

Ginza Graphic Gallery
DNP Ginza Bldg, 7-7-2 Ginza. **Map** 5 B3. **Tel** (03) 3571-5206.

Karakuri Museum
King Bldg 2F, Shibuya 2-9-10. **Map** 1 C5. **Tel** (03) 3599-3313.

Koransha
6-14-20 Ginza. **Map** 5 B3. **Tel** (03) 3543-0951.

Loft
21-1 Udagawacho, Shibuya. **Map** 1 B5. **Tel** (03) 3462-3807.

Matsuya
See Department Stores.

NTT InterCommunication Center
Tel (0120) 144-199.

Plus Minus Gallery
2F, TEPCO Ginza-kan, 6-11-1 Ginza. **Tel** (03) 3575-0456.

Tokyo Opera City Gallery
Tel (03) 5353-0770.

Tokyu Hands
See Department Stores.

Tolman Collection
2-2-18 Shiba Daimon. **Map** 5 A4. **Tel** (03) 3434-1300.

Yoseido Gallery
5-5-15 Ginza. **Map** 5 B2. **Tel** (03) 3571-1312.

BOOKS, MUSIC, AND MANGA

Cisco
11-1 Udagawacho, Shibuya. **Map** 1 A5. **Tel** (03) 3462-0366.

Crayon House
3-8-15 Kita-Aoyama. **Map** 1 C5. **Tel** (03) 3406-6409.

Disk Union
3-31-4 Shinjuku. **Map** 1 B5. **Tel** (03) 3352-2691.

Good Day Books
1-11-2 Ebisu. **Map** 4 F3. **Tel** (03) 5421-0957.

Isseido
1-7 Kanda Jimbocho. **Map** 3 B5. **Tel** (03) 3292-0071.

Kinokuniya
5-24-2 Sendagaya. **Map** 1 B1. **Tel** (03) 5361-3301.

Mandarake
Shibuya Beams B2, 31-2 Udagawacho, Shibuya. **Map** 1 A5. **Tel** (03) 3477-0777.

Maruzen
See Traditional Arts and Crafts.

Sekaido
3-1-1 Shinjuku. **Map** 1 B1. **Tel** (03) 5379-1111.

Tower Records
1-22-14 Jinnan, Shibuya. **Map** 1 B5. **Tel** (03) 3496-3661.

SPECIALTY SHOPS

Isetatsu
2-18-9 Yanaka. **Map** 3 B1. **Tel** (03) 3823-1453.

Nakatsuka
1-37-1 Asakusa. **Map** 4 F3. **Tel** (03) 3843-4455.

Nishijima Umbrellas
1-30-1 Asakusa. **Map** 4 F3. **Tel** (03) 3841-8560.

Puppet House
1-8 Shimomiyabi-cho, Shinjuku. **Tel** (03) 5229-6477.

Sagemonoya
Yabane KK, 4-28-20-704 Yotsuya. **Tel** (03) 3352-6286.

Sanbido
1-33-3 Asakusa. **Map** 4 F3. **Tel** (03) 5827-0070.

Tokiwado
1-3-2 Asakusa. **Map** 4 E3. **Tel** (03) 3841-5656.

Clothing

The pace of change in a city where everything seems temporary is perfectly suited to Tokyo's fast-moving fashion world. Extensive media coverage of the fashion industry, relatively high disposable incomes among the young, and an active nightlife have made Tokyo one of the trendiest, most visible fashion centers on the globe. Snapping at the heels of the fashion establishment with their Paris and New York outlets are brat packs of emerging, young Japanese designers creating a host of trendy labels. Some of the leading fashion houses in the world now call Tokyo their home.

Young shoppers browsing through readymade Western wear, Shibuya 109

FASHION BUILDINGS

Fashion buildings house exclusive boutiques, often with a collective theme, target age group, or approach to design. The modern, innovative architecture of the buildings themselves adds much interest to the entire shopping experience.

Shibuya 109 is a silver, circular tower housing several boutiques renowned for teen fashions. It also stages fashion promotion events in front of the building. **Mark City**, a towering modern building connected by passageways to Shibuya Station, is a more ambitious project. Labyrinthine floors of boutiques and accessory stores aimed at the 20s and 30s age group, provide a social setting with restaurants, bakeries, and trendy cafés. The **LaForet Building**, a Harajuku landmark, is strictly for teen shoppers. **Venus Fort** (see p82), a retail outlet targeted at women in Odaiba, looks more like an Italian film set than a fashion store.

Food courts, cafés, trinket stalls, and trendy shops create a faux Italian street scene.

WOMEN'S FASHIONS

Ginza has always been synonymous with high chic and prices to match. Large department stores such as **Mitsukoshi** and **Matsuzakaya** (for both, see p145) have always been the arbiters of taste here, offering classic design cuts, which appeal to women in their 30s upwards. Luxury foreign brands such as Gucci and Chanel have

Trendy women's wear, Dolce and Gabbana showroom, Omotesando

opened super-modern outlets, providing designer shoes, handbags, cosmetics, and other chic accessories.

Aoyama's **Comme des Garçons** store, the brainchild of radical designer Rei Kawakubo, is well worth a look for the building alone. Also in the contiguous Aoyama/Omotesando/Jingumae districts, **Prada Aoyama**, the latest addition to Minami-Aoyama's high-end fashion scene, is another shopping-plus-architecture experience. The flowing fabrics and colorful embroidery that characterize **Tsumori Chisato** designs, on show in her Shibuya store, enjoy an almost cult following among women. The more radical but fun **Hysteric Glamour** has had a similar effect on the tastes of punk-inclined customers not afraid to wear T-shirts with provocative messages. For a good mix of women's fashions, accessories, and cosmetics, **Daikanyama Address Dixsept**, a retail complex with an open-air plaza and interesting interior consisting of suspension bridges, makes for a great half-day fashion shopping trip. The complex is a little to the northwest of Daikanyama Station.

MENSWEAR

Young Japanese males are almost as fashion conscious as women, though there are not as many exclusive menswear shops in Tokyo. The following recommendations also feature women's fashions. **Muji** design aesthetics – cool, simple, understated – are well known the world over.

Besides clothes and accessories, its Roppongi store has a good line in simple homeware designs.

The singular and arresting designs of **Yohji Yamamoto**, another household name in the Japanese fashion cosmos, seem to go from strength to strength. The interior of the bronze-faced store in Omotesando is well worth a look. The name **Issey Miyake** needs no introduction. The anarchist designer burst onto

Western wear for men, Uniqlo store, Aoyama

the scene in the 1980s with his innovative use of fabrics, design forms, and shapes to create expensive but highly regarded work. The window displays are a joy. Nearby **Undercover** is the brainchild of Jun Takahashi, a punk musician whose designs are inspired by the music his band plays.

The menswear at **Uniqlo**, a popular clothing chain with branches overseas, is simple, contemporary, and bottom-line for many shoppers at this store along Jingumae's Meiji-dori. The fashions here target all age groups.

TEXTILES AND KIMONOS

Silk, cotton, linen, and hemp all feature in Japan's long and rich textile history. While some traditional techniques are fading, most are alive and well. Department stores are often the best places to find a range of textiles. **Matsuzakaya** *(see p145)* grew from a Nagoya kimono merchant and stocks bolts of kimono cloth made in Kyoto and textured *furoshiki* (square wrapping cloths). The shop at the **Tokyo National Museum** *(see pp50–53)* has a good selection of *furoshiki* and scarves made using traditional techniques. Also good is **Bengara**. **Miyashita Obi** on Nakamise-dori at Senso-ji

temple *(see pp56–7)* has wonderful *obi* sashes, used to wrap a kimono at the waist. **Hayashi Kimono** in Yurakucho, sells classic outfits but also a light cotton summer version called *yukata*, which can be comfortable house wear. The **Oriental Bazaar** *(see p143)* and **Uniqlo** offer a good range of *yukata*. Asakusa's **Nakamise-dori** *(see p56)* has a lot of less expensive fabric kimonos in bright colors, the assumption being that foreigners like brilliant, gaudy designs. And do not forget that there are some terrific kimonos and textile bargains to be found at the eclectic Sunday flea markets *(see p143)*.

Kimono with an *obi* sash

A colorful *kimono* with traditional floral motifs

Gifts, Gizmos, and Toys

Handmade combs

In the first months after the Second World War, de-mobbed men and displaced persons would spread a towel or newspaper on the incinerated wasteland around main stations, and display a saucepan or worn kimono in the hope of finding a customer. These were the tentative beginnings of the black markets. Since then, consumers have long moved from desiring just basic necessities to acquiring gifts, gizmos, and the novelties that flood Tokyo's markets.

GIFT SHOPS

The Japanese are not only avid buyers of souvenirs when they venture overseas, but excellent customers for the interesting products of their own country. The result is countless gift shops.

The traditional and modern stationery, origami paper, and calligraphy tools sold at **Itoya** in Ginza, make light, affordable, and portable gifts. The articles at **Japan Sword**, the oldest dealer in authentic Japanese blades, are a little heavier and more expensive, not to mention dangerous. Replicas of the swords are also sold. The shop and exhibition space are located in the business district of Toranomon.

Right in the heart of Shibuya, **Do** is the stylish Claska Hotel's gift shop. The hotel is known for its design, and the gift shop follows the same model. Occasionally, it also shows works by local artists.

Craft and gift sections of reputed department stores (*see p142*) are logical places

An eye-catching chopsticks box, a traditional souvenir

to do one-stop shopping. Large railroad terminuses, especially Tokyo Station, are crammed with souvenir and gift shops.

FOOD AND DRINK

Department store basements have the largest and most interesting single selections of ready-to-go Japanese foods of the kind that make interesting gifts. Markets (*see p143*) and even supermarkets have

interesting and unfamiliar food items as well, from *sembei* (rice crackers) to traditional Japanese confections. The main ingredient of Japanese sweets is *anko*, red bean paste, which may be an acquired taste for some Westerners. These beautifully made confections are called *wagashi* in Japanese, and are often taken with green tea. **Toraya** is famous – it supplies to the imperial family. This Akasaka institution changes its sweet motifs to reflect the seasons. Branches of **Akebono** selling exquisite sweets can be found in the food basements of some of the best Tokyo department stores. The origins of **Iidabashi Mannendo** in Iidabashi, date back to the 17th century, when it began making sweets based on recipes from the old imperial city of Kyoto.

Alcohol is freely available in Tokyo. Individual sake shops and, once again, department store basements have shelves full of *nihonshu* (the word "sake" can actually refer to all alcoholic drinks). The choice, though, can be quite bewildering, involving some knowledge of grades and provenance. For an initiation into the mysteries of the drink, **Sake Plaza** in Shimbashi has excellent displays. Entrance to the plaza is free, and for a small fee visitors can enjoy a five-cup sampling.

GADGETS AND GIZMOS

Tokyu Hands, a treasure trove of inventive and original household goods, is a good place to start for general items from fancy dress costumes to trick store treats evoking a sense of fun. The **Don Quixote** stores, such as the popular one in Shinjuku, are stuffed to the ceilings with novelty, "character" goods, costume wear, mixed in with snacks, camping gear, and ironing boards. For a combination of electronics and eccentricities, **Akihabara** (*see p45*) is hard to beat. **Ishimaru** and **Sofmap**

Bewildering variety of sweets in a store on Nakamise-dori, Akihabara

Electronics store stacked with low-priced gadgets, Akihabara

are two huge electronic department stores here. **Akky** and **Takarada Musen** are also duty-free stores. **Sato Musen** and **Onoden** are other names to look out for in this "Electric Town." Young women dressed as anime characters from classic series such as *Sailor Moon* and *Neon Genesis Evangelion* greet customers outside **AsoBitCity**, which, in addition to software games and peripherals, sells "character" goods and large model train sets. More Akihabara wonders await at **Tsukumo Robocon Magazine Kan**, where the specialty are cute, owner-friendly robots – mechanized turtles, cats, dogs, insects, and fictitious creatures.

TOYS

One of the nice things about Tokyo toy stores is that nobody seems to mind if you pick things up and play with them, even if you are a lone adult. Customers are treated with a measure of tolerance and indulgence in Tokyo. And surprising numbers of adults shop for themselves in the toy stores, a reminder that a sense of playfulness is alive and well among the hard-working Tokyoites. These places are among the best in the world to pick up souvenirs and the latest craze among children before it hits the international market.

Hakuhinkan Toy Park in Ginza has always been a Mecca for toys and still is, with several crowded floors to prove it. Try not to go on a weekend. The six floors of toys, games, and novelties at **Kiddyland** in Jingumae are a wonder to behold. Besides conventional toys, kits, and games, all the popular anime characters are here too, from Pokemon to Hello Kitty. For a slightly more personal experience, **Astro Mike** in Harajuku has many loyal followers. The store traces the history of toy making, both Japanese and Western, from the action figures and models of the 1960s, up to the present day.

Stuffed toys in all sizes at Kiddyland, a major kids' toy store in Jingumae

ENTERTAINMENT IN TOKYO

Entertainment in Tokyo is a wonderful mix of the old world and the cutting-edge modern. Traditional performing arts span the vibrancy of Kabuki theater to the haunting tones of a *shakuhachi* recital. Tokyo is the best place to catch the latest in movies and music from around the world. The abundance of live music on offer ranges from jazz and blues to pop

Man playing a traditional *shakuhachi* **instrument**

and techno, and even Western classical music. Tokyo enjoys a pulsating and truly international club culture; at many places, you can dance till dawn. Sports fans have a choice between baseball and soccer, or the more traditional forms of martial arts, as well as sumo. At night, the city puts on a different face, and the brightly lit leisure districts show how serious Tokyo is about fun.

Kabuki performance in Kabuki-za Theater

INFORMATION SOURCES

Metropolis, a free weekly magazine and website is a good source of information on leisure activities in the city. **Japanzine**, another free magazine, also covers other cities in Japan if you plan to travel out of the city. The **Japan Times**, *Asahi Shimbun*, *Daily Yomiuri*, and **Japan Today** also have comprehensive listings. All of these publications are available at station kiosks and major stores including **Kinokuniya** (see p60), **Tower Records** (see p67), and **Maruzen** (see p145). Information on current events in and around Tokyo is also given on the **JNTO** (see p163) website. Other useful online resources include **Japan Visitor**, **Realtokyo**, and **Tokyo Food Page**.

BOOKING TICKETS

Popular traditional Japanese entertainment, such as Kabuki and sumo, are best reserved ahead of time through a travel

agent or hotel travel desk. For concerts and sporting events, the two major ticket agencies are **Ticket PIA** and **CN Play-guide**. They can be hard to reach by phone. It is easier to book in person; a convenient office is Ticket PIA at Ginza's Sony Building (see p38). Department and convenience stores also have ticket desks, sometimes with English-speaking assistants. Alternatively, book directly by phoning the venue; payment is made when the tickets are picked up. Most agencies speak only Japanese, so

having a Japanese-speaker at hand will help. Reservations can also be made online, at convenience stores such as **Lawson**, or through the *Metropolis* website.

CINEMA

There are several specialist cinemas that screen movies from Asia, as well as Europe and the US. However, most non-Japanese films are shown in the original language with Japanese subtitles. The **Tokyo International Film Festival** (see p30) is becoming increasingly high profile. There are also several other interesting film festivals, showcasing both domestic and international movies.

Cinema prices are not cheap, averaging around ¥1,800. On Cinema Day, usually the first of each month, tickets are reduced. In Shibuya, **Bunkamura** (see p66) sometimes shows Japanese films with English subtitles and is known for screening independent and European films. Also in Shibuya, **Theater Image**

Movie poster in Shinjuku, one of Tokyo's centers for cinema

Ebisu Garden Cinema, a popular
cinema hall for foreign films

Forum uses the most
advanced digital technology.
The more centrally located
Toho Cinemas Chanter shows
art-house and independent
films. **Marunouchi Piccadilly**,
in the Mullion Building in
Yurakucho *(see p38)*, has five
screens, while **Ebisu Garden
Cinema** *(see p76)* has two.
Currently, the most comfortable cinema in the city is at
the nine-screen complex in
Roppongi Hills *(see p69)*,
part of the **Toho Cinema**
group, with an in-house bar
and late-night screenings.
Anyone with an interest
in classic Japanese cinema
should visit the superb
National Film Center *(see p42)*.
Fans of animation should visit
Ghibli Museum; it displays the
work of pioneering anime
director Hayao Miyazaki,
whose films include *Spirited
Away* (2001) and *Howl's
Moving Castle* (2004).

INTERNATIONAL THEATER

The international theater
scene in Tokyo encompasses
everything from Shakespeare
and Broadway musicals to
comedy, classical ballet, and
modern dance. The main venues are in Shinjuku, Shibuya,
and Marunouchi. Although
some foreign touring companies come through Tokyo,
most shows are in Japanese,
with local actors of a consist-
ently high standard. The
Tokyo Comedy Store offers
non-Japanese and Japanese the
chance to exhibit their comedy
skills in English on the fourth
Friday of the month at the
Crocodile club in Harajuku.

LIVE MUSIC

The finest venues for orchestral
concerts are the **New National
Theater**, **Suntory Hall**, **NHK
Hall**, **Orchard Hall** in Bunkamura *(see p66)*, **Sumida
Triphony Hall**, and the two
halls of the **Tokyo International
Forum** *(see p43)*. The New
National Theater and Orchard
Hall also stage opera and
ballet performances.
Tokyo has a vibrant jazz
scene too, reflected in the
large number of clubs and
the quality of the visiting
artists. **Blue Note Tokyo** is the
best-known club (although
prices are high and sets
are short). Other places
that attract world-class
performers include
B Flat, **Shinjuku Pit
Inn**, and the **Cotton
Club**. **STB139** offers
an eclectic mix of
music, with mostly
Japanese artists.
Blues Alley Japan
is a small club
featuring blues
and jazz artists.
Ever since the
Beatles played at
Nippon Budokan
in 1966, Tokyo
has been an essential stop on
the world itinerary of pop and
rock bands. Both the aging
Budokan and the cavernous
Tokyo Dome stadium have
poor acoustics. Smaller and
far better venues include
Koseinenkin Kaikan, **Shibuya
AX**, the inconveniently
located **Zepp Tokyo**, **Nakano
Sun Plaza**, and **Liquid Room**.
As with jazz, though, it is the
more intimate venues where

Street musician giving
a live performance

gigs come alive. **Club Quattro**
can be claustrophobic but
gets top international acts;
Duo Music Exchange and **O-
West** often specialize in techno
and J-pop. **Eggman** and the
ever-eclectic **SuperDeluxe**
showcase experimental, fringe,
and upcoming talent. Live
bands also play at many of
the Irish pubs as well as
the **Pink Cow**, a casual, artsy
hangout, popular with expats.

KARAOKE

The boom for belting out
popular hits to backing music
tracks dates from the 1960s
but remains as popular as
ever today in Japan, the
birthplace of
karaoke. Trans-
lated as "empty
orchestra," karaoke
is enjoyed in tradi-
tional bars, lively
pubs, at home,
and in major enter-
tainment districts,
at karaoke "boxes."
These complexes range
from small, cozy rooms
for couples to much
larger spaces for
groups of friends or
office parties. Food
and drinks can be ordered.
The most performed numbers
are local pop songs, current
and classic; *enka*, the Japanese equivalent of French
chanson; and some Western
pop hits. **Karaoke-kan** in
Shibuya *(see pp66–7)* is the
famed location used in the
movie *Lost in Translation*.
For the best selection of
songs in English follow the
expats to **Smash Hits**.

An extravagant opera performance in New National Theater

Sumo wrestlers compete at Tokyo's National Sumo Stadium

SUMO

Three sumo tournaments (*basho*) are held in Tokyo each year, in January, May, and September, all at the impressive 10,000-seat **National Sumo Stadium** in Ryogoku *(see p74)*. The 15-day tournaments begin on a Sunday, with each wrestler fighting one bout a day. The action starts at 2:30pm with the lowest-ranking wrestlers; the top ranked appear from 5 to 6pm. The highest-ranking wrestler, usually a *yokozuna* (grand champion) will compete in the last bout.

The best views are on the north side of the stadium. Seating in the main auditorium is Japanese-style, in individual boxes. These are cramped and more expensive than the seats upstairs, but much closer to the action. Tickets should be booked in advance. Easiest to get are midweek tickets in the first week of a tournament. If you cannot buy tickets via an agency, try asking your hotel to check for returns, or just line up at the stadium itself.

It is possible to watch practice sessions at sumo stables, or *beya*. They are open to anyone who wants to watch, with a few basic rules – do not eat or use a camera flash, and be silent. Most of the *beya* are situated near Ryogoku station. Visitors can make a trip to the **Kasugano Beya**, a tall building with a green copper gable over the entrance, the **Izutsu Beya**, or the **Dewanoumi Beya**.

OTHER MARTIAL ARTS

The center for martial arts in Japan is the **Nippon Budokan**, and this is where the top tournaments in judo, karate, and *kendo* (wooden sword fighting) are held. There are *dojo* (practice halls) for the various martial arts throughout Tokyo. Not all are open to non-Japanese as observers or participants. Contact **Tokyo TIC** *(see p163)* for a list of *dojos* that allow spectators. To participate in martial arts training, contact one of the national regulatory bodies.

Nippon Budokan, an important center for all martial arts

BASEBALL AND SOCCER

Baseball is regarded as Japan's de facto national sport. Professional baseball teams are split between the Central League and the Pacific League. The Tokyo-based Yomiuri Giants (Central League) are Japan's most popular team. Their engaging games in the soaring **Tokyo Dome** are always sold out. The Yakult Swallows (also

Central League) play at the beautiful **Jingu Stadium**. Book tickets ahead of time.

Soccer fans may want to visit the **Nissan Stadium**, Japan's largest stadium and host to the 2002 World Cup final. It is the home of the J-League's Yokohama F. Marinos. The **Ajinomoto Stadium** is home to FC Tokyo and Tokyo Verdy 1969, both J-League teams. Tickets are available at the stadium on the day of the match.

OTHER SPECTATOR SPORTS

Other sports with a significant presence include rugby, tennis, volleyball, swimming, athletics, basketball, cycling, and motor sports. Racing (horses, speedboats, or cycling) generates fervent interest, especially since gambling is allowed through official channels. Details of competitions are given in the sports pages of *Metropolis*.

PACHINKO

Pachinko *(see p67)* is like an electronic vertical pinball and its practitioners appear hypnotized by the bright lights and trance-inducing electronic music. Not just a pastime, it is a form of gambling. Winnings are exchanged for goods, which are then bought back (off the premises, to remain within the law). To experience pachinko firsthand, try the **Maruhan Pachinko Tower** in Shibuya. Here, each floor has a different theme and there are love seats for couples.

Sportsgear on display at the Baseball Hall of Fame, Tokyo Dome

DIRECTORY

INFORMATION SOURCES

Japanzine
www.japanzine.com

Japan Times
www.japantimes.co.jp/
entertainment.html

Japan Today
www.japantoday.com

Japan Visitor
www.japanvisitor.com

Metropolis
www.metropolis.co.jp

Realtokyo
www.realtokyo.co.jp/
english

Tokyo Food Page
www.bento.com/
tokyofood.html

BOOKING TICKETS

CN Playguide
Tel (03) 5802-9999.
www.cnplayguide.com

Lawson
www.i-tike.com

Ticket PIA
Tel (0570) 02-9999.
www.pia.co.jp

CINEMA

Bunkamura
2-24-1 Dogenzaka,
Shibuya-ku. **Map** 1 A5.
Tel (03) 3477-9111.

Ghibli Museum,
1-1-83 Shimorenjaku,
Mitaka-shi.
Tel (0570) 05-5777.

**Theater Image
Forum**
2-10-2 Shibuya,
Shibuya-ku. **Map** 1 C5.
Tel (03) 5766-0114.

Toho Cinema
Keyakizaka Complex,
6-10-2 Roppongi, Minato-
ku. *Tel (03) 5775-6090*
(press 9 for English).

**Toho Cinemas
Chanter**
1-2-2 Yurakucho, Chiyoda-
ku. *Tel (03) 3591-1511.*

INTERNATIONAL THEATER

Tokyo Comedy Store
www.tokyocomedy.com

LIVE MUSIC

B Flat
6-6-4, Akasaka, Minato-
ku. **Map** 2 F4.
Tel (03) 5563-2563.

Blue Note Tokyo
Raika Building, 6-3-16
Minami-Aoyama,
Minato-ku. **Map** 2 D5.
Tel (03) 5485-0088.

Blues Alley Japan
Hotel Wing International
Meguro, 1-3-14 Meguro,
Meguro-ku. **Map** 1 B1.
Tel (03) 5496-4381.

Club Quattro
Parco Quattro 4F,
32-13 Udagawa-cho,
Shibuya-ku. **Map** 1 A5.
Tel (03) 3477-8750.

Cotton Club
2 F Tokia Tokyo Building,
2-7-3 Marunouchi,
Chiyoda-ku. **Map** 5 B2.
Tel (03) 3215-1555.

**Duo Music
Exchange**
2-14-8 Dogenzaka,
Shibuya-ku. **Map** 1 A5.
Tel (03) 5459-8716.

Eggman
1-6-8 Jinnan, Shibuya-ku.
Map 1 B5.
Tel (03) 3496-1785.

Koseinenkin Kaikan
5-3-1 Shinjuku,
Shinjuku-ku. **Map** 1 C1.
Tel (03) 3356-1114.

Liquid Room
3-16-6 Higashi,
Shibuya-ku.
Tel (03) 5464-0800.

Nakano Sun Plaza
4-1-1 Nakano,
Nakano-ku.
Tel (03) 3388-1151.

**New National
Theater**
1-1-1 Honmachi, Shibuya-
ku. **Map** 1 A2.
Tel (03) 5351-3011.

NHK Hall
2-2-1 Jinnan, Shibuya-ku.
Map 1 B4.
Tel (03) 3465-1751.

Nippon Budokan
2-3 Kitanomaru-Koen,
Chiyoda-ku. **Map** 3 A5.
Tel (03) 3216-5100.

Orchard Hall
Bunkamura, 2-24-1
Dogenzaka, Shibuya-ku.
Map 1 A6.
Tel (03) 3477-9111.

O-West
2-3 Maruyama-cho,
Shibuya-ku. **Map** 1 A5.
Tel (03) 5784-7088.

Pink Cow
Villa Moderuna B1, 1-3-18
Shibuya, Shibuya-ku.
Map 1 B5.
Tel (03) 3406-5597.

Shibuya AX
2-1-1 Jinnan,
Shibuya-ku. **Map** 1 B4.
Tel (03) 5738-2020.

Shinjuku Pit Inn
B1 Accord Building, 2-12-
4 Shinjuku, Shinjuku-ku.
Map 1 B1.
Tel (03) 3354-2024.

STB139
6-7-11 Roppongi,
Minato-ku. **Map** 2 E5.
Tel (03) 5474-0139.

**Sumida Triphony
Hall**
1-2-3 Kinshi, Sumida-ku.
Tel (03) 5608-1212.

Suntory Hall
1-13-1 Akasaka,
Minato-ku. **Map** 2 F4.
Tel (03) 3584-9999.

SuperDeluxe
B1F 3-1-25 Nishi-Azabu,
Minato-ku. **Map** 2 E5.
Tel (03) 5412-0515.

Zepp Tokyo
Palette Town, 1-3-15
Aomi, Koto-ku. **Map** 2 E5.
Tel (03) 3599-0710.

KARAOKE

Karaoke-kan
K&F Building, 30-8
Udagawa-cho, Shibuya-ku.
Map 1 B5.
Tel (03) 3462-0785.

Smash Hits
M2 Building B1F, 5-2-26
Hiroo, Shibuya-ku.
Tel (03) 3444-0432.

SUMO AND OTHER MARTIAL ARTS

Dewanoumi Beya
2-3-15 Ryogoku,
Shibuya ku.
Map 4 E5.

Izutsu Beya
2-2-7 Ryogoku,
Sumida-ku.
Map 4 E5.

Kasugano Beya
1-7-11 Ryogoku,
Sumida-ku.
Map 4 E5.

**National Sumo
Stadium**
1-3-28 Yokoami,
Sumida-ku.
Map 4 E4.
Tel (03) 3623-5111.

Nippon Budokan
See Live Music

BASEBALL AND SOCCER

Ajinomoto Stadium
376-3 Nishimachi,
Chofu City.
Tel (0424) 40-0555.

Jingu Stadium
3-1 Kasumigaoka,
Shinjuku-ku.
Map 2 D4.
Tel (03) 3404-8999.

Nissan Stadium
3300 Kozukue-cho,
Kohoku-ku, Yokohama
City 222-0036.
Tel (045) 477-5000.
www.nissan-stadium.jp/
english/index.php

Tokyo Dome
1-3-61 Koraku,
Bunkyo-ku. **Map** 3 A3.
Tel (03) 5800-9999.

PACHINKO

**Maruhan Pachinko
Tower**
28-6 Udagawa-cho,
Shibuya.
Tel (03) 5458-3905.

Traditional Performing Arts

Despite Tokyo's ultra-modern exterior, its heart still moves to a traditional beat. The rarified, otherworldly court music known as *gagaku* dates back much further than the city itself, as does the Noh Theater *(see p16)*. It is, however, the performing arts of the Edo period *(see p25)*, especially Kabuki and the Bunraku puppet theater *(see p17)*, that capture the rich, vibrant cultural life of premodern Japan. Such displays are not hard to find – at the Kabuki-za Theater, for example, just walk in off the street, buy a one-act ticket, and travel back in time.

An elegant cypress performance stage, Noh National Theater

TRADITIONAL THEATER

Kabuki and Noh, the two best-known forms of traditional theater *(see pp16–17)*, are well represented in Tokyo. Of the two traditions, Kabuki provides a much more flamboyant spectacle, with rousing stories, elaborate sets, and amazing costumes. However, dramatic action sequences can often be interspersed with extended soliloquies. The **Kabuki-za** Theater *(see p40)* is the main venue for Kabuki, with almost daily performances starting mid-morning and lasting three or more hours. It is also possible to buy a ticket to see just one act if you are short of time. Prices range from around ¥2,500 to as much as ¥16,000; one-act tickets are around ¥700. Earphone guides giving explanations and commentary in English are available to hire. The **National Theater** also stages Kabuki performances in January, March, October, November, and December. A number of unorthodox versions of Kabuki have been developed to make it more contemporary. Super Kabuki, introduced in 1985 and staged at the **Shinbashi Enbujo**, adds high-tech special effects (such as actors flying through the air) to the traditional plots. Cocoon Kabuki, a project launched in 1994, brings the traditional plays and costumes each summer to the **Theater**

A Kabuki performance at the Kabuki-za Theater, Ginza

Cocoon in Shibuya, which is also known for visiting foreign theatrical productions.

In contrast, a Noh performance can be heavy going for those unprepared for its slow pace. As a theatrical experience, however, it can be exceptionally powerful. The **Noh National Theater** near Sendagaya JR station usually has weekend performances. Tickets vary from ¥2,300 to ¥4,300. It is also possible to see plays at a Noh school, for instance **Kanze Nohgakudo**. Outdoor Noh performed by torchlight (*Takigi Noh*) can be wonderfully atmospheric, especially when staged in front of an ancient shrine or temple, such as with the annual fall performances at the Kamakura-gu shrine, in the hills of Kamakura. More information is readily available from **JNTO** *(see p163)* or the **Kamakura Tourist Association**.

The puppet theater, Bunraku, predates Kabuki, and many of its plays were later adapted to the stage. The black-robed puppeteers are so skillful, you soon ignore their presence and just watch the lifelike movements of the puppets themselves. Performances can be seen at the National Theater's Small Hall.

Kyogen (short comic farces) is one of Japan's oldest forms of drama, and includes acrobatics and juggling. Now played to comic effect, Kyogen is often performed as part of Noh, or as individual plays between Noh plays. Another lighthearted theatrical tradition is Rakugo. Dressed in a kimono and sitting on a *zabuton* (cushion), the storytellers act out comic situations, often retelling old and well-loved stories. Held at intimate theaters such as **Suzumoto** in Ueno or **Suehirotei** in bustling Shinjuku, they give great insight into characteristic Japanese traditional humor, even without understanding the language. A few Rakugo artists have also started doing occasional shows in English.

A giant Bunraku puppet

Takarazuka Theater, a venue for dance and theater performances

TRADITIONAL AND CONTEMPORARY DANCE

Performances of traditional dance are staged regularly by the **Nihon Buyo Kyokai**. The Azuma Odori, an annual production of dance and drama usually held at the end of May, brings Tokyo's geisha community on stage at **Shinbashi Enbujo**.

A unique theater experience is Takarazuka, a company divided into five troupes and composed entirely of women. With their own state-of-the-art **Takarazuka Theater** in Yurakucho, they perform traditional adaptations in Japanese of Western musicals and historical love stories, and are famed for their extravagant productions.

Butoh is a distinct and compelling form of contemporary dance developed in the 1960s that draws on elements of mime and traditional ascetic practice. Often shaven-headed and almost naked with body makeup, the dancers follow a slow choreography that seeks to create beauty out of self-imposed grotesqueness. Look out for performances by established troupes such as Dairakudakan or Buto-sha Tenkei, staged at **Setagaya Public Theater** but more often at small fringe theaters in outlying areas.

TRADITIONAL MUSIC

The oldest Japanese musical traditions are those of the *matsuri* or festivals *(see pp28–31)*, featuring instruments such as drum and flute. Performances of captivating ancient court music, known as *gagaku*, are given occasionally at the **National Theater** or at major temples in the city. The **Ono Gagaku Kai** holds major concerts featuring other regional instruments such as the stringed *koto* and *shamisen*, and the *shakuhachi* (flute). Do not miss a chance to catch a concert by one of the troupes of Japanese drummers, performing on *taiko* drums ranging from the size of small snares to huge barrels two meters or more in diameter. The most dynamic of the performing groups is Kodo, which plays an annual series of concerts at venues such as the popular Bunkamura *(see p66)* in Shibuya each December.

A woman playing a *shamisen* instrument

(see pp28–31)

DIRECTORY

TRADITIONAL THEATER

Kabuki-za Theater
4-12-5 Ginza, Chuo-ku.
Map 5 C3.
Tel (03) 3541-3131.

Kamakura Tourist Association
Tel (0467) 23-3050.

Kanze Nohgakudo
1-16-4 Shoto, Shibuya-ku.
Map 1 A5.
Tel (03) 3469-5241.

National Theater
4-1 Hayabusa-cho, Chiyoda-ku.
Map 2 F3.
Tel (03) 3265-7411.

Noh National Theater
4-18-1 Sendagaya, Shibuya-ku.
Map 1 C3.
Tel (03) 3423-1331.

Shinbashi Enbujo
6-18-2 Ginza, Chuo-ku.
Map 5 C3.
Tel (03) 3541-2600.

Suehirotei
3-6-12 Shinjuku, Shinjuku-ku.
Map 1 B1.
Tel (03) 3351-2974.

Suzumoto
2-7-12 Ueno, Taito-ku.
Map 3 C3.
Tel (03) 3834-5906.

Theater Cocoon
Bunkamura, 2-24-1 Dogenzaka, Shibuya-ku. **Map** 1 A5.
Tel (03) 3477-9999.

TRADITIONAL AND CONTEMPORARY DANCE

Nihon Buyo Kyokai
2-18-1 Kachidoki, Chuo-ku.
Map 5 D4.
Tel (03) 3533-6455.

Setagaya Public Theater
4-1-1 Taishido, Setagaya-ku.
Tel (03) 5432-1526.
www.onoteru.com

Takarazuka Theater
1-1-3 Yurakucho, Chiyoda-ku.
Map 5 B2.
Tel (03) 5251-2001.

TRADITIONAL MUSIC

Ono Gagaku Kai
2-13-14 Shitaya, Taito-ku.
Tel (03) 3873-2780.

Japanese women performing traditional opera dance

Nightlife

Evening does not signal any let-up in the pace of life in Tokyo. If anything, it seems to intensify, especially in areas where the neon burns brightest. Fashionable Ginza, the cosmopolitan party district of Roppongi, sophisticated Nishi-Azabu, youthful Shibuya or vibrant Shinjuku – there are plenty of choices. Tokyo is rapidly becoming an all-night city, and it is one of the most exciting places in the world to party. It is not just the clubs and cabarets, many restaurants, bars, and traditional *izakaya (see p120)* now stay open until 2am or later.

A DJ performing at La Fabrique, Shibuya

HIGH-RISE BARS

The best place to get into the mood for an evening out is at one of the city's high-rise hotel bars. The Conrad's **TwentyEight Bar** has a brilliant view over the Rainbow Bridge and the Odaiba waterfront. In Shibuya, there is the Cerulean Tower Hotel, with its 40th-floor **Bello Visto Bar**. Best of all is the Park Hyatt Hotel's *(see p116)* luxurious 52nd-floor **New York Bar**, as seen in the film *Lost in Translation*. Cradle a cocktail,

New York Bar offers superb views of the city below

watch the dusk fall and the lights come on, then descend to street level and plunge into the neon night.

CLUBS AND BARS

Ginza remains one of Tokyo's most exclusive and priciest nightlife districts. But alongside the costly hostess bars, there are also more affordable spots, such as the standing-only **300 Bar**, where the food or drink all cost around ¥300. The Ginza Corridor, a row of bars and restaurants built right under the expressway between Ginza and Shinbashi, also offers good options.

Central to the city's nightlife since postwar occupation, Roppongi stays lively through the night. Popular places to start the evening include **Hobgoblin**, Tokyo's largest British pub, and longtime Irish pub **Paddy Foley's**. For more recreation, catch one of the retro-themed shows at **Kaguwa** *(see p181)*, a unique dinner theater (entrance

Logo of British pub, Hobgoblin

¥3,500). Dance the night away at **Salsa Sudade** or **El Café Latino**. Smoke a Havana cigar and sip premium aged tequila at **Agave** or rub shoulders with celebrities at **NewLex Edo**.

The scene is more relaxed in nearby Nishi-Azabu. **The Baron** offers tapas and weekend DJ events. **SuperDeluxe** is an eclectic bar-cum-event space with performance art and live music. The enduringly lively bar **Acaraje Tropicana** swings to a Brazilian rhythm.

Shibuya is the center of Tokyo youth culture and the Center-Gai pedestrian alley is its promenade and fast-food kitchen. Good watering holes in the area include **Tasu-Ichi**, a standing bar with very reasonable prices; and **The Aldgate**, an Anglophile pub with an extensive selection of ales on draught.

Chic, upscale Akasaka also has a good range of clubs and bars. Shinjuku's Kabukicho, with its maze of streets and future-world feel, boasts numerous restaurants and clubs. It is also the city's most notorious red-light district. It is safe to explore, but beware of pickpockets and venues that do not post their prices. A more restful neighborhood is Shinjuku Sanchome, close to Isetan Department Store. Recommended watering holes include the **Marugo** wine bar.

If sightseeing in Asakusa leaves you thirsty, cross the Sumida River to the **Flamme D'Or** bar in the premises of the Asahi Breweries headquarters. Close to Kaminarimon gate is the **Kamiya Bar**, the oldest bar in Tokyo. Near the sumo stadium, look for **Beer Station Ryogoku**, a German-style bierkeller.

DJ AND DANCE CLUBS

Tokyo's clubbing scene has exploded in the last decade, attracting top DJs from around the world. Roppongi, Shinjuku, and Shibuya offer a wealth of options. In terms of scale, the top spot is **AgeHa**, in Shin-Kiba, on the other side of Odaiba.

A row of clubs and bars, Shinjuku Sanchome

The leading online magazine **Cyberjapan** carries up-to-date listings. Dance clubs warm up around 11pm and keep going all night. Expect a cover charge of between ¥2,000 and ¥4,000.

GAY AND LESBIAN

The undisputed center of Tokyo's gay world is the concentration of bars, clubs, and saunas in the small area of Shinjuku called Ni-Chome ("2nd Block"). Many of the venues here cater exclusively to the local gay community, but there are still a good

number of bars that are open to non-Japanese speakers. The most popular places to meet are **GB** and **Advocates Café**, a tiny, lively venue where the action spills out onto the street. The second-floor **Kinsmen** bar is more sedate, attracting a mix of all persuasions. Its lesbian counterpart, the women-only **Kinswomyn**, is equally relaxed and welcoming. Ni-Chome is also the location for the mega-scale **24 Kaikan** bathhouse complex which also has branches in Asakusa, Ueno, and Shinjuku. A good source of online information is the **Utopia Asia** website.

Other substantial venues include favorite **Feria**; hip **Air**; cavernous **Womb**; long-time stalwart **Club Asia**; and **Club Harlem**. On a more manageable scale, **La Fabrique** and **Loop** are also worth checking out.

DIRECTORY

HIGH-RISE BARS

Bello Visto Bar
26-1, Sakuragaoka-cho, Shibuya-ku.
Tel (03) 3476-3000.

TwentyEight Bar
1-9-1 Higashi-Shinbashi, Minato-ku. **Map** 5 B4.
Tel (03) 6388-8000.

CLUBS AND BARS

300 Bar
5-9-11 Ginza, Chuo-ku. **Map** 5 B3.
Tel (03) 3572-6300.

Acaraje Tropicana
1-1-25 Nishi-Azabu, Minato-ku. **Map** 2 E5.
Tel (03) 3479-4690.

Agave
7-15-10 Roppongi, Minato-ku. **Map** 2 E5.
Tel (03) 3497-0229.

Beer Station Ryogoku
1-3-20 Yokoami, Sumida-ku. **Map** 4 E5.
Tel (03) 3623-5252.

El Café Latino
3-15-24 Roppongi, Minato-ku. **Map** 2 E5.
Tel (03) 3402-8989.

Flamme D'or
1-23-1 Azumabashi, Sumida-ku. **Map** 4 F3.
Tel (03) 5608-5381.

Hobgoblin
3-16-33 Roppongi, Minato-ku. **Map** 2 E5.
Tel (03) 3568-1280.

Kamiya Bar
1-1-1 Asakusa, Taito-ku. **Map** 4 F3.
Tel (03) 3841-5400.

Marugo
3-7-5, Shinjuku, Shinjuku-ku. **Map** 1 B1.
Tel (03) 3350-4605.

NewLex Edo
3-13-14 Roppongi, Minato-ku. **Map** 2 E5.
Tel (03) 5575-6600.

Paddy Foley's
5-5-1 Roppongi, Minato-ku. **Map** 2 E5.
Tel (03) 3423-2250.
www.paddyfoleystokyo.com

Salsa Sudade
Palette Bldg 3F, 7-13-8 Roppongi, Minato-ku.
Map 2 E5.
Tel (03) 5474-8806.

SuperDeluxe
B1, 3-1-25 Nishi-Azabu, Minato-ku. **Map** 2 E5.
Tel (03) 5412-0515.

Tasu-Ichi
33-14 Udagawa-cho, Shibuya-ku. **Map** 1 B5.
Tel (03) 3463-0077.

The Aldgate
30-4 Udagawa-cho, Shibuya-ku. **Map** 1 B5.
Tel (03) 3462-2983.

The Baron
1-8-21 Nishi-Azabu, Minato-ku. **Map** 2 D5.
Tel (03) 6406-4551.

DJ AND DANCE CLUBS

AgeHa
2-2-10 Shin-Kiba, Koto-ku.
Tel (03) 5534-1515.

Air
Hikawa Bldg, B1, 2-11 Sarugaku-cho, Shibuya-ku.
Tel (03) 5784-3386.

Club Asia
1-8 Maruyamacho, Shibuya-ku.
Tel (03) 5458-2551.

Club Harlem
Dr. Jeekahn's Bldg 2-3F, 2-4 Maruyamacho, Shibuya-ku.
Tel (03) 3461-8806.

Cyberjapan
www.cyberjapan.tv

Feria
7-13-7 Roppongi, Minato-ku. **Map** 2 E5.
Tel (03) 5785-0656.

La Fabrique
Zero Gate B1F, 16-9 Udagawa-cho, Shibuya-ku.
Map 1 A5.
Tel (03) 5428-5100.

Loop
2-1-13 Shibuya, Shibuya-ku. **Map** 1 B5.
Tel (03) 3797-9933.

Womb
2-16 Maruyama-cho, Shibuya-ku.
Map 1 A5.
Tel (03) 5459-0039.

GAY AND LESBIAN

24 Kaikan
2-13-1 Shinjuku, Shinjuku-ku.
Map 1 C1.
Tel (03) 3354-2424.

Advocates Café
2-18-1 Shinjuku, Shinjuku-ku.
Map 1 C1.
Tel (03) 3358-8638.

GB
2-12-16 Shinjuku, Shinjuku-ku.
Map 1 C2.
Tel (03) 3352-8972.

Kinsmen
2-18-5 Shinjuku, Shinjuku-ku.
Map 1 C1.
Tel (03) 3354-4949.

Kinswomyn
Dai-ichi Tenka Bldg 3F, 2-15-10 Shinjuku, Shinjuku-ku. **Map** 1 B1.
Tel (03) 3354-8720.

Utopia Asia
www.utopia-asia.com

SURVIVAL GUIDE

PRACTICAL INFORMATION

Tokyo is much easier for foreign visitors to negotiate than is generally believed. Being unable to speak or read Japanese is rarely a serious problem in the city, since many everyday signs at tourist attractions and in major suburbs are displayed in Roman script as well as in Japanese characters. English-speaking locals are generally quick to offer assistance, and the infrastructure for tourism

Logo of the Japan
National Tourism
Organization (JNTO)

(public transportation, accommodations, sightseeing) is highly developed. Where problems can arise for visitors is in the surprising clashes in Tokyo's unique East–West culture – for instance, the contrast between the ease with which even tourists can get around on the efficient rail network compared with the difficulty everyone, including the Japanese, has with locating an address in the city (see p175).

WHEN TO GO

The best times to visit Tokyo are spring (April–May) and fall (October–November). July and August tend to be hot and humid. The rainy season runs from early June to mid-July, while typhoon season, which may bring heavy rainfall and strong winds, peaks in August and September.

Tokyo hosts many festivals throughout the year (see pp28–31). Cherry-blossom season (usually late March to early April) draws large crowds to the parks. Peak vacation periods for the Japanese are New Year (December 29– January 3/4), Golden Week (April 29–May 5), the period around Obon (the Buddhist Festival of the Dead; mid-August), and Silver Week (mid-September, approximately every six years). At these times, flights and accommodations fill up fast. However, the only big shutdown of tourist attractions occurs at New Year.

WHAT TO BRING

Keep luggage to a minimum, with items that are easy to carry. Train stations often have many steps and no porters.

Modern buildings tend to be overheated in winter and overcooled in summer, so take a range of clothes that you can layer. Casual clothing is acceptable everywhere, even in smart restaurants. Footwear often has to be removed when entering tourist attractions, so wear shoes that can be easily slipped on and off.

Picnics in Tokyo's Ueno Park at cherry-blossom time

During rainy and typhoon seasons an umbrella is a must; cheap ones are available from convenience stores (konbini). Almost anything you need can be bought in Tokyo. Items may be expensive, but ¥100 stores, found in larger neighborhoods, sell a great range of goods, mostly costing just ¥100. Be aware that clothes and shoes may be available only in smaller sizes.

A colorful display of practical and souvenir fans for sale

VISAS AND PASSPORTS

Citizens of most Western countries may enter Tokyo for short visits (up to 90 days) as Temporary Visitors with only a valid passport; no visa is needed. US journalists are an exception and must always obtain a visa before traveling to Tokyo on business. Temporary Visitors are not allowed to undertake paid employment.

Citizens of some countries, including the UK, may extend their Temporary Visitor by up to a further 90 days at the **Tokyo Regional Immigration Bureau** at least 10 days before the original expiration date.

If you wish to undertake paid or voluntary work or long-term study in Tokyo, you must obtain a visa from a Japanese embassy before traveling. Foreigners who stay in Tokyo for more than 90 days must also apply for a Certificate of Alien Registration from the

Ward Office of the area in which they live within 90 days of arrival in Japan. This certificate, or your passport, must be carried at all times – not doing so can occasionally lead to arrest. Visa holders who want to leave the country and return within the duration of their visa need a re-entry permit from the Tokyo Regional Immigration Bureau. For up-to-date information, contact the nearest Japanese embassy or consulate ahead of travel.

On the plane, you will be given a landing card. Fill in the first part; the second part will be attached to your passport to be completed upon departure. All foreigners are required to be fingerprinted and photographed upon arrival in Japan. A refusal to cooperate may result in being denied entry into the country.

CUSTOMS INFORMATION

For non-residents, duty-free allowances are 400 cigarettes or 18 oz of tobacco or 100 cigars; three 0.76-liter bottles of alcohol; 2 oz (57 g) of perfume; and gifts and souvenirs of a total value up to ¥200,000 (excluding items less than ¥10,000). Prohibited articles include narcotic drugs or stimulants (including Vicks inhalers, some medicines for allergies and sinus problems, and painkillers containing codeine); counterfeit money; articles that infringe on patents or copyrights; pornography; and firearms and ammunition. Animals and plants are subject to quarantine inspection.

For guidelines on tax-free shopping in Tokyo, see page 142. Guns, swords, and some personal computers require an export license from the **Ministry of Economy, Trade, and Industry**. Art objects may be subject to restrictions.

TOURIST INFORMATION

Before traveling, request leaflets and brochures from the **Japan National Tourism Organization** (JNTO) in your own country. The JNTO does not make recommendations or reservations, nor does it

An "i" tourist information office, with multilingual staff

sell Japan Rail Pass Exchange Orders *(see p179)*, but it can suggest travel agents that do.

Tokyo's **Tourist Information Center** (TIC) offers literature and advice on tour itineraries in and outside the city; it does not make transport bookings. The TIC also has a counter for the Welcome Inn Reservation Center *(see pp106–7)*, where staff will arrange hotel reservations at locations beyond Tokyo for free.

Most towns outside Tokyo have a tourist information office, usually in or near the main train station. Nearly 100 of these are designated "i" tourist information offices, which have multilingual staff and carry pamphlets in English.

Details of attractions and events in Tokyo can be found in such free local publications as *Metropolis* (also online at http://metropolis.co.jp) and *Japanzine*. Free listings brochures are also available at the TIC, most bookstores, and hotels. Hotel staff will usually help reserve tickets

for local events and shows. Ticket-agency booths, located near train stations and inside department and convenience stores, also book seats in advance and sell tickets up to the last minute. CN Playguide, Ticket PIA *(see p153)*, and **Ticket Saison** are the main agencies.

ADMISSION PRICES

Admission to Tokyo temples and shrines is free, however, in historical towns and cities, such as Kamakura, a fee (¥200–500) is often charged. Some attractions may cost over ¥1,000.

For discounts on tourist facilities and services, invest in a **Welcome Card**. There are several types to choose from, offering different benefits and discounts at museums, sights, hotels, and restaurants, for example. Visit the website for further details *(see Directory on p163)*.

OPENING HOURS

Buddhist temples are typically open 8 or 9am–4pm (until 5pm in summer), but times may vary. Shinto shrines are often open 24 hours. Museums, art galleries, and many tourist attractions are usually open 10am–4 or 5pm daily except Monday (Tuesday if Monday is a public holiday). Most attractions close for the New Year holiday period.

Shopping hours are mostly 10am–8pm, though many supermarkets stay open until midnight. For banking hours, see page 168; for post offices, see page 171.

Kencho Temple in Kamakura, where an admission fee is charged

PUBLIC CONVENIENCES

Toilets in Japan range from basic to highly sophisticated. Japanese-style toilets are simple troughs over which one squats, facing the end with the hood. Many public places, including trains, have both traditional and western-style facilities. Toilet paper and hand towels may not be provided, so it is wise to carry some tissues with you.

Modern toilets may have a panel that, when pressed, plays a tune or produces a flushing sound to discreetly mask natural noises. They may also have heated seats, automatic seat covers, bidets, and hot-air-drying facilities. For protocol on toilet slippers, see page 165.

At many train stations, it is not possible to use the toilets unless you have first paid for your ticket and passed through the ticket barrier. For those in need, public toilet facilities can usually be found in major stores, fast-food outlets, and, in quieter neighborhoods' convenience stores.

TRAVELERS WITH SPECIAL NEEDS

Facilities for the disabled in Tokyo are of mixed quality: the visually impaired are well provided for, but people in wheelchairs may face problems with subway and train stations and pedestrian overpasses, which often have no escalators or elevators. However, barrier-free access and universal design are slowly becoming implemented, so the situation is improving. Most modern buildings have excellent toilet facilities. For detailed information on disabled facilities, contact **Accessible Tokyo**.

TRAVELERS WITH CHILDREN

Children are welcome in most places, including restaurants, and parents need have few worries about their offspring's safety. Discreet breastfeeding in public is accepted, and baby food, formula, and disposable diapers are easily obtainable. Top hotels usually

Japanese children playing on the sidewalk

offer babysitting services and nurseries, while at traditional inns, a maid may be willing to babysit.

Many theme parks and museums are great fun for kids, but some temples and galleries may have age restrictions. At most attractions, children get reduced rates, which are typically half the adult price. Children under 6 can ride for free on buses and trains; those aged 6 to 11, pay half-fare. It is unwise to travel on rush-hour trains with small children. Care should be taken with little ones in hot *onsen* pools.

If your children are curious about their forthcoming trip to Japan, **Kids Web Japan** is full of child-friendly information about the country.

STUDENT AND SENIOR TRAVELERS

Upon presentation of an International Student Identity Card or ISIC (www.isic.org), students can enjoy reductions of up to 50 percent at a number of locations in Tokyo, including major museums, a couple of hotels and ferries, and some eateries, such as the Hard Rock Café. At several other places that do

International Student Identity Card (ISIC), great for discounts

not formally recognize the ISIC, students may receive a discount with their regular student identity cards, or simply with a verbal claim to being a student.

The general safety of the country makes Japan a popular choice among senior travelers. People aged 60 and above often receive discounts on admission fees. However, not many facilities are adapted to support the needs of those with mobility issues *(see also Travelers with Special Needs)*.

GAY AND LESBIAN TRAVELERS

Same-sex couples traveling around Japan are unlikely to encounter many problems. Open displays of affection may be frowned upon by some Japanese, but attitudes are broader in Tokyo, which has an active gay scene and a small but lively gay quarter *(see p157)*. However, even this only really comes out at night. **Magnet Tours** is a gay-owned tour operator specializing in gay vacations. For more information on the local gay and lesbian scene, visit the **Utopia Asia** website.

TIME AND THE CALENDAR

Tokyo is 9 hours ahead of Greenwich Mean Time and 14 hours ahead of US Eastern Standard Time. There is no daylight-saving time: when countries that use daylight-saving time switch to summer time, the time difference is an hour less.

Years are numbered both by the Western system and the reign of the current emperor. The present era, Heisei (meaning "achieving peace"), began when Emperor Akihito came to the throne in 1989, which became Heisei 1; 2013 is Heisei 25. The Japanese system of years is generally used within the country, especially on official documents; the Western system is often used in international contexts.

ELECTRICITY

The electric current in Tokyo is 100 volts, AC, 50 cycles – a system similar to that in the US. The country has two different cycles: 50 cycles in eastern Japan (including Tokyo) and 60 cycles in western Japan. Plugs with two flat pins are standard, so US appliances can be used, but sometimes at reduced efficiency.

European appliances can be used only with transformers suitable for US voltage. If in doubt, consult the appliance instructions. Some international hotels have two outlets – 110 and 220 volts – although these accept only two-pin plugs. Adapters are available from electrical stores.

CONVERSIONS

Metric to US/UK Standard
1 millimeter = 0.04 inch
1 centimeter = 0.4 inch
1 meter = 3 feet 3 inches
1 kilometer = 0.6 mile
1 gram = 0.04 ounce
1 kilogram = 2.2 pounds
1 liter = 2.1 US/1.8 UK pints

RESPONSIBLE TOURISM

As might be expected from the country that produces the world's best-selling hybrid car, environmental consciousness is quite strong in Japan. For decades, the Japanese have been separating their garbage into burnable and non-burnable types. Containers for recycling Styrofoam food trays, PET bottles, and paper drink cartons in addition to other categories stand outside most supermarkets. This kind of eco-thinking does not, however, extend to the use of disposable wooden chopsticks *(waribashi)*, which are the most common implements in eateries serving Japanese food. Tourists can do their bit to avoid this waste of wood by taking their own reusable chopsticks to restaurants. Organic food has not really taken off in Japan as it has in the West. However, there are certainly some decent organic restaurants in Tokyo.

Separate recycling bins can be found outside most supermarkets

DIRECTORY

VISAS AND PASSPORTS

Tokyo Regional Immigration Bureau
www.moj.go.jp

UK Embassy
ukinjapan.fco.gov.uk/eng

US Embassy
http://japan.usembassy.gov

CUSTOMS INFORMATION

Ministry of Economy, Trade, and Industry
www.meti.go.jp

TOURIST INFORMATION

Japan National Tourism

Organization (JNTO)
10F Tokyo Kotsu Kaikan Bldg, 2-10-1 Yurakucho, Chiyoda-ku, Tokyo.
Tel (03) 3201-3331.
www.jnto.go.jp

Australia:
Tel (02) 9279-2177.
www.jnto.org.au

Canada:
Tel (416) 366-7140.
www.ilovejapan.ca

UK:
Tel (020) 7398-5670.
www.seejapan.co.uk

US:
Tel (212) 757-5640 (New York) or (213) 623-1952 (Los Angeles).
www.japantravelinfo.com

Ticket Saison
Tel (03) 3341-1824.

Tourist Information Center (TIC)
Marunouchi Trust Tower North 1F, 1-8-1 Marunouchi, Chiyoda-ku, Tokyo.
Tel (03) 5220-7055.
www.tictokyo.jp/en/

Welcome Card
www.jnto.go.jp/eng/arrange/essential/welcome.html

TRAVELERS WITH SPECIAL NEEDS

Accessible Tokyo
http://accessible.jp.org/tokyo/en

TRAVELERS WITH CHILDREN

Kids Web Japan
http://web-japan.org/kidsweb

GAY AND LESBIAN TRAVELERS

Magnet Tours
2F Sereno Nishishinbashi Bldg, 2-11-14 Nishishinbashi, Minato-ku, Tokyo.
Tel (03) 3500-4819.
www.magnettours.jp

Utopia Asia
www.utopia-asia.com/tipsjapn.htm

USEFUL WEBSITES

Eventful
http://eventful.com/tokyo/events

Japan Guide
www.japan-guide.com/

Seek Japan
www.seekjapan.jp/

Etiquette and Language

Etiquette is important in Tokyo – the social lubricant for a crowded community. In recent decades, attitudes have relaxed, yet even the most apparently rebellious Tokyoite will not break certain rules. What constitutes correct behavior often varies according to the situation and status of the individuals involved. Foreigners will be forgiven most gaffes, but good manners will earn them respect. The best approach is to be as sensitive as possible to situations, avoid loud or dogmatic behavior, and follow the lead of those around you.

TABOOS

Few allowances are made even for foreigners on certain points, mainly relating to Japanese standards of hygiene. It is considered unforgivable to get soap or shampoo in a bathtub; washing belongs to the shower area (see p109).

At one time, eating while walking and on local trains and buses was frowned upon. Such constraints have become more relaxed, though some older people would still never engage in such practices. Eating on longer train trips is fine.

Bodily emissions are considered very rude, though anything drawn inward is acceptable. Thus, sniffing is fine, but blowing your nose in public is reviled. Gauze face masks are worn in public to prevent the spread of colds.

THE HIERARCHY

Respect for seniors is fundamental to Japanese society. Seniors include not only parents, grandparents, company bosses, and teachers, but even those a year or two senior in school or employment. The term *sensei* (teacher) is used as a term of respect for those with high professional status, such as doctors. Many Japanese regard the emperor as being at the pinnacle of the social hierarchy and show him great respect, but stop short of veneration.

Social attitudes are reflected in the Japanese language, which has a special form of honorific speech. This is vitally important in many social situations to indicate the speaker's respect, humility, and politeness.

The Japanese wear gauze masks to prevent the spread of colds

BOWING

The formal greeting in Tokyo is a bow, its depth reflecting the relative status of the participants. However, visitors rarely need to bow – a hand-shake is fine. In department stores, restaurants, and hotels, bows are part of the service, and they can be ignored or met with a brief smile. If you wish to bow, hold your arms and back straight, and bend from the waist, pausing for a moment at the low point.

SMOKING

In a number of Tokyo's wards, smoking on the street (except in specially designated areas) is punishable by on-the-spot fines. There is often a small smoking zone outside major stations. Smoking is banned on buses and trains (except for some long-distance trains, such as the *shinkansen*, which has smoking cars), as well as all stations. Lighting up is usually permitted in restaurants and bars, but the number of non-smoking venues is on the rise.

ATTITUDES TO PHYSICAL CONTACT AND SEX

Members of the same sex are physically at ease with each other, and the atmosphere in single-sex public baths is relaxed. Between the sexes, however, public contact is more limited than in the West. Couples hold hands in public, but kissing is not so common; even a kiss on the cheek might cause embarrassment. In general, sex is seen as free from shame, but something to be indulged in discreetly. Homosexual activity is less openly accepted than in many Western nations (see p162). Sadly, the sleazier side of the sex trade includes schoolgirl prostitution, and pornography is widely sold in convenience stores. Nonetheless, everyday life is relatively sanitized, and it is important to remember that geisha and most bar hostesses are not prostitutes.

Bow between business colleagues close in status to each other

Traditional footwear neatly lined up on racks outside a temple

ETIQUETTE AT TEMPLES AND SHRINES

The atmosphere in Buddhist temples and Shinto shrines is casual, and there are no restrictions on clothing. Visitors should show respect and not be noisy, but there are few of the taboos found in some Buddhist nations. If you enter buildings in a shrine or temple, except those with stone floors, leave your shoes at the entrance or carry them with you. Plastic bags may be provided for this, especially if you can use a different exit. Some temples allow photography, some only without flash, and others not at all.

SHOES

It is a serious mistake to wear shoes indoors in all private and many public buildings. The principle is that the clean interior not be contaminated with dirt from the outside. Always remove your shoes if the area immediately beyond the entrance to a room or building is at a higher level than the entrance itself.

When you enter a Japanese house or traditional restaurant, take off your shoes and put on slippers before stepping onto the raised floor. Other people's shoes will usually be evident, or there will be

a rack in which shoes can be stored. If no slippers are provided, go in stockinged feet. In Western-style hotels, the main part of the room is not raised above the entrance, and so shoes can be worn by both guests and staff. Slippers should be removed to walk on *tatami* matting – go in stockinged feet.

Many restrooms, public and private, have special slippers inside the toilet area. Remove your own slippers outside before stepping into the toilet slippers, which are then left behind upon exiting the toilet area.

TAXES AND TIPPING

A consumption tax of 5 percent (planned to double over the next few years) is paid by consumers for goods and services. Shops and service providers include the tax in the prices shown.

Other than for exceptional service, there is no tipping in Japan; indeed, an attempt at tipping might even cause offense.

LANGUAGE

Tokyo is well signposted in English, and it is not hard for visitors to find their way around. Many, especially younger, Japanese do speak at least a little English. It is not uncommon for English-speaking Japanese to offer help to what they perceive as the foreign visitor in distress. However, do not expect too much English to be understood by taxi drivers, policemen, or station clerks.

JAPANESE NAMES

Japanese names are given as family name followed by first name. However, many Japanese automatically reverse this order when giving names to Westerners, so you may need to check which is which. The Japanese

generally call each other by the family name, even if they are close friends, but they will happily call you by your first name if you prefer.

When speaking to or about an adult, add "-san," which stands for Mr., Mrs., or Ms., to their name – for instance, Smith-san or John-san. For babies and young girls, add "-chan," for young boys "-kun." However, one should never refer to oneself as "-san."

GIFT-GIVING

Gift-giving is an important aspect of social etiquette in Japan. Any trip means bringing home souvenirs for friends and colleagues, usually something edible. Small gifts may be exchanged at a first business meeting, and if you visit someone's home, you should buy a luxury food item or take a small gift from your home country. Keep gifts small to avoid placing an obligation on the recipient. Gifts are often not opened in front of the giver. Note that it is regarded as unlucky to give four of anything.

Box of cookies elegantly gift-wrapped in paper, then cloth

LINING UP AND JAYWALKING

When waiting, such as for a train, people line up neatly. To get off a crowded train, gently push your way through. If you are stuck and cannot reach the door in time, call out *"orimass"* ("I'm getting off") as you attempt to push your way toward the exit.

Jaywalking is heavily discouraged. Pedestrians in Tokyo invariably wait for the crossing lights, even when there is no traffic coming.

Personal Security and Health

Medical facilities and general hygiene standards are high and crime rates in Tokyo are low, though pickpockets occasionally operate in crowds. *Koban* (manned police boxes) are found in every neighborhood, usually near the train station; their presence helps to keep crime down. Due to its vulnerable position at the juncture of several tectonic plates, Japan is particularly prone to earthquakes and volcanic eruptions, some of which cause extreme devastation. The country also lies in the path of typhoons, which can wreak enormous damage.

POLICE

Japanese police are generally helpful. Those at the *koban* are accustomed to dispensing directions, though their English may be limited. Keep your passport with you at all times as the police can legally demand visitors to produce their passport or Certificate of Alien Registration *(see p161)*. Failure to do so could result in arrest and 23 days' detention while the case is investigated. Under questioning, which can last many hours, detainees will not have access to a lawyer. Interviews are not recorded.

WHAT TO BE AWARE OF

Tokyo is widely regarded as a safe city, though episodes of pickpocketing and bag-snatching sometimes take place in crowded areas, on trains, and at airports. It is generally safe to walk around at night, but take extra care in the Roppongi district. There have been reports of drinks being spiked with drugs that leave the victim unconscious for hours, allowing fraudulent billings to be made to their credit card.

Due to the nuclear accident that occured in 2011, follow government advice by not going within a 49-mile (80-km) radius of the Fukushima Daiichi nuclear facility.

Sex crimes tend to go unreported or unprosecuted in Tokyo. Women should take sensible precautions regarding where they go and with whom. Be wary of men outside train stations who try to start a conversation – it may lead to an unwanted advance. These can usually be shaken off with a simple "no."

A uniformed Tokyo policeman

IN AN EMERGENCY

Emergency calls are free. The Tokyo **police** operates a help line for foreign visitors; your hotel, embassy, or consulate may also be able to help. The **Tokyo Metropolitan Health and Medical Information Center** offers information in English, Spanish, Chinese, Korean, and Thai. In case of language difficulties regarding medical matters, contact the **Emergency Medical Translation Services**.

Japan Helpline is a great resource for 24-hour assistance in English with all manner of problems. The **Tokyo English Life Line** offers an excellent free counseling service.

NATURAL DISASTERS

Each year, Japan experiences more than 1,000 earthquakes large enough to be felt; most are nothing to worry about. Tremors are more noticeable in tall buildings, which sway markedly but usually have mechanisms to absorb the motion. In a larger earthquake, especially in an old building, open the doors (to prevent them from buckling and jamming) and turn off any gas. Do not rush outside, where debris may be falling, but shelter under a reinforced doorway or a sturdy table. Don't sleep close to heavy furniture not securely fixed to the wall or under air-conditioning units. The Tokyo Government has issued a useful bilingual **Earthquake Survival Manual**, and the **Japan Meteorological Agency** provides early warnings.

The peak months for typhoons are August and September. Typhoons may cause flooding or landslides; the worst bring violent winds too. Active volcanoes are usually fenced off so that no one can get close, but toxic fumes occasionally seep from the crater or its vicinity; look out for warning notices.

In the event of a natural disaster, you can reassure your loved ones that you are safe by calling the **Disaster Emergency Message Dial**.

LOST AND STOLEN PROPERTY

The Japanese are very honest people, and found items are often handed in to the authorities, so it pays to

Schoolchildren practicing an earthquake drill

report the loss of any item at the nearest *koban* or with the transport authorities. For items lost on the JR network, call the number given in the Directory on page 179. Lost or stolen passports should be reported at the local police station, which will provide an official report. This can be presented at the embassy or consulate in order to obtain a replacement or emergency passport.

HOSPITALS AND PHARMACIES

Medical facilities in Japan are excellent, but you will be expected to pay the cost of any treatment you receive. If you are sick, go to a hospital; for minor problems, try consulting a pharmacist first.

If you need to find a hospital or another medical institution, contact the Tokyo Metropolitan Health and Medical Information Center, which has multilingual staff. The **AMDA (Asian Medical Doctors Association) International Medical Information Center** offers free medical consultations over the telephone in eight languages and a free telephone interpreter service.

The hospitals listed in the Directory below have English-speaking staff and deal with 24-hour emergencies.

Medicines are dispensed at pharmacies, though there may be problems in carrying out a prescription from abroad. Western brands are available, if expensive, at international pharmacies, such as Tokyo's **American Pharmacy**. Contact lenses can be obtained with relative ease, and Western-brand lens solutions are reasonably priced. The prevalence of mosquitoes in the warmer months calls for insect repellents and soothing lotions for mosquito bites, sold in pharmacies. Mu-hi is a popular brand. Chinese herbal medicine is widely available.

Illuminated pharmacy sign

MINOR HAZARDS

Despite the nuclear accident in Fukushima in 2011, there should be no danger to food and water in Tokyo and surrounding regions. Tap water is drinkable, and food poisoning is rare thanks to good hygiene standards. An upset stomach is likely to be due only to a change in diet.

Raw seafood in sushi and sashimi is not a risk. Though extremely toxic if inexpertly prepared, *fugu* (blowfish) is safe, since all the fish served in restaurants and on sale in supermarkets is prepared by licensed chefs, who undergo the most rigorous training. Eat raw meat only in good restaurants. Insecticides are widely used, so always wash or peel fruit before eating.

TRAVEL AND HEALTH INSURANCE

It is advisable to take out comprehensive travel insurance in advance of the trip. It is important to confirm that it covers medical costs, since these can be very high in Japan. Insurance should also cover such areas as loss of belongings, theft, cancellation of journey, and repatriation.

DIRECTORY

IN AN EMERGENCY

Emergency Medical Translation Services
Tel (03) 5285-8185.
Open 5–8pm Mon–Fri, 9am–8pm Sat, Sun, & public hols.

Fire/Ambulance
Tel 119
(English rarely spoken).

Japan Helpline
Tel 0570-000-911.

Police
Tel 110 (emergencies; English rarely spoken).
Tel (03) 3501-0110 (English help line).

Tokyo English Life Line
Tel (03) 5774-0992.
Open 9am–11pm.

Tokyo Metropolitan Health and Medical Information Center
Tel (03) 5285-8181.
Open 9am–8pm daily.

NATURAL DISASTERS

Earthquake Survival Manual
www.metro.tokyo.jp/
ENGLISH/POLICY/security.
htm

Disaster Emergency Message Dial
Tel 171 (voice message).
www.ntt-east.co.jp/
saigai_e/voice171

Japan Meteorological Agency
www.jma.go.jp/jma/en/
Activities/eew.html

HOSPITALS AND PHARMACIES

AMDA International Medical Information Center
Tel (03) 5285-8088.

American Pharmacy
B1 Marunouchi Bldg,
2-4-1 Marunouchi,
Chiyoda-ku, Tokyo.
Tel (03) 5220-7716.

Japanese Red Cross Medical Center
4-1-22 Hiroo,
Shibuya-ku, Tokyo.
Tel (03) 3400-1311.

St. Luke's International Hospital
9-1 Akashicho,
Chuo-ku, Tokyo.
Tel (03) 3541-5151.

Seibo International Catholic Hospital
2-5-1 Naka-Ochiai,
Shinjuku-ku, Tokyo.
Tel (03) 3951-1111.

Tokyo Medical and Surgical Clinic
32 Shiba-koen Building 2F,
3-4-30 Shiba-koen,
Minato-ku, Tokyo.
Tel (03) 3436-3028.

Banking and Currency

Logo of Mizuho Bank

For visitors used to easy and instant cash access 24 hours a day, Japan's banking system can prove frustrating. Credit cards are accepted at a growing number of shops (including convenience stores), restaurants, most hotels, and major railway stations, but Japan is still largely a cash society. Make sure you always have some cash at hand. Payments can be made using debit cards where the appropriate sign (such as VISA or MasterCard) is displayed; however, cash withdrawals using debit cards are possible only at a limited number of ATMs. Personal checks are unknown.

BANKS AND BUREAUX DE CHANGE

Buying yen, exchanging traveler's checks, and other regular banking transactions can be easily conducted via major Japanese banks, including **Bank of Tokyo-Mitsubishi UFJ**, **Sumitomo Mitsui**, and **Mizuho Bank**. Some foreign banks, such as **Citibank**, offer a similar range of services.

Most banks open 9am–3pm on weekdays and are closed on weekends and national holidays. The exchange rate is posted at about 10am for US dollars; later, for other currencies. Banks usually exchange currency between 10am and 3pm; some city banks, however, offer this service from as early as 9am.

It is possible to change cash and traveler's checks at banks, major hotels (which offer the same rates as banks), main post offices, *ryokan*, and some city department stores. Bureaux de change are often near major train stations.

At major international airports, currency exchange counters may keep longer hours than banks; at Tokyo International, for example, the counter is open from 6:30am to 11pm. Rates at airports are not very competitive, though.

Even leading city banks may be unfamiliar with foreign currency other than dollars, so be prepared for bank tellers to check with their superiors if they have not experienced such notes before. In city centers, staff may speak English, and forms are often supplied in English; if not, staff will show you where to write. Transactions are relatively simple but may be time-consuming. Always carry your passport with you.

It is illegal for public transportation, stores, and restaurants to accept payment in foreign currencies, so you will need some Japanese yen on arrival to cover any immediate needs. It is always wise to obtain cash before traveling anywhere outside of Japan's major cities.

Some banks and post offices also offer money transfer facilities.

ATMS

Automatic Teller Machines (ATMs) are easily available in large urban areas throughout Japan. However, many do not take foreign credit or cash cards – for example, Cirrus, Maestro, Link, and Delta cash cards are not widely accepted. Most Japanese post offices and all 7-Eleven stores (more than 17,000 in the Tokyo area) have ATMs that will accept VISA, MasterCard, American Express, Maestro, Plus, Cirrus, and JCB cards; they also provide an English menu for users. ATMs at 7-Eleven stores

ATM typically found in a post office

are open 24 hours. The operating hours of post office ATMs vary: those at major post offices are typically open 7am–11pm Monday to Friday, with shorter hours at weekends; those at minor post offices are usually open 9am–4pm during the week and closed at weekends. The ATMs at the main post offices – **Tokyo Central Post Office**, **Shibuya Post Office**, and Shinjuku *(see p171)* – are open around the clock (except 8pm–midnight on Sundays and public holidays). Some Citibank ATMs are open 24 hours, though Citibank branches are not so numerous in the Tokyo area. Visit the Citibank website for a list of locations.

CREDIT AND DEBIT CARDS

International credit cards, such as **American Express**, **VISA**, **MasterCard**, and **Diners Club**, are generally accepted by leading banks, hotels, and stores in larger cities in Japan. They can be used to buy train tickets at major JR stations, and they are also accepted by some taxis. Note that there may be a charge to use a credit card.

Obtaining cash with credit or debit cards is not always possible – even if a machine displays the sticker for your card, it may have a problem reading it *(see also ATMs)*.

Traveler's checks are usually accepted only in major city banks and large hotels.

Travelex, American Express, and VISA checks are the most widely recognized.

If your credit or debit card gets stolen or lost, contact your bank to cancel the card.

CURRENCY

The Japanese currency is the yen (¥). Coins come in denominations of ¥1, ¥5, ¥10, ¥50, ¥100, and ¥500. Bank notes are printed in denominations of ¥1,000, ¥2,000 (very rare), ¥5,000, and ¥10,000.

Japanese bank notes (but not coins) can be reconverted to foreign currency at the point of departure; the amount is limited only by the funds carried by the airport exchange center.

Bank Notes
Each of the bank note denominations carries a portrait of a historical figure, such as the novelist Ichiyo Higuchi on the ¥5,000 note.

¥10,000 note

¥5,000 note

¥2,000 note

¥1,000 note

¥500 coin

Coins
The denominations of Japan's coins are all marked in Arabic numerals, except for the ¥5. On the reverse side of most of the coins is a design of a flower or plant design; on the ¥10 it is a temple.

¥100 coin

¥50 coin

¥10 coin

¥5 coin

¥1 coin

Communications and Media

Tokyo basks in the image of being a high-tech megalopolis, and though there is some truth in this – the Japanese were accessing the Internet on their mobile phones long before anyone else – the city is far from being the wired, computer-geek capital one might suppose. Just about everyone has mobile phones, while Internet cafés and free Wi-Fi hotspots are still surprisingly rare. Public phones are easy to find, though not all are suitable for making international calls. English-language newspapers and magazines are readily available, and the postal system is fast and efficient.

A green public telephone, used for making only local calls

INTERNATIONAL AND LOCAL TELEPHONE CALLS

Some public phones accept international credit cards as well as phone cards. The call will be routed via **NTT Communications**, unless you purchase a phone card issued by one of the other major telecom companies offering international calls, such as **KDDI** (KDDI Super World Card) and **SoftBank Telecom** (Super Moshi Moshi Card). Each company has a toll-free number for information on charges and services. To make a call, dial the relevant company's access code, then the country code, area code (minus the initial zero), and the desired number.

All major hotels in Tokyo offer international direct dialing, but there may be a surcharge for calls from your room. NTT Communications and KDDI offer international collect calls; simply dial the relevant access code, then ask the operator to place a collect call. The cheapest times for making international calls are

11pm–8am daily, though the rates between 7 and 11pm are also off-peak.

The charge for a local call is ¥10 per minute. Use small coins or phone cards in a public phone; unused coins will be returned to you. In this guide, the area code is given in parentheses; omit it if calling from within the area.

MOBILE PHONES

Some foreign mobile phones may work in Japan if the operator is an inbound roaming partner of **SoftBank Mobile** or **NTT DoCoMo**. Check with your service provider before traveling.

As an alternative, visitors can rent a mobile phone from companies like **Rentafone Japan**. Payment is typically made by credit card. Prepaid phones (though not prepaid SIM cards) are also available from such mobile operators as KDDI and SoftBank. The operator's conditions may differ, but a passport as ID and a hotel address usually suffice.

PUBLIC TELEPHONES

Public phones are found in train stations, often outside convenience stores, and on some busy streets. Green public phones, which accept coins and phone cards, are for domestic calls only. For international calls, use the gray public phones, which have a button for English-language information and another for the emergency services. They also have digital jacks for data transmission. Old-style pink phones, occasionally found in restaurants, are for local calls and accept ¥10 coins only.

USEFUL DIALING CODES AND NUMBERS

- Domestic directory enquiries, **104**
- Domestic operator, **100**
- International directory enquiries, **0051**

Use these codes after the international access codes to dial the following countries:
Australia **61**, Brazil **55**, Canada **1**, China **86**, France **33**, Germany **49**, Hong Kong **852**, India **91**, Indonesia **62**, Ireland **353**, Israel **972**, Italy **39**, Republic of Korea **82**, Malaysia **60**, Netherlands **31**, New Zealand **64**, Peru **51**, Philippines **63**, Russia **7**, Singapore **65**, Spain **34**, Sweden **46**, Switzerland **41**, Taiwan **886**, Thailand **66**, United Kingdom **44**, and US **1**.

A phonecard dispenser and a gray public telephone that provides local and international dialing access

INTERNET AND EMAIL

Internet cafés are not as plentiful as might be expected, but access to the Internet is slowly on the rise. **Kinko's** provides Internet access at its branches throughout the city. Some computer stores, including **Apple**, also provide free Internet access.

For a list of Wi-Fi hotspots, check www.hotspot-locations.com and www.freespot.com/users/map-e/map_tokyo.html; however, bear in mind that many of the entries may be out of date. The lobbies of large hotels sometimes have free Wi-Fi access.

POSTAL SERVICES

Post offices *(yubin-kyoku)* and mailboxes can be identified by a character looking like the letter "T" with an extra horizontal bar across the top. Main post offices are usually open 9am–5pm on weekdays and 9am–12:30pm on Saturdays. Smaller post offices may open 9am–4:30pm on weekdays, but they are often closed on weekends. Stamps are also sold at convenience stores and larger hotels.

All post offices provide **EMS** express mail services. For urgent mail, the **Tokyo Central Post Office** and **Shinjuku Post Office** both provide all-night counters.

Several door-to-door delivery services *(takkyubin)*, including Yamato and Sagawa-Kyubin, offer prompt and efficient services throughout Japan. Small packages can be sent via these courier services from convenience stores and other shops. International courier services include **FedEx** and **DHL**.

NEWSPAPERS AND MAGAZINES

Three English language daily newspapers – *The Japan Times*, the *International Herald Tribune-Asahi Shimbun*, and *The Daily Yomiuri* – are sold at kiosks in train stations, major hotels, foreign-language bookstores, and in some convenience

Selection of local newspapers at a Tokyo newsstand

stores. These newspapers and *The Mainichi Daily News* are also available online. The best publication for business and technology is the *Nikkei Weekly*.

Imported magazines can be found at foreign-language bookstores. Free English-language magazines are also easily available. In particular, *Metropolis* and *Japanzine* have extensive listings and classified ads. *Metropolis* is also available online (http://metropolis.co.jp); another useful website is Japan Today (www.japantoday.com).

TELEVISION AND RADIO

The state public broadcaster, NHK, has two terrestrial and two satellite TV channels. Its 7pm and 9pm news bulletins (7pm on weekends) can be heard in English on bilingual TV stations, which are often available in hotels. Other networks include Nippon TV, TBS, Fuji TV, and TV Asahi. Check *Metropolis* for English-language programs. Overseas networks are widely available via cable or satellite.

NHK Radio airs news and classical music on both AM and FM. There are several commercial radio stations in Tokyo: J-Wave (www.j-wave.co.jp) and Inter FM (www.interfm.co.jp) offer some programs in English.

DIRECTORY

INTERNATIONAL AND LOCAL TELEPHONE CALLS

KDDI
Tel 001 (access code).
Tel 0057 (toll-free info).
www.kddi.com

NTT Communications
Tel 0033 (access code).
Tel 0120 54-0033 + 8#
(toll-free info).
http://506506.ntt.com/
english/service/p_card

SoftBank Telecom
Tel 0061 (domestic long-distance access code).
Tel 0041 (international call service access code).

Tel 0066-11 & 0088-41
(toll-free info).
http://tm.softbank.jp/
english

MOBILE PHONES

NTT DoCoMo
www.nttdocomo.com

Rentafone Japan
www.rentafonejapan.com

SoftBank Mobile
http://mb.softbank.jp/en

INTERNET AND EMAIL

Kinko's
http://english-fedex kinkos-cojp.presencehost.net

Apple
3-5-12 Ginza,
Chuo-ku, Tokyo.
Tel 104-0061.
www.apple.com/jp

POSTAL SERVICES

DHL
Tel 0120-39-2580, then 0.
www.dhl.co.jp/en.html

EMS
www.post.japanpost.jp/
int/ems/index_en.html

FedEx
Tel 0120-00-3200
(toll-free).
www.fedex.com/
jp_english

Shinjuku Post Office
1-8-8 Nishi-Shinjuku,
Shinjuku-ku, Tokyo.
Tel (03) 3340-1093.

Toyko Central Post Office
2-7-2 Marunouchi,
Chiyoda-ku, Tokyo.
Tel (03) 3284-9539
(domestic mail); (03) 3284-9540 (international mail).

TRAVEL INFORMATION

Tokyo is served by flights from across the world, most of them arriving at Narita Airport. Although Narita is a long way from the city center, this gives visitors their first introduction to the prompt and highly efficient public transportation system that makes traveling so easy in Japan. Tokyo can be used as the hub for travel to other parts of the country, either by air from Haneda Airport or by *shinkansen* bullet train

A Japan Airlines airplane taking off

(see p178). There are direct bus and train connections from Narita to Haneda. The Japan National Tourism Organization (JNTO) website *(see p163)* provides useful travel information for visitors, including lists of travel agents that can make reservations and sell travel tickets and Rail Pass vouchers *(see p179)*. In Tokyo, the JNTO has a tourist information center that provides travel information in English *(see p163)*.

ARRIVING BY AIR

All major international airlines fly to Tokyo. Most flights land at Narita Airport, formally known as Tokyo New International Airport. Tokyo's other airport, Haneda (also, confusingly, referred to as Tokyo International Airport) is served by a growing number of international flights and is also the major hub for domestic flights. The two airports are linked by an efficient network of train, bus, and helicopter services.

TICKETS AND FARES

Japan Airlines (JAL) and **All Nippon Airways (ANA)** are Japan's main airlines. They fly nonstop between London and Tokyo, along with **Virgin** and **British Airways**. The flying time is around 12 hours. **Qantas**, **Air New Zealand**, and JAL operate nonstop flights between Tokyo and Australia

(flying time: about 10 hours) and New Zealand (12 hours). JAL and **United** are the main carriers between Tokyo and North America, but Northwest, American, Delta, and ANA also link Tokyo with several US cities.

Prices are highest over the major holiday periods of New Year and Golden Week, and in the summer (July and August).

ON ARRIVAL

Immigration forms are handed out on the plane in advance of landing. Immigration procedures tend to go more smoothly for the Japanese. All foreigners entering the country are photographed and fingerprinted on arrival. With both immigration and customs, a neat appearance and politeness help. For more details regarding customs, see p161. Both Narita and Haneda airports are well signposted in English.

GETTING TO AND FROM NARITA AIRPORT

Narita Airport, 35 miles (60 km) northeast of the center of Tokyo, has two terminals linked by a free shuttle bus. There is a **Tourist Information Center** in the arrival lobby of each terminal.

Holders of a Japan Rail Pass Exchange Order *(see p179)* should have it validated at the Japan Railways (JR) counter; they can then use it to travel into Tokyo by JR train. Airport **Limousine Buses** are frequent and have drop-offs at most major hotels within Tokyo, Yokohama, and other nearby cities. Traveling to Tokyo by taxi will cost at least ¥22,000.

The most convenient fast link to Tokyo is the **Narita Express (N'EX)** train, which departs from beneath the terminal buildings and travels nonstop to Tokyo Station in 53 minutes, and then on to Shinjuku, Shinagawa, Shibuya, and Ikebukuro in the capital, or to Yokohama and Ofuna. You can use the Japan Rail Pass on the N'EX, but you must reserve a seat (free of charge) at the ticket booth before traveling. All signs and announcements are in Japanese and English.

Travelers without a Japan Rail Pass can take the **Keisei Skyliner** from the station under the terminal buildings. This train takes 36 minutes to get to Nippori Station and 41 minutes to Ueno Station.

Local Keisei trains offer the cheapest but slowest link between Narita and Tokyo.

Check-in area of Tokyo New International Airport, at Narita

Entrance to Terminal 2, Haneda Airport

GETTING TO AND FROM HANEDA AIRPORT

Lying just to the south of central Tokyo, Haneda Airport has three terminals, only one of which handles international flights. The terminals are linked by a free shuttle bus and an underground walkway.

Limousine Buses run to several destinations in central Tokyo, including major hotels. The Keikyu private train line (see p179) departs from underneath the airport and connects with the JR network at Shinagawa Station (about 11 minutes). The Tokyo Monorail (see p175) links Haneda with Hamamatsucho Station, on the JR Yamanote Line (about 20 minutes). It is pretty cramped at rush hour, but it gives a fascinating view over parts of Tokyo Bay. A taxi into Tokyo will cost at least ¥5,000.

DOMESTIC FLIGHTS

An extensive flight network run by JAL and ANA covers Japan's four main islands and many of the smaller ones, too. For trips up to around 350 miles (600 km), *shinkansen* bullet trains (see p178) may be faster and more convenient than planes; in addition, there is often little difference in price. Domestic flights have both economy seats and, at an extra cost, a "Super Seat" service, which combines first and business class. The domestic low-cost airline **Skymark** connects Haneda and Narita to various cities in Hokkaido and Kyushu, and to Naha in Okinawa.

LUGGAGE DELIVERY

It is possible to have your luggage delivered from the airports to any address in the city and beyond. You can also have your luggage picked up for delivery to the airport, though this has to be ordered two days in advance. Companies offering this service operate counters at Narita and Haneda airports. Among the service providers are **JAL ABC** and **ANA Sky Porter**. The cost is about ¥2,000 for one large bag.

ON DEPARTURE

It can take up to 90 minutes to reach Narita Airport from central Tokyo, so set out about 4 hours before your departure time. If traveling by the Narita Express, reserve seats well in advance, especially during Golden Week and the New Year holiday. All trains stop at Terminal 2 first, and terminate at Terminal 1. The departure lobbies of both terminals are on the 4th floor. Many flights from Terminal 2 are boarded at the satellite terminal, reached via a shuttle train. Other flights require shuttle bus connections in order to board the plane.

Luxurious N'EX, traveling from Narita Airport to central Tokyo

DIRECTORY

TICKETS AND FARES

Air New Zealand
www.airnewzealand.com

All Nippon Airways (ANA)
Tel 0120-029-222
(toll-free).
www.ana.co.jp

British Airways
www.britishairways.com

Japan Airlines (JAL)
Tel 0120-25-5931
(toll-free; international reservations); or

0120-25-5971 (toll-free; domestic reservations).
www.jal.co.jp/en/

UK:
Tel (0845) 7-747-700.
www.uk.jal.com/ukl/en/

USA and Canada:
Tel 1-800 525 3663.
www.ar.jal.com/arl/en/

Qantas
www.qantas.com.au

United
www.united.com

Virgin
www.virgin-atlantic.com

NARITA AIRPORT

Keisei Skyliner
www.keisei.co.jp

Limousine Buses
www.limousinebus.co.jp/en

Narita Airport
www.narita-airport.jp/en/index.html

Narita Express (N'EX)
www.jreast.co.jp/e/nex

Tourist Information Center
Terminal 1.
Tel (0476) 30-3383.

Terminal 2.
Tel (0476) 34-6251.

DOMESTIC FLIGHTS

Skymark
Tel 050-3116-7370.
www.skymark.jp/en

LUGGAGE DELIVERY

ANA Sky Porter
www.ana.co.jp/eng/amc/reference/tameru/other/delivery/skyporter.html

JAL ABC
www.jalabc.com/english/index.html

Getting Around Tokyo

Equipped to handle a daytime population swelling to well over 10 million every weekday, Tokyo's public transportation system is remarkably diverse. Besides using the very efficient subway system, visitors can explore the city by bus, overground train (notably the Japan Railways Yamanote and Chuo lines, and the private railway lines), tram, monorail, boat, taxi, bicycle, or even rickshaw. Buses are good for areas not reached by subway or train, though the lack of English signage can pose a difficulty. Taxis are numerous and can be easily hired for short trips within the city. Maps are available at the Tourist Information Center *(see p163)*.

"Himiko" water bus speeding along the skyscraper-lined Sumida River

GREEN TRAVEL

Travel in Tokyo is pretty green. The superb public transportation network means that this is the one metropolis in the world where you would feel least inclined to drive your own car. Very efficient mass transportation – albeit sometimes very packed – is the rule in this city, and this results in a very small carbon footprint per passenger mile.

As indicated by the huge numbers of bikes parked on city streets, the bicycle is an extremely popular way of getting around parts of Tokyo, even though there are no cycle paths to speak of. In fact, for distances of up to around 6 miles (10 km), the bicycle is the fastest way of getting around. Eco-friendly velotaxis can be seen in the more touristy parts of Tokyo. In such areas, rickshaws are also frequently an option for those who prefer a more leisurely and traditional form of transportation. An increasing number of regular taxis now use hybrid cars.

BUSES

Bus companies such as **Keio**, **Toei Bus**, and **Tokyu Bus** connect many parts of Tokyo. Buses are much slower than trains and, with no information in English, difficult to use for people who do not read Japanese. Buses in central Tokyo have a flat-fare system. As you enter, place your fare in the box beside the driver. Suica and Pasmo cards *(see p177)* can be used on most forms of public transportation. If you travel often by bus, you can buy a prepaid card from the driver or from bus sales offices around Tokyo.

MONORAIL

The **Tokyo Monorail** starts at Haneda Airport, skirts along Tokyo Bay, and terminates at Hamamatsucho Station (on the JR Yamanote Line). The journey takes 20 minutes.

Though technically not a monorail, the driverless **Yurikamome Line** offers fabulous views as it crosses the Rainbow Bridge over Tokyo Bay. You can buy a one-day Open Pass (¥800) for unlimited travel on this line; a combined ticket with the Water Bus costs ¥900.

WATER BUS

The most popular water bus *(suijo basu)* route is the **Tokyo Cruise Ship Company**, operated Sumida River Water Bus, between Asakusa and the Hama Detached Palace Garden. Other routes ply to various points along the waterfront. All services depart from Hinode Pier, close to Hinode Station (Yurikamome Line) and a 10-minute walk from Hamamatsucho JR Station (Yamanote Line). Boats run approximately every half-hour.

TRAMS

Tokyo's two tramlines are somewhat removed from most tourist haunts. The **Arakawa Line** *(see p73)* trundles through the backstreets of northern Tokyo. The stations at either end have subway connections, and the tram can also be boarded at Otsuka, where it crosses the JR Yamanote Line.

In the west of the city, the **Setagaya Line** links Sangenjaya (Denentoshi Line) and Shimotakaido (Keio Line).

Visitors on a city tour of Tokyo in an open-topped sightseeing bus

CAR RENTAL

Renting a car in Tokyo is not recommended; few roads are signposted in English, and although rental cars usually feature sat nav systems, the on-screen text is in Japanese.

If you wish to explore Japan by car, head out of Tokyo by train and rent a vehicle in a smaller town. The **Japan Automobile Federation (JAF)** offers details about car rental companies such as **Nippon Rent-a-Car**, **Toyota Rent-a-Car**, and **Nissan Rent-a-Car**.

TAXIS

Taxis can be hailed on major thoroughfares and found at large hotels and at railway stations. A red light in the front window indicates availability. Few taxi drivers speak English, so have your destination written in Japanese. **Nihon Kotsu** offers a 24-hour taxi ordering service with English-speaking operators.

Taxi fares start at ¥600–700 for the first mile (2 km), and then cost around ¥100 for each additional 1,640 ft (500 m). Fares increase by about 30 percent between 11pm and 5am. Tipping is not required.

RICKSHAWS

The rickshaw (*jinriki-sha*) is a popular, if expensive, vehicle for sightseeing. Look for the rickshaw men, in their *happi* coats and shorts, in front of the Kaminarimon Gate in Asakusa. They will pull two slender Japanese people at a time, but they may ask bigger-built foreigners to ride solo.

CYCLING

Cycling is a popular way of covering short distances around Tokyo. Most streets have no sidewalks, so cars, bikes, and pedestrians essentially share the same space. It is perfectly permissible to cycle on sidewalks if they are available. **Tokyo Rent a Bike** (¥1,000/day) caters to visitors, offering information and maps in

A ride on an old-fashioned rickshaw

English; it also organizes bike tours. The **Muji** store in Yurakucho, close to the Imperial Palace, also rents bicycles (¥525/day; ¥1,050 holidays and weekends).

WALKING

Walking is an excellent way of exploring parts of Tokyo. The **City of Tokyo Walking Tours** (in various languages) are free and depart from Shinjuku. The city also arranges tours that focus on such themes as sumo, traditional gardens, the tea ceremony, and architecture. Each tour lasts about three hours and costs ¥650–3,540.

FINDING AN ADDRESS

Only the main thoroughfares in Tokyo have street names. In an address – for example, 2-3-4 Otemachi – the first number refers to the *chome*, or main block. The second number indicates a smaller block of buildings within the *chome*. The last is the number of a yet smaller block of buildings. There is no logical order to this system. Officers at police boxes are used to helping people find their destinations.

DIRECTORY

BUSES

Keio
www.keio-bus.com/bus/
index.html (*Japanese*)

Toei Bus
www.kotsu.metro.tokyo.
jp/eng/index.html

Tokyu Bus
www.tokyubus.co.jp/top/
index.shtml (*Japanese*)

MONORAIL

Tokyo Monorail
www.tokyo-monorail.
co.jp/english

Yurikamome Line
www.yurikamome.co.jp/en/

WATER BUS

Tokyo Cruise Ship Company
www.suijobus.co.jp

TRAMS

Arakawa Line
www.kotsu.metro.tokyo.
jp/eng/services/streetcar.
html

Setagaya Line
www.setagaya-line.com
(*Japanese*)

CAR RENTAL

Japan Automobile Federation (JAF)
www.jaf.or.jp/e/index.htm

Nippon Rent-a-Car
Tel 0800-500-0919
(*toll-free*)
or (03) 3485-7196.
www.nipponrentacar.
co.jp/service/general.htm

Nissan Rent-a-Car
Tel 0120-00-4123
(*toll-free*).

http://nissan-rentacar.
com (*Japanese*)

Toyota Rent-a-Car
Tel 0070-8000-10000
(*toll-free*)
or (03) 5954-8008.
http://rent.toyota.co.jp/en/
index.html

TAXIS

Nihon Kotsu
Tel (03) 5755-2336.

CYCLING

Muji
Yurakucho Building
3-8-3 Marunouchi,
Chiyoda-ku, Tokyo.
Tel (03) 5208-8241.
www.mujiyurakucho.
com/info/index.asp
(*Japanese*)

Tokyo Rent a Bike
3-5-11 Nakameguro,
Meguro-ku, Tokyo.
Tel 080-3209-9996.
www.tokyorentabike.com

WALKING

City of Tokyo Walking Tours
www.tourism.metro.
tokyo.jp/english/tourists/
guideservice/guideservice/
index.html

Using Trains in Tokyo

The fastest way of getting around Tokyo is by train. The various systems that make up Tokyo's train network – Toei Subway and Tokyo Metro lines, overground Japan Railways (JR) lines, and a number of private lines – are clean, efficient, and punctual. Some of Tokyo's huge stations can be daunting, but the system is safe and fairly straightforward to negotiate, with color-coded train lines and maps, directional arrows, and bilingual signs. Trains run 5am–midnight daily; on some lines, trains run approximately every 5 minutes at peak times. Avoid rush hour (8–9am and 6–8pm) if possible, especially if you are carrying luggage or traveling with small children.

Well-designed and comfortable interior of a metro car

Uniformed subway staff assisting train commuters

RAILWAY NETWORK

The Japan Railways' (JR) Yamanote Line forms a loop encircling most of central Tokyo. Many of its stations act as hubs, linking with long-distance JR lines, suburban private rail lines, and subway stations. Four other JR lines run through the city. The Sobu Line (yellow) cuts east–west across the center of the loop, from Shinjuku to Akihabara and then farther eastward. Next to it is the express Chuo Line (orange), linking Tokyo JR Station with Shinjuku and the western suburbs. The Keihin Tohoku Line (turquoise) runs north–south along the eastern side of the Yamanote Loop. The Saikyo Line (green) runs parallel with the Yamanote Line between Osaki and Ikebukuro before extending north beyond Tokyo to Saitama Prefecture. These JR lines offer fascinating above-ground glimpses of the metropolis and its suburbs.

For more on JR trains beyond Tokyo, see pages 178–9.

The private railway lines generally run from hubs along the Yamanote Line to other points in Tokyo and beyond. The most useful private railway lines for visitors are the Keihin Electric Express Railway (from Shinagawa to Haneda Airport) and the Odakyu Electric Railway (from Shinjuku to Odawara and Hakone). There are also the Rinkai Line and Yurikamome, both of which can be used to reach Odaiba. For more on private railway lines, see page 178.

SUBWAY NETWORK

Tokyo's subway network consists of the **Tokyo Metro** (nine lines) and **Toei Subway** (four lines) systems. Tokyo Metro and Toei Subway have different symbols (a white "M" on a blue background and a green fan-shaped symbol respectively), but they share the same subway

sign (a blue train on its track), which is usually prominent at the street-level entrance to the subway. Besides being color-coded, each subway line is designated a letter (G for the Ginza Line, for example), and each station is assigned a number. Hence, Shibuya, the western terminal of the Ginza Line, is G-01 *(see also Back Endpaper)*. Metro maps in English are available at all major train and metro stations, tourist hotels, and the TIC *(see p173)*.

ROUTES AND FARES

For an online route planner, visit the **Jorudan** website.

On both JR and subway lines, directions to various platforms are indicated with appropriate color codes; sometimes the distance is given in meters. Prominent signs in Japanese and English give the name of the station, as well as the next and previous stations on the line. Inside many trains, there are

Metro platform with prominent signs displaying station names

bilingual (or quadrilingual) indicators above the doors showing the name of the next station. On some trains, route maps and the current position are displayed on screens above the exit doors. Announcements may also be made in English before arrival at the next station.

Tickets are dispensed from automatic vending machines, usually located close to the entrance gates at each station. Most accept both bank notes and coins; they also dispense change. Electronic touch-screen vending machines have instructions in English.

To access the platform, feed the ticket into the slot in the automatic ticket gate. Retrieve your ticket and retain it until your final destination, as you will need it when you exit.

Fares are charged according to distance traveled, starting at ¥160 (¥170 on Toei lines), with children aged 6 to 11 charged half-fares; children

under 6 ride for free. Some stations have route maps showing the fares and place names in Roman script. If you are unsure or cannot work out the exact fare to your destination, buy the cheapest ticket available and pay the difference when you arrive. There are fare adjustment machines by the exit gates: you insert your ticket, the amount due is indicated, you pay the difference in fare, and a new ticket is dispensed.

For those who intend to do a lot of travel on the subway, the Toei One-Day Economy Pass *(Toei marguto kippu)* is a good option. It costs ¥700 and offers unlimited use of subways, city buses, and the Arakawa tram. The **Tokyo Tour Ticket** (¥1,580) allows unlimited use for one day on JR trains within the 23 wards of Tokyo, subway lines, city buses, and the Arakawa tram.

Subway turnstile at entry and exit points at a train station

SMART CARD SYSTEM

Suica and **Pasmo** are inter-operable smart cards that can be used for virtually all forms of public transportation in Tokyo and surrounding areas. They cost ¥2,000, including a ¥500 refundable deposit. Suica cards can be bought at JR stations, and Pasmo cards at Tokyo Metro and Toei Subway stations, where they can subsequently be charged in ¥1,000 increments.

The cards can also be used for making purchases at many stores around town, as well as at vending machines and station baggage lockers.

Hold your card over the sensor at the ticket barrier; an acoustic signal will tell you that the card has been registered and the minimum fare deducted; the balance (if any) is deducted on exit at your destination.

Strips of yellow tiles on the floor marking the routes to the ticket barriers

COMMUTER CULTURE
Commuters packed into trains are a common sight morning and evening at Tokyo's major train stations. High urban land prices force families to look farther out of the city for affordable housing. A commute of at least an hour each way is practically the standard. The majority of commuters are men, since they still tend to be the prime earners in most families. The commute effectively removes them from family life – they leave before the children get up, come back after they are in bed, and collapse on weekends with fatigue. The other major group on the trains is unmarried younger women (after marriage, women are often expected to stay home and raise the children). An entire industry has grown up around these commuters: dozens of magazines are produced for killing time, and stand-up restaurants offer cheap meals to those with a long ride ahead.

DIRECTORY

SUBWAY NETWORK
Toei Subway
www.kotsu.metro.tokyo.jp
Tokyo Metro
www.tokyometro.jp

ROUTES AND FARES
Jorudan
www.jorudan.co.jp/english
Tokyo Tour Ticket
www.jreast.co.jp

SMART CARD SYSTEM
Pasmo
www.pasmo.co.jp/en
Suica
www.jreast.co.jp/e/pass/suica.html

Traveling Beyond Tokyo

With roads often clogged with traffic, trains are the best way of exploring Tokyo and the surrounding area. Japan's rail system leads the world in terms of safety, efficiency, and comfort. The city and surrounding area are served by a bewildering complexity of lines. In addition to the Japan Railways (JR) trains, there are many private railway companies serving suburban areas. For many destinations, such as Nikko, travelers have a choice of lines. Fares on private lines tend to be cheaper than on JR trains. Even in the most rural areas, the names of stations are given in Roman script.

People buying tickets at Shinjuku JR Station

THE RAILWAY NETWORK

The main operator in the country is the Japan Railways Group (JR), which includes all the *shinkansen* super expresses (bullet trains) and a nation-wide network of almost 17,000 miles (27,350 km) of tracks. JR is divided into regional groups, and operations in Tokyo and the surrounding area are run by **JR East**. Many private railway lines link smaller communities in more remote regions.

THE SHINKANSEN: BULLET TRAIN

The first "bullet train," as the *shinkansen* was quickly nicknamed by the marveling media worldwide, drew out of Tokyo Station in 1964, the year of the Tokyo Olympics. Symbolic of Japan's economic recovery and future drive, it became, and remains, a source of national pride.

Shinkansen are no longer the world's fastest trains, but their efficiency, as proved by the punctuality of the long-distance journeys (within six seconds of the scheduled time was recorded in 2003), is legendary. There are five *shinkansen* lines serving Tokyo. The Tokaido Line runs south to Nagoya, Kyoto, and Osaka (continuing as the Sanyo Line to Hiroshima and Fukuoka). The Tohoku Line runs north via Sendai and Morioka to Aomori. The Joetsu Line serves Niigata. In addition, there are *shinkansen* lines to Nagano and Yamagata. All *shinkansen* services start from Tokyo Station. Many Tokaido Line trains can also be boarded at Shinagawa. Trains on the Tohoku, Joetsu, Nagano, and Yamagata *shinkansen* lines stop briefly at Ueno. Announcements in English and clear signs make the *shinkansen* an appealing form of transportation, often more convenient than flying, though there is little room for large suitcases.

It is advisable to reserve a seat, especially during a holiday period, as the non-reserved carriages can get very crowded.

PRIVATE RAILWAY LINES

Private train lines, which tend to be cheaper than JR, also operate express trains, some of which try to rival the *shinkansen* for luxury.

The **Odakyu Railway** (from Shinjuku) runs the luxury Romancecar service to the tourist area of Hakone; it also has trains to Enoshima, on the Shonan coast, close to Kamakura. **Tobu Railway** operates the fastest and most economical route to Nikko from Asakusa. Take the **Tokyu Railway** (from Shibuya) if you are going to Yokohama's port area or the city's Chinatown. Other private lines include **Seibu Railway** (destinations include the mountainous area of Chichibu), **Keisei Railway** (to Narita), and **Keikyu** (Yokohama and Yokosuka).

STATION SIGNS AND FACILITIES

Tokyo's Shinjuku Station (*see p63*) is the world's busiest, and several others – including Tokyo JR Station – are vast warrens built on several levels. Finding a particular line or exit during rush hour can be intimidating for newcomers with heavy baggage. If you can, find out which named or numbered exit is best for your destination before arriving at one of the major stations.

Shinkansen lines are clearly marked, and signs for other lines are color-coded. The yellow bobbled tracks on the floor are intended to help visually impaired people navigate, but the tracks do

Aerodynamic nose of the fabled *shinkansen*, or "bullet train"

Ticket barriers for the Tobu Railway at Tobu Asakusa Station

DIRECTORY

THE RAILWAY NETWORK/ PRIVATE RAILWAY LINES

JR East
Tel (03) 3423-0111 (English info).
www.jreast.co.jp/e

Keikyu
www.keikyu.co.jp

Keisei Railway
www.keisei.co.jp

Odakyu Railway
www.odakyu.jp/english/

Seibu Railway
www.seibu-group.co.jp/railways/
tourist/english/index.html

Tobu Railway
www.tobu.co.jp/foreign/tobu.html

Tokyu Railway
www.tokyu.co.jp/global/index.html

RAIL PASSES

Japan Rail Pass
www.japanrailpass.net

JR East Rail Pass
www.jreast.co.jp/e/eastpass/

not make it easy for those pulling suitcases with wheels. Escalators are readily available for commuters.

Note that many trains, especially the *shinkansen*, stop only briefly in order to maintain their timetables. Thus, travelers are encouraged to line up on some platforms. Floor markings on the platform indicate where the train doors will open; however, these are written in Japanese, so they can be difficult for most visitors to decipher.

On trains with reserved seats, such as the *shinkansen* and the N'EX, the car number is the first of the two numbers that appear on the ticket. This is followed by a letter, which indicates the actual seat. Again, this information is in Japanese.

Stations in major tourist areas have baggage lockers and information booths where staff may speak English.

ON-BOARD FACILITIES

On *shinkansen* and other long-distance routes, trolleys serving snacks, beverages, *bento* lunchboxes, and edible *omiyage* (local specialties) are wheeled up and down the length of the train. There is often a choice of Western- (sit-down) and Japanese style (squat) toilets. Washrooms and toilets may be electronically operated, requiring a hand to be passed in front of a panel for flushing, or use a lever.

THE JAPAN RAIL PASS

In a country with some of the world's highest train fares, the **Japan Rail Pass** is a wonderful deal. Specially devised for tourists, the pass is not for sale inside Japan and must be purchased from an agent abroad before your visit.

The pass gives unlimited travel on all JR lines and affiliated buses, including the N'EX *(see p172)* between Narita Airport and Tokyo, city-center JR trains (including the Yamanote Line), and

The Japan Rail Pass

shinkansen, except Nozomi and Mizuho trains. Also included is the ferry to the island of Miyajima, near Hiroshima. Subways and private railways are not included. You may have to reserve a seat on long-distance trains, but the reservation will be free.

You can choose a 7-day (¥28,300), 14-day (¥45,100), or 21-day (¥57,700) pass; there are also more expensive passes that allow travel in Green Cars (equivalent to first class). If you intend to do much traveling by train, the pass will save you money. If you want to explore Japan by train for more than 21 days, or prefer to break up your travels by staying in one place for more than a few days, consider buying more than one pass. JNTO offices *(see p163)* have a full list of rail-pass agents in your country. The agent will issue a Japan Rail Pass Exchange Order, usually at a price based on the day's rate of exchange with the yen.

This voucher is exchanged for the actual Japan Rail Pass at designated JR Travel Service Centers in Japan, including Narita Airport and major train stations. When you get your pass, you must specify the date on which you wish to start using it; the date has to be within three months of the issue of the exchange order. After the start date of the pass, the cost cannot be refunded, neither can the exchange order or pass be replaced if lost or stolen.

OTHER PASSES

There are also other, less expensive regional rail passes. The **JR East Rail Pass**, which can be bought both outside Japan and within the country, covers Honshu, northeast of Tokyo. A 5-day pass costs ¥20,000 (children ¥14,000) and a 10-day pass costs ¥44,800 (children ¥22,400). Tobu Railway issues two-day and four-day passes for Nikko. Odakyu offers various passes to Kamakura and the Hakone area. Seibu issues passes for the popular spots of Chichibu and Kawagoe.

TOKYO STREET FINDER

Tokyo is notoriously hard for visitors to find their way around, due to the scarcity of street names and the complex numbering system for buildings. The Tokyo sights covered in this guide, plus Tokyo hotels (*see pp110–17*), restaurants (*see pp132–41*), and many of the city's key landmarks are plotted on the maps on the following pages. Transportation points are also marked, and indicated by the symbols listed in the key below. When map references are given, the first number tells you which Street Finder map to turn to, and the letter and number that follow refer to the grid reference. The map below shows the area of Tokyo covered by the six Street Finder maps. The Street Finder index opposite lists street names, buildings, and stations. For a map of the Tokyo subway system, see the inside back cover.

KEY

■ Major sight		🚓 Police station	
■ Other sight		卍 Temple	
■ Other building		⛩ Shrine	
S Subway station		✝ Church	
🚋 Train station		⊠ Post office	
🚌 Long-distance bus station		━ JR Rail line	
🚢 River boat		━ Other rail line	
ℹ Tourist information		━ Expressway	
✚ Hospital		— Pedestrian street	

0 kilometers   2

0 miles   1

SCALE OF MAPS 1–6

0 meters   500

0 yards   500

Street Finder Index

1

A   **B**   **C**

SHOKUAN-DORI

Higashi-shinjuku

SHOKUAN-DORI

YOCHOMAC

SHINJUKU-KU

Seibu-shinjuku

OME-KAIDO

NISHI-SHINJUKU

Koma Theater

Club Complex Code

KABUKICHO

BUNKA CENTERDORI

TOMIHISACHO

1

Nishi-shinjuku

Shinjuku-nishiguchi

Shinjuku Ward Office

Hotel Sunlite Shinjuku

Tokyo Medical College Hospital

Golden Gai

Hanazono Shrine

Hilton Tokyo

Nomura Building

Yakitori Yokocho

Studio Alta

KITA-DORI

Island Tower

Yasuda Kasai Kaijo Building

SHINJUKU

Isetan

Bosphorus Hassan

Koseinenkin Kaikan

Dai-Ichi Seimei Building

Mitsui Building

Suehirotei

Marugo

Kinsmen Bar

Sumitomo Building

Shinjuku Center Building

Shinjuku-sanchome

Shinjuku Pit Inn

GB

Advocate Bar

24 Kaikan

YASUKUNI-D

Century Hyatt Hotel

Kuu

Shinjuku Station

Tsunahachi

SHINJUKU

SHINJUKU CENTRAL PARK

Tochomae

Keio Plaza Hotel

Wa Cafe Yusoshi

Shinjuku-gyoenmae

Tokyo Metropolitan Government Offices

PLAZA-DORI

KOSHU-KAIDO

SHINJUKU-DORI

YOTSU

NISHI-SHINJUKU

KDD Building

Hotel Sunroute Shinjuku

Takashimaya Dept Store

MINAMI-DORI

The Washington Hotel

SHINJUKU GYOEN GARDEN

2

Park Hyatt Tokyo

Hotel Century Southern Tower

Yuuan

Bunka Gakuen Costume Museum

Tokyo Railway Hospital

YOYOGI

Yoyogi

SENDAGAYA

Tokyo Opera City

Minami-shinjuku

Angkor Wat

Chuo Line

Sendagaya

Sword Museum

Odakyu Line

EXPRESSWAY NO. 4

Noh National Theater

Kokuritsu-kyogijo

Sangubashi

Meiji Shrine Treasure Museum

3

SHIBUYA-KU

Meiji Shrine

SENDAGAYA

National Stadium

YOYOGI

Yamanote Line

MEIJI-DORI

GAIEN-NISHI-DORI

YOYOGI PARK

Fonda de la Madrugada

Natural Harmony Angolo

Togo Shrine

JINGUMAE

Yoyogi-uehara

Harajuku

TAKESHITA-DORI

Museum of Contemporary Art

Muji

4

Yoyogi-koen

Ukiyo-e Ota Memorial Museum of Art

Meiji-jingumae

INOKASHIRA-DORI

LaForet

Gesshinkyo

Maisen

Reikyo

NHK Hall

Fuji-Torii

Kiddyland

OMOTESANDO-DORI

Omotesando Hills

The Orbient

TOMIGAYA

INOKASHIRA-DORI

Olympia Stadiums

Uniqlo

Oriental Bazaar

Heirokuzushi

AOYAMA-DORI

MINAM AOYAM

NHK Broadcasting Station

Shibuya AX

Hysteric Glamour

JINGUMAE

Hanae Mori Building

Crayon House

Comme des Garcons

Issey Miyake

JINNAN

Astro Mike

Omotesando

Prada Aoyama

Purple Clock Tower

Eggman

Crocodile Club

KITI-AOYAMA

Spiral Building

Undercover

UDAGAWACHO

Tobacco and Salt Museum

Tokyo Metropolitan Children's Hall

National Children's Castle

Yohji Yamamoto

Arimax Hotel

Shibuya Tobu Hotel

Shibuya Parco Part 1

Beacon

Blue Note Club

Creston Hotel

La Fabrique

Tower Records

The Pink Cow

KOTTO-DORI

5

Kanze Nobgakudo

Tokyu Hands

Marui Jam Dept Store

SHIBUYA

Loop Club

SHOTO

Mandarake

Tasu-ichi

CENTER GAI

Shibuya Tokyu Inn

Sushi Ouchi

Bunkamura

The Akigate

Karaoke-Kan

Seibu Dept Store

MIYAMASU-ZAKA

Theater Image Forum

SHIBUYA-KU

Shibuya City Hotel

Duo Music Exchange

Shibuya 109

KONNO-ZAKA

SAKAE-DORI

O-West Hall

DOGEN-ZAKA

Mark City

Excel Hotel

ROPPONGI-DORI

EXPRESSWAY NO. 3

HIGASHI

MARUYAMACHO

Club Womb

Capsule Land Shibuya

Shibuya

A Shinsen   **B**   **C**

General Index

Acknowledgments

Dorling Kindersley would like to thank the many people whose help and assistance contributed to the preparation of this book.

Main Contributors
Jon Burbank is a travel writer and photographer who lives in Chiba prefecture, to the east of Tokyo, with his family.

Emi Kazuko is a writer and broadcaster who moved to London from Japan in the 1980s. She is the author of several books about the cuisine of her home country.

Stephen Mansfield is a British photojournalist and author based in the Tokyo region. His work has appeared in over 60 magazines, newspapers, and journals worldwide, including *The Geographical, South China Morning Post, The Traveller, Japan Quarterly,* and *Insight Japan.* He is a regular book reviewer for *The Japan Times.* His pieces cover a variety of subjects such as travel, contemporary issues, and cultural and literary themes. His photographs have appeared in several books. He has authored eight books and is currently working on a book on the cultural history of Tokyo. He is also the author of *Japan: Islands of the Floating World, Birmanie: Le Temps Suspendu,* and *China: Yunnan Province.*

Robbie Swinnerton moved to Japan in 1980, impelled by his fascination for sake, seaweed, and soba noodles, plus all other aspects of the traditional Japanese diet and culture. For the past 26 years, he has been based in Kamakura, balancing his life by the ocean in the old Japanese capital with writing assignments around Japan and East Asia. While writing extensively on foods of all flavors – his restaurant review column Tokyo Food File has run in the *Japan Times* for over a decade – it is Japanese cuisine in all its intricate simplicity that remains his first and abiding love.

Fact Checker Yumi Shigematsu

Proofreader Gowri Mohanakrishnan

Design and Editorial
Publisher Douglas Amrine
Publishing Manager Jane Ewart
Managing Editor Kathryn Lane
Project Editor Mani Ramaswamy
Project Art Editor Kate Leonard
Senior Cartographic Editor Casper Morris

DTP Designer Natasha Lu
Picture Researcher Ellen Root
Production Controller Shane Higgins

Deisgn and Editorial Assistance
Marta Bescos, Imogen Corke, Stephen Forster, Emily Grigg-Saito, Katrina Grigg-Saito, Sumita Khatwani, Priya Kukadia, Hayley Maher, Nicola Malone, Sonal Modha, Ellen Root, Sands Publishing Solutions, Susana Smith

Additional Photography
Stephen Bere, Demetrio Carrasco, Katrina Grigg-Saito, Martin Hladik, Ian O'Leary, Clive Streeter, Linda Whitwam, Peter Wilson.

Additional Illustrations
Gary Cross, John Fox, Nick Gibbard, David Harris, Kevin Jones Associates, Claire Littlejohn, Mel Pickering, John Woodcock.

Special Assistance
Bunka Gakuen Costume Museum; Dolce & Gabbana Showroom, Omotesando; Drum Museum; Goto Art Museum; Isetan Department Store; Isetatsu; Japan Folk Craft Museum; Mikimoto, Ginza; Mitsukoshi, Mitsukoshimae; National Museum of Western Art; National Science Museum, Ueno; Noh National Theater; Shibuya 109; Sony Showroom, Ginza; Tosho-gu Museum of Art

Picture Credits
a-above; b-below/bottom; c-centre; f-far; l-left; r-right; t-top.

The Publishers are grateful to the following individuals, companies and picture libraries for permission to reproduce their photographs:

ALAMY: Ablestock 148c; allOver photography 95tl; AM Corporation 29cl; Jonah Calinawan 147bc; Chromepix.com 14bc; Corbis Collection 2–3; Alan King Etching 07 9c, 159c; Michele Falzone 46; FantasticJapan 163cr; Frederick Fearn 85b; Jeremy Sutton-Hibbert 125c, 126cl, 168c; Peter Horree 58, 168crb; Jon Arnold Images 15bl, 28c, 30ca, 41b, 148bl; Look Die Bildagentur der Fotografen GmbH 143bl; Iain Masterton 87tr, 151c, 161tl; Megapress 19bc; Pacific Press Service 125tl, 130tr; Peter Arnold, Inc. 16c; Photo Japan 16clb, 27crb, 126br; Rollie Rodriguez 4br, 10bc; Eitan Simanor 160; Jochen Tack 1c; Tribaleye Images/J Marshall 105c; Chris Willson 127br; EVE ASTRID ANDERSSON: 102clb; AXIOM PHOTOGRAPHIC AGENCY: Steve J

Berbow 107bl; Mitchell Coster 18–19c, 18br; Jim Holmes 18tl, 165tl; Paul Quayle 19cr, 19bl.

DAVE BARTRUFF: 17bc, 18tr, 19br; BRIDGEMAN ART LIBRARY: British Museum, London, Katsu-shika Hokusai (1760–1849) *Fuji in Clear Weather* from the series *36 Views of Mount Fuji* pub by Nishimura Eijudo in 1831, 25br; Fitzwilliam Museum, University of Cambridge, Katsushika Hokusai (1760–1849) *Block Cutting and Printing Surimono*, 1825 5cl, 55bc; Private Collection Ando or Utagawa Hiroshige (1797–1858) *Mountains and Coastline*, two views from the series *36 Views of Mount Fuji* pub by Kosheihei in 1853, 97crb; Victoria & Albert Museum, London, Utagawa Kuniyoshi (1798–1861) *Mitsukini Defying the Skeleton Spectre* c.1845, 55crb; BRITISH LIBRARY: Maps Collection Maps 63140 (2) *Map of Yedo Japan*, 1707, 25clb.

CHRISTIE'S IMAGES LTD: 21c, 23t, 25tc, 55tc, 55clb; CORBIS: 27tl; Jon Arnold 171lc; Asian Art & Archaeology, Inc. 16tr, 55cl; B.S.P.I. 28br, 36; Morton Beebe 128tr; Bettmann 26cb; Burstein Collection 22cr; Christie's Images 8–9; Dex Image 155c; EPA/Andy Rain 28tc,/Frank Robichon 30clb,/Akio Suga 30bc; Ric Ergenbright 96tr; Eye Ubiquitous/Frank Leather 98bl,/Paul Thompson 86cl; Jon Hicks 70; Historical Picture Archive 97br; Image Plan 87br; Robbie Jack 16crb; Richard T. Nowitz 82bc; Philadelphia Museum of Art 26tl; Photo & Co./Stephane Reix 19cb; Jose Fuste Raga 83tr, 104–5; Reuters/Kimimsa Mayama 154bl; Ken Straiton 142cr; Liba Taylor 164c; TWPhoto 152bl; Werner Forman 16bc, 16br, 17tr; Michael S. Yamashita 3c, 17c, 17clb, 17crb, 18cl, 19tc, 96bc, 109cb, 150cl.

ARON DANBURG: 93cr; DREAMSTIME.COM: Radzian 178cl. FAST RETAILING CO. LTD 2007: 147tl; STEPHEN FORSTER: 170tr; FOTOLIA: targezed 167c. GETTY IMAGES: AFP/Stringer 27c; Stone/Thierry Cazabon 18clb,/Paul Chesley 166br,/Chad Ehlers 84,/Charles Gupton 119br, 124cl, 164br; Kyoshi Ota 173cr; MARTIN HLADIK: 15tl; HOBGOBLIN JAPAN LTD: 156cb. IKJELD.COM:

Kjeld Duits 150tc; JAPAN AIRLINES: 172tc; JAPAN NATIONAL TOURIST ORGANISATION: Japan Convention Services, Inc 178br, 179tl.

MASTERFILE: Allen Birnbach 69tl; R. Ian Lloyd 32–3; Jeremy Woodhouse 158–9. NARITA INTERNATIONAL AIRPORT CORPORATION: 172bl; NATIONAL AERONAUTICS AND SPACE ADMINISTRATION: 12tr; NEW NATIONAL THEATRE, TOKYO: Chikashi Saegusa 151br.

PARK HYATT TOKYO: 156bl; PHOTOGRAPHERSDIRECT. COM: Mantis Metalworks/Jonathan Christopher Roberts 11tr; PHOTOLIBRARY: Jtb Photo Communications Inc. 155bl; PRIVATE COLLECTION: 33c.

REUTERS: Toshiyuki Aizawa 31bl; Issei Kato 29br, 174cr; Yuriko Nakao 31c; Susumu Toshiyuki 149tl.

HOTEL SEIYO GINZA, A ROSEWOOD HOTEL: 106cr; STA TRAVEL GROUP: 162bc; SUPERSTOCK: age fotostock 67cla.

TIC TOKYO: 161tc; TREASURES FROM THE TOKUGAWA ART MUSEUM: 24tl; TOKYO NATIONAL MUSEUM COLLECTION: 10tc, 20, 22tl, 22cb, 23c, 35cr, 50bl, 51tl, 51ca, 51cra, 50cl, 50bc, 51cb, 52tr, 52cl, 52cr, 52clb, 52clb, 53u, 53cla, 53crb, 53bc

WERNER FORMAN ARCHIVE: Victoria & Albert Museum, London. 55cr; WIKIPEDIA, THE FREE ENCYCLOPEDIA: 27br.

FRONT ENDPAPER: ALAMY IMAGES: Michele Falzone tr, Peter Horree bl, Photo Japan br; CORBIS: Jon Hicks tl; GETTY IMAGES: Stone/Chad Ehlers tc.

JACKET: Front – DORLING KINDERSLEY: Rough Guides/Martin Richardson. Back – ALAMY IMAGES: Prisma Bildagentur AG/Vidler Steve cl; Robert Harding Picture Library Ltd/Eitan Simanor bl; CORBIS: JAI/ Michele Falzone cla; DORLING KINDERSLEY: Martin Hladik tl.

SPECIAL EDITIONS OF DK TRAVEL GUIDES

DK Travel Guides can be purchased in bulk quantities at discounted prices for use in promotions or as premiums. We are also able to offer special editions and personalized jackets, corporate imprints, and excerpts from all of our books, tailored specifically to meet your own needs.

To find out more, please contact:
(in the United States) **SpecialSales@dk.com**
(in the UK) **travelspecialsales@uk.dk.com**
(in Canada) DK Special Sales at **general@tourmaline.ca**
(in Australia)
business.development@pearson.com.au

Phrase Book

The Japanese language is related to Okinawan and is similar to Altaic languages such as Mongolian and Turkish. Written Japanese uses a combination of three scripts – Chinese ideograms, known as *kanji*, and two syllable-based alphabet systems known as *hiragana* and *katakana*. These two latter are similar, *katakana* functioning as italics are used in English. Traditionally, Japanese is written in vertical columns from top right to bottom left, though the Western system is increasingly used. There are several romanization systems; the Hepburn system is used in this guide. To simplify romanization, macrons (long marks over vowels to indicate longer pronunciation) have not been used. Japanese pronunciation is fairly straightforward, and many words are "Japanized" versions of Western words. This Phrase Book gives the English word or phrase, followed by the Japanese script, then the romanization, adapted to aid pronunciation.

Guidelines For Pronunciation

When reading the romanization, give the same emphasis to all syllables. The practice in English of giving one syllable greater stress may render a Japanese word incomprehensible.

Pronounce vowels as in these English words:

a   as the "a" in "cat"
e   as in "red"
i   as in "big"
o   as in "solid"
u   as the "oo" in "wood"

When two vowels are used together, give each letter an individual sound:

ai   as in "pine"
ae   as if written "a-eh"
ei   as in "pay"

Consonants are mostly pronounced as in English. The letter *g* is always hard as in "gate," and *j* is always soft as in "joke." *R* is pronounced something between *r* and *l*. *F* is sometimes pronounced as *b*. "*Si*" always becomes "*shi*," but some people pronounce "*shi*" as "*hi*." *V* in Western words (e.g., "video") becomes *b*. If followed by a consonant, *n* may be pronounced as either *n* or *m*.

All consonants except *n* are always followed by a vowel unless they are doubled; however, sometimes an *i* or *u* is barely pronounced. In this Phrase Book, to aid pronunciation, apostrophes are used where an *i* or *u* is barely pronounced within a word, and double consonants where this occurs at the end of a word.

Dialects

Standard Japanese is used and understood throughout Japan by people of all backgrounds. But on a colloquial level, there are significant differences in both pronunciation and vocabulary, even between the Tokyo and Osaka-Kyoto areas, and rural accents are very strong.

Polite Words and Phrases

There are several different levels of politeness in the Japanese language, according to status, age, and situation. In everyday conversation, politeness levels are simply a question of the length of verb endings (longer is more polite), but in formal conversation entirely different words (*keigo*) are used. As a visitor, you may find that people try to speak to you in formal language, but there is no need to use it yourself; the level given in this Phrase Book is neutral yet polite.

In an Emergency

Help!	たすけて！	Tas'kete!
Stop!	とめて！	Tomete!
Call a doctor!	医者をよんで ください！	Isha o yonde kudasai!
Call an ambulance!	救急車を よんでください！	Kyukyusha o yonde kudasai!
Call the police!	警察を よんでください！	Keisatsu o yonde kudasai!
Fire!	火事！	Kaji!
Where is the hospital?	病院はどこに ありますか？	Byoin wa doko ni arimass-ka?
police box	交番	koban

Communication Essentials

Yes/no.	はい／いいえ	Hai/ie.
… not …	・・・ない／ちがい ます。	… nai/ chigaimass.
I don't know.	しりません。	Shirimasen.
Thank you.	ありがとう。	Arigato.
Thank you very much.	ありがとう ございます。	Arigato gozaimass.
Thank you very much indeed.	どうもありがとう ございます。	Domo arigato gozaimass.
Thanks (casual).	どうも。	Domo.
No, thank you.	結構です。 ありがとう。	Kekko dess, arigato.
Please (offering).	どうぞ。	Dozo.
Please (asking).	おねがいします。	Onegai shimass.
Please (give me or do for me).	・・・ください。	… kudasai.
I don't understand.	わかりません。	Wakarimasen.
Do you speak English?	英語を 話せますか？	Eigo o hanasemass-ka?
I can't speak Japanese.	日本語は 話せません。	Nihongo wa hanasemasen.
Please speak more slowly.	もう少し ゆっくり 話して ください。	Mo s'koshi yukkuri hanash'te kudasai.
Sorry/Excuse me!	すみません。	Sumimasen!
Could you help. me please? (not emergency)	ちょっと手伝って いただけません か？	Chotto tets'datte itadakemasen- ka?

Useful Phrases

My name is ….	わたしの 名前は・・・ です。	Watashi no namae wa … dess.
How do you do, pleased to meet you.	はじめまして、 どうぞ よろしく。	Hajime-mash'te, dozo yorosh'ku.
How are you?	お元気ですか？	Ogenki dess-ka?
Good morning.	おはよう ございます。	Ohayo gozaimass.
Hello/ Good afternoon.	こんにちは。	Konnichiwa.
Good evening.	こんばんは。	Konbanwa.

Good night.	おやすみなさい。	Oyasumi nasai.
Good-bye.	さよなら。	Sayonara.
Take care.	気をつけて。	Ki o ts'kete.
Keep well (casual).	お元気で。	Ogenki de.
The same to you.	そちらも。	Sochira mo.
What is (this)?	(これは)何ですか？	(Kore wa) nan dess-ka?
How do you use this?	これをどうやって使いますか？	Kore o doyatte ts'kaimass-ka?
Could I possibly have ...? (very polite)	…をいただけますか？	... o itadake-mass-ka?
Is there ... here?	ここに…がありますか？	Koko ni ... ga arimass-ka?
Where can I get ...?	…はどこにありますか？	... wa doko ni arimass-ka?
How much is it?	いくらですか？	Ikura dess-ka?
What time is ...?	…何時ですか？	... nan-ji dess-ka?
Cheers! (toast)	乾杯！	Kampai!
Where is the restroom/toilet?	お手洗い／おトイレはどこですか？	Otearai/otoire wa doko dess-ka?
Here's my business card.	名刺をどうぞ。	Meishi o dozo.

Useful Words

I	わたし	Watashi
woman	女性	josei
man	男性	dansei
wife	奥さん	ok'san
husband	主人	shujin
daughter	むすめ	musume
son	むすこ	mus'ko
child	こども	kodomo
children	こどもたち	kodomo-tachi
businessman/woman	ビジネスマン／ウーマン	bijinessuman/wuman
student	学生	gakusei
Mr./Mrs./Ms. ...	…さん	...-san
big/small	大きい／小さい	okii/chiisai
hot/cold	暑い／寒い	atsui/samui
cold (to touch)	冷たい	tsumetai
warm	温かい	atatakai
good/not good/bad	いい／よくない／悪い	ii/yokunai/warui
enough	じゅうぶん／結構	jubun/kekko
free (no charge)	ただ／無料	tada/muryo
here	ここ	koko
there	あそこ	asoko
this	これ	kore
that (nearby)	それ	sore
that (far away)	あれ	are
what?	何？	nani?
when?	いつ？	itsu?
why?	なぜ？／どうして？	naze?/dosh'te?
where?	どこ？	doko?
who?	誰？	dare?
which way?	どちら？	dochira?

Signs

Open	営業中	eigyo-chu
closed	休日	kyujitsu
entrance	入口	iriguchi
exit	出口	deguchi
danger	危険	kiken
emergency exit	非常口	hijo-guchi
information	案内	annai
restroom, toilet	お手洗い／手洗い／おトイレ／トイレ	otearai/tearai/otoire/toire
free (vacant)	空き	aki
men	男	otoko
women	女	onna

Money

Could you change this into yen please.	これを円に替えてください。	Kore o en ni kaete kudasai.
I'd like to cash these travelers' checks.	このトラベラーズチェックを現金にしたいです。	Kono toraberazu chekku o genkin ni shitai dess.
Do you take credit cards/travelers' checks?	クレジットカード／トラベラーズチェックで払えますか？	Kurejitto kado/toraberazu chekku de haraemass-ka?
bank	銀行	ginko
cash	現金	genkin
credit card	クレジットカード	kurejitto kado
currency exchange office	両替所	ryogaejo
dollars	ドル	doru
pounds	ポンド	pondo
yen	円	en

Keeping in Touch

Where is a telephone?	電話はどこにありますか？	Denwa wa doko ni arimass-ka?
May I use your phone?	電話を使ってもいいですか？	Denwa o ts'katte mo ii dess-ka?
Hello, this is	もしもし、…です。	Moshi-moshi, ...dess.
I'd like to make an international call.	国際電話、お願いします。	Kokusai denwa, onegai shimass.
airmail	航空便	kokubin
e-mail	イーメール	i-meru
fax	ファクス	fak'su
postcard	ハガキ	hagaki
post office	郵便局	yubin-kyoku
stamp	切手	kitte
telephone booth	公衆電話	koshu denwa
telephone card	テレフォンカード	terefon kado

Shopping

Where can I buy ...?	…はどこで買えますか？	... wa doko de kaemass-ka?
How much does this cost?	いくらですか？	Ikura dess-ka?
I'm just looking.	見ているだけです。	Mite iru dake dess.
Do you have ...?	…ありますか？	... arimass-ka?
May I try this on?	着てみてもいいですか？	Kite mite mo ii dess-ka?
Please show me that.	それを見せてください。	Sore o misete kudasai.
Does it come in other colors?	他の色もありますか？	Hoka no iro mo arimass-ka?
black	黒	kuro
blue	青	ao
green	緑	midori
red	赤	aka
white	白	shiro
yellow	黄色	kiiro
cheap/expensive	安い／高い	yasui/takai
audio equipment	オーディオ製品	odio seihin
bookstore	本屋	hon-ya
boutique	ブティック	butik
clothes	洋服	yofuku
department store	デパート	depato
electrical store	電気屋	denki-ya
fish market	魚屋	sakana-ya
folk crafts	民芸品	mingei-hin
ladies' wear	婦人服	fujin fuku
local specialty	名物	meibutsu
market	市場	ichiba
menswear	紳士服	shinshi fuku
newsstand	新聞屋	shimbun-ya

pharmacist	薬屋	kusuri-ya
picture postcard	絵葉書	e-hagaki
sale	セール	seru
souvenir shop	お土産屋	omiyage-ya
supermarket	スーパー	supa
travel agent	旅行会社	ryoko-gaisha

Sightseeing

Where is …?	…はどこ ですか？	… wa doko dess-ka?
How do I get to …?	…へは、どうやって いったらいいですか？	… e wa doyatte ittara ii dess-ka?
Is it far?	遠いですか？	Toi dess-ka?
art gallery	美術館	bijutsukan
reservations desk	予約 窓口	yoyaku madoguchi
bridge	橋	hashi/bashi
castle	城	shiro/jo
city	市	shi
city center	街の 中心	machi no chushin
gardens	庭園／庭	tei-en/niwa
hot spring	温泉	onsen
information office	案内所	annaijo
island	島	shima/jima
monastery	修道院	shudo-in
mountain	山	yama/san
museum	博物館	hakubutsukan
palace	宮殿	kyuden
park	公園	koen
port	港	minato/ko
prefecture	県	ken
river	川	kawa/gawa
ruins	遺跡	iseki
shopping area	ショッピング街	shoppingu gai
shrine	神社／神宮／宮	jinja/jingu/gu
street	通り	tori/dori
temple	お寺／寺	otera/tera/dera/ji
tour, travel	旅行	ryoko
town	町	machi/cho
village	村	mura
ward	区	ku
zoo	動物園	dobutsu-en
north	北	kita/hoku
south	南	minami/nan
east	東	higashi/to
west	西	nishi/sei
left/right	左／右	hidari/migi
straight ahead	真っ直ぐ	mass-sugu
between	間に	aida ni
near/far	近い／遠い	chikai/toi
up/down	上／下	ue/sh'ta
new	新しい／新	atarashii/shin
old/former	古い／元	furui/moto
upper/lower	上／下	kami/shimo
middle/inner	中	naka
in	に／中に	ni/naka ni
in front of	前	mae

Getting Around

bicycle	自転車	jitensha
bus	バス	basu
car	車	kuruma
ferry	フェリー	feri
baggage room	手荷物一時 預かり所	tenimotsu ichiji azukarijo
motorcycle	オートバイ	otobai
one-way ticket	片道切符	katamichi kippu
return ticket	往復切符	ofuku kippu
taxi	タクシー	takushi
ticket	切符	kippu
ticket office	切符売場	kippu uriba

Trains

What is the fare to …?	…までいくら ですか？	… made ikura dess-ka?
When does the train for… leave?	…行きの電車 は、何時に 出ますか？	… iki no densha wa nan-ji ni demass-ka?
How long does it take to get to …?	…まで時間は、 どのぐらい かかりますか？	… made jikan wa dono gurai kakarimass-ka?
A ticket to …, please.	…行きの切符 をください。	… yuki no kippu o kudasai.
Do I have to change?	乗り換えが 必要ですか？	Norikae ga hitsuyo dess-ka?
I'd like to reserve a seat, please.	席を予約 したいです。	Seki o yoyaku shitai dess.
Which platform for the train to …?	…行きの 電車は、 何番ホーム から出ますか？	… yuki no densha wa nanban homu kara demass-ka?
Which station is this?	この駅は、 どこですか？	Kono eki wa doko dess-ka?
Is this the right train for …?	…へは、この 電車でいい ですか？	… e wa kono densha de ii dess-ka?
bullet train	新幹線	shinkansen
express trains:		
"limited express" (fastest)	特急	tokkyu
"express" (second)	急行	kyuko
"rapid" (third)	快速	kaisoku
first-class	一等	itto
line	線	sen
local train	普通／各駅 電車	futsu/kaku-eki-densha
platform	ホーム	homu
train station	駅	eki
reserved seat	指定席	shitei-seki
second-class	二等	nito
subway	地下鉄	chikatetsu
train	電車	densha
unreserved seat	自由席	jiyu-seki

Accommodations

Do you have any vacancies?	部屋があります か？	Heya ga arimass-ka?
I have a reservation.	予約をして あります。	Yoyaku o sh'te arimass.
I'd like a room with a bathroom.	お風呂つきの 部屋、お願い します。	Ofuro-ts'ki no heya, onegai shimass.
What is the charge per night?	一泊いくら ですか？	Ippaku ikura dess-ka?
Is tax included in the price?	税込みですか？	Zeikomi dess-ka?
Can I leave my luggage here for a little while?	荷物を ちょっとここに 預けてもいい ですか？	Nimotsu o chotto koko ni azukete mo ii dess-ka?
air-conditioning	冷房／エアコン	reibo/eakon
bath	お風呂	ofuro
check-out	チェックアウト	chekku-auto
hair drier	ドライヤー	doraiya
hot (boiled) water	お湯	oyu
Japanese-style inn	旅館	ryokan
Japanese-style room	和室	wa-shitsu
key	鍵	kagi
front desk	フロント	furonto
single/twin room	シングル／ツイン	shinguru/tsuin

shower	シャワー	shyawa
Western-style hotel	ホテル	hoteru
Western-style room	洋室	yo-shitsu

Eating Out

A table for one/two/three, please.	一人／二人／三人、お願いします。	Hitori/futari/sannin, onegai shimass.
May I see the menu.	メニュー、お願いします。	Menyu, onegai shimass.
Is there a set menu?	定食がありますか？	Teishoku ga arimass-ka?
I'd like ….	私は・・・がいいです。	Watashi wa … ga ii dess.
May I have one of those?	それをひとつ、お願いします。	Sore o hitotsu, onegai shimass?
I am a vegetarian.	私はベジタリアンです。	Watashi wa bejitarian dess.
Waiter/waitress!	ちょっとすみません。	Chotto sumimasen!
What would you recommend?	おすすめは何ですか？	Osusume wa nan dess-ka?
How do you eat this?	これはどうやって食べますか？	Kore wa doyatte tabemass-ka?
May we have the check please.	お勘定、お願いします。	Okanjo, onegai shimass.
May we have some more …	もっと・・・、お願いします。	Motto …, onegai shimass.
The meal was very good, thank you.	ごちそうさまでした。おいしかったです。	Gochiso-sama desh'ta, oishikatta dess.
assortment	盛りあわせ	moriawase
boxed meal	弁当	bento
breakfast	朝食	cho-shoku
buffet	バイキング	baikingu
delicious	おいしい	oishii
dinner	夕食	yu-shoku
to drink	飲む	nomu
a drink	飲みもの	nomimono
to eat	食べる	taberu
food	食べもの／ごはん	tabemono/gohan
full (stomach)	おなかがいっぱい	onaka ga ippai
hot/cold	熱い／冷たい	atsui/tsumetai
hungry	おなかがすいた	onaka ga suita
Japanese food	和食	wa-shoku
lunch	昼食	chu-shoku
set menu	セット／定食	setto (snack)/teishoku (meal)
spicy	辛い	karai
sweet, mild	甘い	amai
Western food	洋食	yo-shoku

Places to Eat

Cafeteria/canteen	食堂	shokudo
Chinese restaurant	中華料理屋	chuka-ryori-ya
coffee shop	喫茶店	kissaten
local bar	飲み屋／居酒屋	nomiya/izakaya
noodle stall	ラーメン屋	ramen-ya
restaurant	レストラン／料理屋	resutoran/ryori-ya
sushi on a conveyor belt	回転寿司	kaiten-zushi
upscale restaurant	料亭	ryotei
upscale vegetarian restaurant	精進料理屋	shojin-ryori-ya

Foods *(see also Reading the Menu pp122–3)*

apple	りんご	ringo
bamboo shoots	たけのこ	takenoko
beancurd	とうふ	tofu
bean sprouts	もやし	moyashi
beans	豆	mame
beef	ビーフ／牛肉	bifu/gyuniku
beefburger	ハンバーグ	hanbagu
blowfish	ふぐ	fugu
skipjack tuna/tuna	かつお／ツナ	katsuo/tsuna
bread	パン	pan
butter	バター	bata
cake	ケーキ	keki
chicken	とり／鶏肉	tori/toriniku
confectionery	お菓子	okashi
crab	かに	kani
duck	あひる	ahiru
eel	うなぎ	unagi
egg	たまご	tamago
eggplant/aubergine	なす	nasu
fermented soybean paste	みそ	miso
fermented soybeans	納豆	natto
fish (raw)	さしみ	sashimi
fried tofu	油揚げ	abura-age
fruit	くだもの	kudamono
ginger	しょうが	shoga
hamburger	ハンバーガー	hanbaga
haute cuisine	会席	kaiseki
herring	ニシン	nishin
hors d'oeuvres	オードブル	odoburu
ice cream	アイスクリーム	aisu-kurimu
jam	ジャム	jamu
Japanese mushrooms	まつたけ／しいたけ／しめじ	mats'take/shiitake/shimeji
Japanese pear	なし	nashi
loach	どじょう	dojo
lobster	伊勢えび	ise-ebi
mackerel	さば	saba
mackerel pike	さんま	sanma
mandarin orange	みかん	mikan
meat	肉	niku
melon	メロン	meron
mountain vegetables	山菜	sansai
noodles:		
buckwheat	そば	soba
Chinese	ラーメン	ramen
wheatflour	うどん／そうめん	udon (fat)/somen (thin)
octopus	たこ	tako
omelet	オムレツ	omuretsu
oyster	カキ	kaki
peach	もも	momo
pepper	こしょう	kosho
persimmon	柿	kaki
pickles	つけもの	ts'kemono
pork	豚肉	butaniku
potato	いも	imo
rice:		
cooked	ごはん	gohan
uncooked	米	kome
rice crackers	おせんべい	osenbei
roast beef	ローストビーフ	rosutobifu
salad	サラダ	sarada
salmon	鮭	sake
salt	塩	shio
sandwich	サンドイッチ	sandoichi
sausage	ソーセージ	soseji
savory nibbles	おつまみ	otsumami
seaweed:		
laver	のり	nori
kelp	こんぶ	konbu

shrimp	えび	ebi
soup	汁／スープ	shiru/supu
soy sauce	しょうゆ	shoyu
spaghetti	スパゲティ	supageti
spinach	ほうれんそう	horenso
squid	いか	ika
steak	ステーキ	suteki
sugar	砂糖	sato
sushi (mixed)	五目寿司	gomoku-zushi
sweetfish/smelt	あゆ	ayu
taro (potato)	さといも	sato imo
toast	トースト	tosuto
trout	鱒	masu
sea urchin	ウニ	uni
vegetables	野菜	yasai
watermelon	すいか	suika
wild boar	ぼたん／いのしし	botan/inoshishi

Drinks

beer	ビール	biru
coffee (hot)	ホットコーヒー	hotto-kohi
cola	コーラ	kora
green tea	お茶	ocha
iced coffee:		
black	アイスコーヒー	aisu-kohi
with milk	アイスオーレ	kafe-o-re
lemon tea	レモンティー	remon ti
milk	ミルク／牛乳	miruku/gyunyu
mineral water	ミネラルウォーター	mineraru uota
orange juice	オレンジジュース	orenji jusu
rice liquor	酒	sake
(non-alcoholic)	（甘酒）	(ama-zake)
tea (Western-style)	紅茶	kocha
tea with milk	ミルクティー	miruku ti
water	水	mizu
whiskey	ウイスキー	uis'ki
wine	ワイン／ぶどう酒	wain/budoshu

Health

I don't feel well.	気分が よくないです。	Kibun ga yokunai dess.
I have a pain in …	・・・が痛いです。	… ga itai dess.
I'm allergic to …	・・・アレルギーです。	… arerugi dess.
asthma	喘息	zensoku
cough	せき	seki
dentist	歯医者	haisha
diabetes	糖尿病	tonyo-byo
diarrhea	下痢	geri
doctor	医者	isha
fever	熱	netsu
headache	頭痛	zutsuu
hospital	病院	byoin
medicine	薬	kusuri
Oriental medicine	漢方薬	kampo yaku
pharmacy	薬局	yakkyoku
prescription	処方箋	shohosen
stomachache	腹痛	fukutsu
toothache	歯が痛い	ha ga itai

Numbers

0	ゼロ	zero
1	一	ichi
2	二	ni
3	三	san
4	四	yon/shi
5	五	go
6	六	roku
7	七	nana/shichi
8	八	hachi
9	九	kyu
10	十	ju
11	十一	ju-ichi
12	十二	ju-ni
20	二十	ni-ju
21	二十一	ni-ju-ichi
22	二十二	ni-ju-ni
30	三十	san-ju
40	四十	yon-ju
100	百	hyaku
101	百一	hyaku-ichi
200	二百	ni-hyaku
300	三百	san-byaku
400	四百	yon-hyaku
500	五百	go-hyaku
600	六百	ro-ppyaku
700	七百	nana-hyaku
800	八百	ha-ppyaku
900	九百	kyu-hyaku
1,000	千	sen
1,001	千一	sen-ichi
2,000	二千	ni-sen
10,000	一万	ichi-man
20,000	二万	ni-man
100,000	十万	ju-man
1,000,000	百万	hyaku-man
123,456	十二万三千 四百五十六	ju-ni-man-san-zen-yon-hyaku-go-ju-roku

Time

Monday	月曜日	getsu-yobi
Tuesday	火曜日	ka-yobi
Wednesday	水曜日	sui-yobi
Thursday	木曜日	moku-yobi
Friday	金曜日	kin-yobi
Saturday	土曜日	do-yobi
Sunday	日曜日	nichi-yobi
January	一月	ichi-gatsu
February	二月	ni-gatsu
March	三月	san-gatsu
April	四月	shi-gatsu
May	五月	go-gatsu
June	六月	roku-gatsu
July	七月	shichi-gatsu
August	八月	hachi-gatsu
September	九月	ku-gatsu
October	十月	ju-gatsu
November	十一月	ju-ichi-gatsu
December	十二月	ju-ni-gatsu
spring	春	haru
summer	夏	natsu
fall/autumn	秋	aki
winter	冬	fuyu
noon	正午	shogo
midnight	真夜中	mayonaka
today	今日	kyo
yesterday	昨日	kino
tomorrow	明日	ash'ta
this morning	今朝	kesa
this afternoon	今日の午後	kyo no gogo
this evening	今晩	konban
every day	毎日	mainichi
month	月	getsu/ts'ki
hour	時	ji
time/hour (duration)	時間	jikan
minute	分	pun/fun
this year	今年	kotoshi
last year	去年	kyonen
next year	来年	rainen
one year	一年	ichi-nen
late	遅い	osoi
early	早い	hayai
soon	すぐ	sugu

Tokyo Subway System

The subway system in Tokyo is fast and efficient. This map shows all the subway lines, plus selected JR (Japan Rail) lines and private rail lines. See the Street Finder maps on pages 180–89 for the location of central subway stations at street level. Many stations have multiple exits; it is often easier to go up to ground level, then orient yourself.